The Art, Literature and Music of Solitude

Bloomsbury Solitude Studies

Series Editors: Julian Stern, Dat Bao, Axel Seemann and Małgorzata Wałejko

Bloomsbury Solitude Studies brings together research on solitude, silence and loneliness to explore these topics from numerous academic perspectives and to consider how they are developed and learned across the lifespan. Each contribution takes a distinctive approach to conceptual and empirical thinking about loneliness and solitude, how people relate loneliness and solitude to physical and mental well-being, how people live with and mitigate experiences of loneliness, and the role of silence in everyday life. The series brings together the work of scholars from many disciplines and includes well-established and newer scholars, all embedded in their own disciplines and all also drawing on other disciplines to inform their research.

Forthcoming in the series:
Solitude, Silence, and Loneliness in Adolescence,
edited by Sandra Leanne Bosacki

The Art, Literature and Music of Solitude

Julian Stern

BLOOMSBURY ACADEMIC
LONDON · NEW YORK · OXFORD · NEW DELHI · SYDNEY

BLOOMSBURY ACADEMIC
Bloomsbury Publishing Plc, 50 Bedford Square, London, WC1B 3DP, UK
Bloomsbury Publishing Inc, 1385 Broadway, New York, NY 10018, USA
Bloomsbury Publishing Ireland, 29 Earlsfort Terrace, Dublin 2, D02 AY28, Ireland

BLOOMSBURY, BLOOMSBURY ACADEMIC and the Diana logo are trademarks of
Bloomsbury Publishing Plc

First published in Great Britain 2024
This paperback edition published in 2025

Series design: Grace Ridge
Cover Image © Kathrin Ziegler / Getty Images

Bloomsbury Publishing Plc does not have any control over, or responsibility for, any
third-party websites referred to or in this book. All internet addresses given in this
book were correct at the time of going to press. The author and publisher regret any
inconvenience caused if addresses have changed or sites have ceased to exist,
but can accept no responsibility for any such changes.

A catalogue record for this book is available from the British Library.

A catalog record for this book is available from the Library of Congress.

ISBN: HB: 978-1-3503-4801-1
PB: 978-1-3503-4805-9
ePDF: 978-1-3503-4802-8
eBook: 978-1-3503-4803-5

Series: Bloomsbury Solitude Studies

Typeset by Newgen KnowledgeWorks Pvt. Ltd., Chennai, India

For product safety related questions contact productsafety@bloomsbury.com.

To find out more about our authors and books visit www.bloomsbury.com
and sign up for our newsletters.

Contents

Series Editors' Foreword

Solitude Studies brings together research on solitude, silence and loneliness; how they are understood from numerous academic perspectives; and how they are developed and learned across the lifespan. Contributions will be from philosophical, sociological, historical, psychological, theological, counselling, social policy and gerontology disciplines, with all taking distinctive approaches to conceptual and empirical thinking about loneliness, silence and solitude; how people relate them to physical and mental well-being; how people live with and mitigate experiences of loneliness; and the role of silence in everyday life. It is a series that explores the many theories and practices concerned with ways of 'being alone' (in different forms) and how they are learned, understood and explored throughout a lifespan and across many cultural and other contexts.

Stimulated by the publication of the *Bloomsbury Handbook of Solitude, Silence and Loneliness*, these books will extend the work of scholars from many disciplines who are increasingly concentrating on both the harmful and beneficial forms of solitude. Scholarship in this field of research is supported by the International Society for Research on Solitude (ISRS http://isrs.usz.edu.pl/), to which this monograph series is affiliated. The ISRS also provides guidance and opportunities for exchanges of views for all participating authors.

Contributors to the series include well-established and newer scholars, all embedded in their own disciplines and all also drawing on other disciplines to inform their research. The series aims to include foundational texts on the meanings and characteristics of solitude, silence and loneliness from within different disciplines, along with texts based in various national settings, and in a wide range of professional and practice settings including formal and informal educational contexts.

Julian Stern, Dat Bao, Axel Seemann and Małgorzata Wałejko

The Art, Literature and Music of Solitude by Julian Stern

The artistic representation of solitude, which endures through time but often stays elusive in academic discourse, had never been so visible to me until I read this work. The book with its vivid narrative voice unveils layers of solitudinous nuances that pervade the arts in stimulating ways.

Dat Bao

Preface

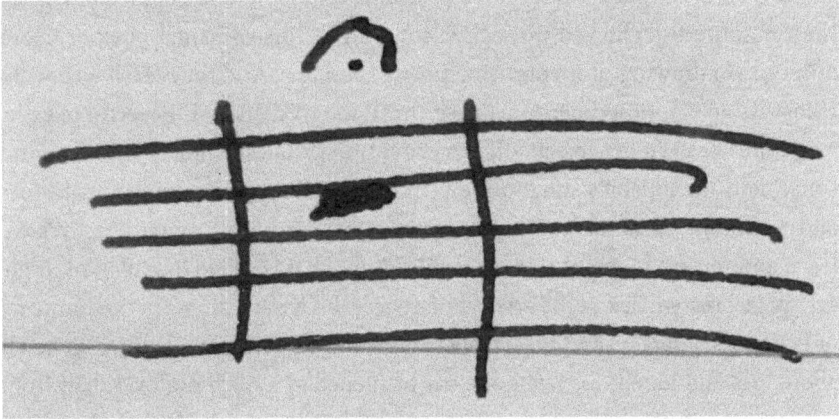

© Julian Stern, 2022

We seek solitude for separation from some, to meet the others:
Escaping from everyone to be with everyone else.

A Personal Solitude

This book presents a thematic analysis of various aspects of solitude, silence and loneliness, seen through the lenses of artistic, literary and musical forms of expression. Why bring together solitude and the arts? Well, both the creation and consumption of the arts are typically intensely solitary activities even while they are intensely dialogic. The arts come out of solitude, and they describe solitude. What is more, the arts themselves help create the very means of experiencing solitude. The emotion called *loneliness*, for example, is not a simple, unchanging and natural (whatever 'natural' may mean) state, universally understood in the same way. It is a complex, changeable, ineffable emotion. The question 'when you have felt lonely, how do you know the feeling is of loneliness, and not of something else?' is one of the hardest questions I have asked in decades of teaching and research (Stern 2014a, p. 23). It is a question I still find hard to answer. Yet my own understanding of loneliness – my own personal experience of loneliness – comes from the poetry of Larkin or Dickinson, the songs of Johnson or Lennon, the pictures of Munch or Lowry, the novels of McCullers or Eliot and more. That is a list personal to me, and yet all of us learn loneliness, learn silence and learn different forms of solitude, and we learn as much as anything from art, literature and music. Forms of solitude are not taught at school, at least not as formal subjects on the curriculum. Yet even at school, the arts provide opportunities for healthy solitude, achieved through silent reading, instrumental practice, close observation drawing or memorising poems, perhaps. And they teach us how to recognise an emotion called loneliness, the power of silence or the terror of exile.

Before we even get to school, storybooks, fairy tales, children's rhymes and songs, and the lullabies sung to the youngest babies tell of estrangements, loss and loneliness as much as happy togetherness. And all through our lives we learn and relearn aloneness, we recognise it in what is called 'popular' or 'high' art, we feel recognised in the arts, we discover who we are, alone, in the company of fictional characters and their real creators and performers. I learned as much about loss and loneliness from one bar of silence in a Bach oratorio than from a bookshelf of psychology texts or a couchful of therapists. (Yes, I know it is the patient who is supposed to be on the couch, with the therapist sitting on a seat, but having a couch full of therapists keeps me entertained.) While seeking solitude, we often manage to find it as a result of being in dialogue with fictional figures and with long-dead artists.

This book will be a personal account, and not a comprehensive survey or systematic history. It is personal in being informed by my own, personal, engagement with art, literature and music. That makes it reasonably typical of an English-speaking middle-class white man brought up in the UK in the second half of the twentieth century. I hope I've escaped some of the traps of my upbringing, helped by the history of exile lived by my parents' generation. My life's been like one long escape room. Indeed a solitudinous escape from a narrow, provincial, background through art is precisely the point of the book. We escape to the rest of the world, if we're lucky. But the book is also personal because it is a personalist account of solitude and the arts. 'Personalism' is a tradition in philosophy, with links in psychology and theology, that puts personhood at the centre of how we think about the world. It is not a single philosophy, a single school of thought, even. It is made up of a cluster of writers from the second quarter of the twentieth century onwards, albeit with allies and sources stretching long into history. Trying to describe personalism is itself an illustration of one of the lessons I have learned from it. Rather than describing personalism as a 'theory', I want to say '*this* person is a personalist, and *this* person', naming Mounier (1952) or Polanyi (1962) or Macmurray (1991). Sacks, himself someone who might be referred to as a personalist, warned against searching always for the universal, the general. We get to universals and generalities only by focusing on individuals. Individual persons, or rather each person, is what matters, is *who* matters. We do not get to generalities and apply them to individuals. Quite the reverse. This is the position Sacks is attacking, a 'paradigm that has dominated Western thought, religious *and* secular, since the days of Plato' (Sacks 2003, p. 19).

> It is the idea that, as we search for truth or ultimate reality we progress from the particular to the universal. Particularities are imperfections, the source of error, parochialism and prejudice. Truth, by contrast, is abstract, timeless, universal, the same everywhere and for everyone. Particularities breed war; truth begets peace, for when everyone understands the truth, conflict dissolves. How could it be otherwise? Is not tribalism but another name for particularity? And has not tribalism been the source of conflict through the ages? (Sacks 2003, p. 19)

Instead, he says, we should respect and explore the 'dignity of difference':

> The dignity of difference is more than a religious idea. It is the overarching theme that links the various strands of the argument I have constructed in the chapters that follow. ... The world is not a single machine. It is a complex, interactive ecology in which diversity – biological, personal, cultural and religious – is of the essence. Any proposed reduction of that diversity through the many forms of fundamentalism that exist today – market, scientific or religious – would result in a diminution of the rich texture of our shared life, a potentially disastrous narrowing of the horizons of possibility. (Sacks 2003, pp. 21–2)

It is that way, I think, that this book will work. The selection of art, literature and music will be mine, a personal selection. It will be informed by many years of watching, reading and listening, and discussions held all around the world with those interested in the arts and/or solitude. But it is a personal selection, a selection of materials that mean something to me. I will not try to force the material into a single 'big universal theory' of solitude and will instead present many-voiced overlapping themes open to further exploration.

Some Contexts and an Origin Story: Alone Together

The literature referred to in this book is mostly written in English, the only language in which I have fluency. There are some materials translated into English – the writings of Hölderlin, for example, or religious texts from Buddhist,

Christian, Hindu and Jewish traditions. The art I have considered is mostly the 'fine art' typically found in major galleries in Europe and North America – the galleries I have been visiting all my life, given the opportunity, but a narrow (if often regarded as canonical) selection. When it comes to music, I draw on two major traditions. One is the primarily European classical tradition roughly from the eighteenth century onwards. This, I learned from my parents' record collection, from my own (classical) piano lessons between the ages of eleven and eighteen, and, from about age fourteen onwards, live classical concerts in my home city of Hull, and later in London and beyond. The second broad musical tradition on which I draw for this book is what can be called 'popular' music, or such popular music I could access from the UK. This included not only 'pop' music from radio stations but also jazz, blues, rock and folk music from the UK, the United States and Canada, from France and Belgium, from Ireland, from West and Southern Africa and more.

I am a slow reader, a rather limited traveller (compared to most of my colleagues and friends) and a rather 'picky' consumer of art who will often go round a gallery at walking pace, rarely stopping to stare at individual exhibits. There are other projects with which I am involved that attempt a somewhat broader – no, a very much broader – survey of the arts and culture as a whole. What I attempt in this book is unlike those bigger, multi-author, projects. This is a narrower, more particular and more personal account of the art of solitude, based on a history of slow and careful reading, watching and listening. Through this particularity I hope to be able to make a specific, coherent, argument for the importance of considering the arts when exploring solitude, and considering solitude when exploring the arts.

Part of my aim is simply to raise the profile of solitude. I am a communitarian, someone who thinks of personhood as only existing in and through community. It was a remark by an eight-year-old child, in a research project exploring schools as learning communities, that led to my own realisation of the importance of solitude and the need to raise its profile (Stern 2009, p. 49). I asked many children, young people and adults in schools in the UK and in Hong Kong, China, 'when do you feel most included, in school?' Just one respondent in my own study (following some similar comments found in Hatfield 2004) said that they felt most included when they were left alone, to work on their own. How odd. But then I thought about how I too value being left alone – at home and at work – and feel 'crowded out' when I'm expected to be permanently active with other people. I wrote a few pages about this, in the book of the project (Stern 2009). That led to more and more discussions with people about the role of solitude in school, and the risk of loneliness. But already two key elements in my argument were in place.

The first two building blocks in my own solitude model were derived from that one research response. One is that solitude is a necessary *part* of community, and not, or not only, an *alternative* to it. Even us communitarians have to understand and value solitude within, as well as beyond, community. The other building block that came to me at this early stage was, in its simplest form, that it takes two to be lonely. Loneliness is a social emotion, and – ironically – not one we have all on our own. To understand loneliness, just as to understand solitude, requires an understanding of communities and other forms of society. The phrase 'alone together' was used as the title of the first conference I organised on solitude. That phrase, used by the novelist Woolf in the 1920s (Woolf 2000a, p. 102), the philosopher Macmurray in the 1970s (Macmurray 2004, p. 169) and the computing guru Turkle in the 2010s (Turkle 2011, title), captures elements of both of these building blocks.

It was fascinating to work on both puzzles: why solitude was important to community and why loneliness requires more than one person. The first arguments I had – that is, the first disagreements I had (the ordinary meaning of 'argument', rather than the academic meaning) – were with a good friend and sometime colleague. He didn't think that children felt lonely, and didn't think it takes two to be lonely. As we argued one day over lunch, he concluded by saying: 'you'll just have to write a book on this, Julian'. I did as he suggested. The resulting book (Stern 2014a) did not persuade him that I was right or that he was wrong, but it helped me realise how hard it is to define solitude or loneliness, and how much insight children and young people had into both those topics. It also led me to see how much better loneliness and solitude were described and explained in art, literature and music than in academic texts in philosophy, psychology or sociology.

In literature, art and music I found answers to many questions about solitude, silence and loneliness. And I found that using art helped children explore their own experiences of solitude in its various forms. Adults, too. What do you think the people in this picture are themselves thinking? Who do you feel you are most like, out of all the characters in the picture, and why? Using the pictures by artists known for their depictions of solitude or loneliness or, in contrast, for their depictions of sociability and community, children and adults found insights in, and were insightful about, these works of art (Stern and Buchanan 2021). These were not research projects in which I simply drew on the views of respondents. The respondents were themselves interpreting and drawing on the work of artists. The respondents were learning themselves, learning about art (and solitude) and learning about themselves *from* art. I was lucky to be there amongst it all, learning about and from art and the lives of my respondents.

Being Creative

Along with this use of the products of artists and writers and musicians, there is a story to be told of the process of creating art, literature and music. It is something of a Romantic stereotype – more of which, later – that artists are or should be lonely and solitary figures. Some arts are more structurally sociable, some more solitary. The poet Larkin was a stereotypical lonely, solitary poet who spent his days working in a busy university library. Another poet said they envied his more sociable day job, as a balance to the solitary writing of poems. Larkin is said to have replied, 'yes, I wake every morning wanting to kill myself; I go to work, and after ten minutes, I want to kill someone else' (Courtenay 2003). Poets tend to be 'structurally' solitary (at least in modern Western cultures), playwrights and violinists more social. But there are many times in the life of all artists (including performers as artists, of course) when solitary work is required. The focus needed to create, repetitive practice or exercises, observation, learning lines: all are solitary in some senses.

I had piano lessons from the age of eleven. Practising and playing the piano was and to an extent remains a huge pleasure. (My fingers are less flexible these days, and I have less incentive to practise for a particular purpose.) Reading sheet music, I am trying to get the right notes in the right order. I am also trying to understand the composer and the piece, and I am trying not only to listen to my performance, to critique it and improve, but also to enjoy the experience of hearing the music. If I am improvising (i.e. composing and performing at the same time), I am listening intently all the time. Most of the time, I play the piano on my own, with no audience – other than more or less reluctant listeners in other rooms in the house, or walking past the house. It seems peculiar as I describe it to spend decades performing music with no-one to hear. But that is what I have done, as have many others who play, or paint, or write without expecting others to witness the results. Solitary practice and performance, learning lines, staring at a blank page – so much of art is created alone, and quite a bit of it never reaches other people. There are plenty of people who sing in the shower and no-one hears, but there are also more substantial unheard and unseen works of art. Near misses include the major works of Kafka. Kafka was not only a solitary in his own right – and there is more about Kafka later in the book – he also asked his executor to destroy all his manuscripts when he died. The world may be grateful to Max Brod for failing to carry out Kafka's instructions, but that doesn't make his actions right. While he was living, Kafka destroyed much of his own work, so he certainly was not being uncharacteristic in wishing for the posthumous bonfire. What is interesting – at this point of my own book (*not* to be destroyed, should I die: it deserves at least to die in its own time on a bookshelf somewhere) – is what Kafka's relationship was with his work, such that he wanted it destroyed.

Fly, My Pretties

I would not say that Kafka was a perfectionist. Perhaps he was, perhaps not. But what I know of perfectionism is that it is a destructive condition. It can help a person improve, and it can sabotage the very success it seeks. A creative person – perfectionist or not – may achieve greater creative success through dissatisfaction with what they have done so far. But if you think that what you have created is perfect and is the 'last word' to be said on the matter, why create more? The creator – perfectionist, dissatisfied or simply plodding on while employed to create (this latter, anti-Romantic yet far more common creative life) – is ambiguously related to what is created. Few say 'fly, my pretties, fly!' (Even the Wicked Witch of the West, to whom this quotation is attributed, did not say it – at least, not in the *Wizard of Oz*, Baum et al. 1939.) Most of the time, what is created is not quite what was wanted, or ends up haunting, or speaking back to, the creator. *The Picture of Dorian Gray* (Wilde 1966) is not just a description of a dissolute life of an artist, it is also a vivid description of the work of art itself telling a story that is somewhat independent of the artist.

Burning one's manuscripts, as Kafka often did and as Brod failed to do, is something like disowning one's children. It tells of a real dialogic relationship with the art. Buber, for whom dialogue – 'real' dialogue, in contrast to technical dialogue and 'monologue disguised as dialogue' (Buber 2002a, p. 22) – was central to all (his) philosophy, is often misunderstood. Dialogue is not always positive or loving, it is not always cuddly and helpful. A real dialogue includes a duel, when two people want to kill each other, in contrast to play-fighting (Buber 2002a, p. 241), and real dialogue can be dialogue with the devil, as it were (addressed in more detail in Chapter 8). Children who grow up in violent and abusive households are likely to be learning this devilish dialogue, and may not be able to recognise or participate in more positive forms of dialogue. *Who's Afraid of Virginia Woolf* (Albee 1962) is a good description of destructive, real, dialogue, too. So an artist's relationship with their creation is dialogic, and the dialogue is not always a happy one. Just ask Kafka, or Mary Shelley.

Kafka's solitude is his own experience as an artist and is the alienated, lost, character at the very centre of so many of his stories. 'Alienation' seems a better word than 'lonely', although that might be a second-hand image of his work, the image of the 'Kafkaesque'. His characters are also portrayed as exiles, albeit exiles within their own countries. Perhaps Kafka's life as part of a German-speaking Jewish community in Prague gave him his sense of exilic alienation. Explaining in a letter that reading should shatter one's skull like an ice axe (quoted in Steiner 1967, p. 67, and followed up in Chapter 7), his is a *breakthrough* form of dialogue. Or is it a break*out*? When Gregor Samsa metamorphoses into an insect (Kafka 1961), his is the solitude of being a different species, even to his own family – or himself, the day before. This is the experience of racism, as a European Jew – the imposition of a species character of 'race' to a subgroup of a single (human) species, a form of pushing people beyond their species. It is an exile from humanity, often reflected in (non-human) animal nouns such as 'vermin'. Kafka is describing this as a subjective experience. What does it feel like to be de-specied? The 'ice axe' of Kafka is not breaking through in the sense of breaking through to a better place. It is a breaking into the experience of alienation, an experience that is both subjective and barely communicable.

A century before Kafka, Mary Shelley was describing the solitude of the created thing, the creature of *Frankenstein* (Shelley 1999). An account of life-giving that fails (echoing Shelley's own lost baby), and a creation that wants to die in a solitary place, as it has found no place in company, Shelley is updating the narratives of Prometheus and of the Golem. Solitude trying and failing to break through into company, this is as much an account of failed art as of failed humanity. It would not have surprised me if Shelley had wanted her manuscript burned, as Kafka wanted his burned, in a doubling of the exile of the work of art. The book survived, and its author continued writing, with a later novel, *The Last Man* (Shelley 2004), describing once again the experience of being separate and an individualist – as 'man' rather than as 'creature'. Shelley's mother, Mary Wollstencraft, opened up the world of women, as an early feminist. Shelley's father taught her, and his was a radically individualist anarchist view of the world. The nineteenth century in Europe, Europe's century of industrialisation and urbanisation, colonialism mixed with revolutionary freedom movements, could hardly be better represented than by the alienated writings of Shelley and, into the twentieth century, Kafka. Artists and works of art shouting their solitude, attempting to communicate the voiceless.

Readers and writers each have their own solitudes, as have musicians and listeners, artists and viewers. Yet all are also brought into dialogue with each other. That is what this book is attempting to capture: the solitudes of art from both sides, a solitude that is both dialogic and, potentially, leads beyond dialogue to a oneness that may also be nothingness. The zero that is nothing yet which is able to make more of any finite thing, and may in turn, as we might say, represent everything. 'Nothing acts faster than Anadin', my father used to tell us, quoting a popular advert for an analgesic of the time, if any of us had a headache and asked for a pill. 'So you can have nothing.'

Chapters and Verses

The following chapters take the reader through a number of themes. All the themes overlap, as good themes should. Initially, I had planned to write this book as a roughly chronological account of the art of solitude, as I had attempted in Stern (2022b). Two issues distracted me from that plan. One was a separate development of a more systematic historical account, the cultural history of solitude. That is planned to be a major six-volume publication, edited by me and a team of period specialists working with authors addressing individual topics. That publication leaves me less in need of a systematic history for this book. The second distraction was the wish to cross historical boundaries in order to explore each of my themes. To take an example, exile and solitude can be illustrated as much from ancient texts as from those of twenty-first-century refugees. I will certainly attempt to put art, literature and music into its proper historical and social contexts. What I will avoid is a chronological ordering of all the thematic chapters. Although exile, ecstasy and enstasy were well established in ancient arts, and loneliness took its modern form much more recently, the former did not die out, and the latter had many precursors, outside those periods.

In Chapter 1, I explore creativity and solitude in history, including the relation-ship between solitude and history (i.e. how solitude seems to change over time, and what does not change). The solitudes of exile are addressed in Chapter 2, as one of the most persistent of all solitude themes in the arts. Chapter 3 looks at ecstasy – going 'beyond the self' – and enstasy – being at peace 'within the self'. Those were developed in religious traditions but have become themes in many arts well beyond the religious. In Chapter 4, the idea of the artist *as* solitary is described. That is an image central to Romantic aesthetics, but can be found in various forms both before and since the period of Romanticism. Aloneness in nature – also popular in Romanticism – is the theme of Chapter 5, with pastoral accounts dating back to ancient times, and regularly reinvented ever since. Chapter 6 covers various forms of alienation as it is portrayed in the arts, and in particular the *emotions* of alienation. Within this chapter there is an emphasis on loneliness as it developed alongside alienation. Loneliness has come to dominate artistic solitudes up to the present day. It can come out of alienation, but it can also come out of conflict more generally – conflict within and between societies, the theme of Chapter 7. Conflict can result in exile or in alienation, the themes of earlier chapters, but conflict itself can directly create solitudes, good and bad – separations within families, between social groups, forms of racism and sexism and much more. However, the artistic movements known as Modernism and Postmodernism tell a distinct story, a story of individualism (often a utopian individualism) and of mortality amidst industrial-scale slaughter, a story worth telling in a separate chapter, Chapter 8, lying somewhere between alienation, conflict and the more personal contemporary loneliness. In the conclusion, Chapter 9, there is an account of new and old solitudes, and some speculative work on the future of the arts and solitude.

In the eleventh century CE, a Japanese novel by Shikibu described courtly life. The *Tales of Genji* (Shikibu 2001) is full of quiet and peaceful moments, along with intensely social times. Poetry has been described by T. S. Eliot as writing with a lot of silence on the page (quoted in Maitland 2008, p. 186, and see Michalski 2017). In the courts of eleventh-century Japan, courtly etiquette expected people to be able to improvise poems in their conversations. This was done at important moments such as arrivals and departures. In the *Tales of Genji*, such poems are scattered throughout the text, along with quotations from and allusions to classic poetry. The form of the poems is most often (in English translations) structured as thirty-one syllables in phrases of seven, five and five syllables for the first line, and seven and seven syllables in the second line. (What counts as a syllable is not quite the same in Japanese and English, but this poetic form – like the more popular *haiku* form – now has its own English tradition.) I describe this poetic form because I attempt at the start of every chapter to give an account of an essential quality of that chapter in such a poem. It is not an attempt to demonstrate poetic artistry but, as in the eleventh-century court, an attempt to summarise important ideas and feelings in a concise way – leaving much unsaid, leaving much silence on the page.

Acknowledgements

Two teachers had a particular influence on my views of music and literature. May Havercroft taught me the piano and had an enthusiasm for phrasing – to *there* – that stays with me, and Nan Grewe taught me literature with an enthusiasm for the words themselves, especially those of Larkin. Putting the book together, I realise the continuing influence of the family I grew up with who were all intensely engaged with music, art and literature, notably my mother Pam Rauchwerger (who had been a piano teacher and a teacher of literature), my father Axel Stern and my oldest brother Karl Stern (who painted/paints). More recently, I have written on literature with Catherine Samiei, Małgorzata Wałejko and Gill Simpson, and their views are some of the most influential on my current work. Anne Pirrie, Maria James, Gavin Graveson, Samir Dyal, Ben Mijuskovic and David Weir are all significant in valuing art, literature and music as contributing to understanding solitude. Tina Grant's work on art with her young students was hugely important for my understanding of solitude and loneliness, and my work with Michael Buchanan using art to explore adult professional views of togetherness and solitude provided more encouragement. Marie Stern and Mike Bottery, and Alison Baker from Bloomsbury, provided support for the whole project, which is published in association with the ISRS: The International Society for Research in Solitude (https://isrs.usz.edu.pl/), with Małgorzata Wałejko (again) and Rafał Iwański. And I'd like to acknowledge the support of all those people who, when I mentioned I was writing a book about the art, literature and music of solitude, said to me, 'but what about …?' Triggering ideas on other examples of the arts of solitude is precisely what I am hoping the book to achieve, so these 'but what about …?' stimuli have not only contributed to the content of this book but will I hope continue long after it has been published.

Introduction: Creativity and Solitude in History

Alone together: our lives are made in both ways, in combination,
But creativity makes many different solitudes.

Summary

Art, literature and music are historically embedded, and the same can be said of various kinds of solitude. Creativity itself is seen quite differently in different times and cultures, with modern forms of creativity particularly emphasising individualism and novelty, which in turn can lead to more isolated artists, less close to the communities in which they are active. The first solitudes we experience are those learned in the earliest years of life. Children's literature, from nursery rhymes onwards, express solitude, loneliness and alienation remarkably clearly, though often not noticed by the adults reading such literature to children.

The solitudes described in art, literature and music are not only historically but also geographically and culturally embedded, and the range and scope of this book, as well as the themes of each of the subsequent chapters, are described here.

Some key artists: Virginia Woolf (1882–1941), Stradivarius (Antonio Stradivari) (1644–1737), Maurice Sendak (1928–2012), Catherine Storr (1913–2001), Hans Christian Andersen (1805–1875), David McKee (1935–2022)

Introduction: History

The art of solitude is historically embedded. Some writers describe solitude, silence, loneliness and other forms of aloneness as timeless and universal. There may indeed be universal elements to being alone, and yet there are many others that change. Think of their opposites. The opposite of solitude is being together with someone. Togetherness has changed over time, as housing and communication change, as social structures and institutions change. Being 'together' in a family home may seem like a universal experience, but houses and homes and families are not now as they were half a century ago, are not the same in England as in other parts of the world. And if the opposite of silence is 'noise', then noise itself has changed and how we expect it to be has changed. People seem to live noisier lives today, with mass media generating sound even when it is not the focus of anyone's attention. (As I write this, a television is on in the background.) And people now celebrate the silence of the countryside, notwithstanding the many noises of the countryside. For example, Woolf, in *The Years*, says how 'all along the silent country roads leading to London carts plodded; the iron reins fixed in the iron hands, for vegetables, fruit, flowers travelled slowly' (Woolf 2000c, p. 118) (in contrast to 'the roar of London', Woolf 2000b, p. 95). In *The Waves* Woolf describes how 'no sound breaks the silence of our house, where the fields sigh close to the door' although 'the wind washes through the elm trees; a moth hits the lamp; a cow lows; a crack of sound starts in the rafter, and I push my thread through the needle and murmur, "Sleep"' (Woolf 2000b, p. 123). Kierkegaard, also aware of the oddity of describing noises as silent, describes the noises of animals in the countryside as *amplifying*, rather than *interrupting*, the silence:

> In the evening, when silence rests over the land and you hear the distant bellowing from the meadow, or from the farmer's house in the distance you hear the familiar voice of the dog, you cannot say that this bellowing or this voice disturbs the silence. No, this belongs to the silence, is in a mysterious and thus in turn silent harmony with the silence; this increases it. (Kierkegaard 2000, p. 335)

It might be that those brought up in a farming community hear those sounds quite differently, and therefore conceive of silence differently. And what is the opposite of loneliness? Some might say intimacy, yet intimacy has also changed over time (Mijuskovic 2022). This all makes for a fascinating, rich and complex history of solitude.

Creativity

Solitudes change over time and across cultures, and the arts of solitude are changing, with that art being both cause and effect of those changes. To be creative today is not the same as being creative in the past. I once attended a 'creative writing' course and asked whether my academic writing was an example of 'creative writing', and was firmly told 'no'. Being creative meant writing poetry and fiction. And what is fiction? I was at a religious education conference many years ago. We were being introduced to the government's new 'literacy hour'. The consultant illustrated her talk with a book (a 'big book', which was all the rage in those days, or hours), and it was a book about St David, the patron saint of Wales. Choosing a religious text was a sensible attempt to bridge literacy hours and religious education. A question came from the audience. 'What genre would you put a book like this in?', the questioner asked, as the literacy hour was intended to teach young children all about genre. 'Why, *fiction*, of course', the consultant unwisely proclaimed. Fiction? Well, at least that settles that debate: religion is fiction. Others may well agree, but what counts as fiction is, as the audience's unsmiling response demonstrated, still *contested*.

The modern sense of 'creativity' was a creation – a fiction, one might say – of the Cold War. The USSR managed to get into space before the United States. One of the American responses to this was to celebrate and promote in schools the 'creativity' that would be needed to compete more successfully with the USSR – which was portrayed as oppressive, communal and over-planned (Cropley 2001, pp. 1–2). American creativity was – in response – very individualistic and 'sellable'. Typically, creativity was then described as an individual person making something that is new (or original) and of value. 'Value' might include any aesthetic value – including the more obvious qualities such as beauty or insight – but also hints at *commercial* value. Of the three elements of creativity – making, newness and value – value has the most straightforward link to the American economic system of the 1950s. What about 'making' and 'newness'?

In most accounts of 'making', this is seen as something done by an individual. That is problematic. Even in film-making, known as a 'teamwork' art, there has been – especially in the 1950s and 1960s – an emphasis on the 'auteur', the single genius controlling the whole film and able to take credit for the whole film. This was a fiction. And even in more solitary arts, the 'making' is rarely altogether solitary. Things are typically made collectively, even if – at a minimum – the collaboration simply involves giving the creative person space and time to create. Having 'a room of one's own' was rightly seen by Woolf as the advantage male writers usually have over female writers (Woolf 1929). Organising a household to allow a person such space and time is often – usually – what women contribute to men being creative, she says. But whoever is advantaged, all have contributed to the creativity. I grew up in a house where one man had a study, a room of his own where his wife and children did not go. There, he read and wrote, creatively I think. And, even closer to home, as it were, I realise that my own writing as a university professor is a collective endeavour, with colleagues and also friends and family contributing in many ways. Publishers too, and reviewers and readers. In earlier times, creativity was more likely to be attributed to the *collective*, to a studio, for example, even if that studio was known by the name of the 'star' artist. Damian Hirst has revived this approach, but he is criticised for 'cheating' – as the price, if not the value, of work produced in such a way is less than that produced by a single certified genius. Hirst responded with a 'renewed focus on painting sans assistance' (Cascone 2018).

Workshops such as that of violin-maker Stradivarius are other good examples of collective making. Stradivarius's workshop is a particularly good example. Not only is it unclear who in the workshop could ever be said to be individually responsible for any one violin, but the workshop collectively had skills that have never been equalled, and never reproduced. Polanyi gives this as an example of 'personal knowledge', that is, knowledge embedded in a community that is so rich, complex and built-in to practices of the community (i.e. 'implicit' rather than 'explicit' knowledge) that if the community is wholly disbanded, the knowledge itself disappears.

> An art which cannot be specified in detail cannot be transmitted by prescription, since no prescription for it exists. It can be passed on only by example from master to apprentice. This restricts the range of diffusion to that of personal contacts, and we find accordingly that craftsmanship tends to survive in closely circumscribed local traditions. … It follows that an art which has fallen into disuse for the period of a generation is altogether lost. … These losses are usually irretrievable. It is pathetic to watch the endless efforts – equipped with microscopy and chemistry, with mathematics and electronics – to reproduce a single violin of the kind the half-literate Stradivarius turned out as a matter of routine more than 200 years ago. (Polanyi 1962, p. 53)

Polanyi says that *all* knowledge is to an extent personal in this way, although some 'communities' are very large and/or very long-lasting. But the example of Stradivarius and his workshop is enough in itself to make wholly individual 'making' a very odd and unviable model of creativity.

'Newness', too, has its communal aspect and its American pragmatist aspect. The history of the United States has had a special relationship with newness. A country like the United States was built on the land of an indigenous population who were mostly slaughtered, and it is comfier to think of the country starting anew. All countries have violent histories, all are built on the bones of the defeated, but the United States has two 'forgotten' histories – the history of its origin in already occupied territory, the other its own first century as an independent nation built with slavery, and its continuing systematic inequalities and exploitation. Embedded in American culture is a sense of everything being new, fresh and forward-looking, with occasional glances at the birth of the nation in 1776 (or 1492, or 1620). The philosophical pragmatism of the late nineteenth and twentieth centuries has some of these same characteristics. One should think afresh what works, now, rather than building on established philosophical traditions. Being new is important, and valorising newness helps us forget the past. So the emphasis on originality-as-newness in definitions of creativity is more than a simple matter of definition. It carries a message that is central to American culture. In educational contexts, novelty is prized over quality: teaching techniques that are 'innovative' are valued above those that are 'good' (however 'good' is measured). In the arts, to be innovative, to create new ways of doing an art and to dismantle established ways are the routes to fame.

This writing seems to be falling into the style of crusty traditionalism, and that is not my intention. I value originality in my own work as in that of others. It is just that an emphasis on novelty may take away from consideration of beauty and insight. Some of the artists I most value were well-embedded in traditions from which they did not break. J. S. Bach was a respected composer in his own time, but his own children – also composers – thought his music very old-fashioned and less valuable for that. Chopin seems to have described Bach as a 'discoverer', not a 'creator', as 'like an astronomer who, with the help of ciphers, finds the most wonderful stars' (Chopin 2004, veracity doubted by Hedley, in Chopin 1962). The poet Larkin (1988) wrote poetry with clear regular forms using language that was readable by a wide audience, rather like poets from earlier in the twentieth century (such as Hardy), and this gave him a reputation for being less original. The landscapes painted by Hockney in the twenty-first century (Hockney and Holzwarth 2021) are, as landscapes, looked down upon by some critics as unoriginal. (Searle (2012) describes how 'all those splodges and patterns, smears and dapples and churnings get very wearying'.) This is not to wage a war on behalf of traditionalists but to acknowledge that some music, writing and art may be creative without always being regarded as 'new'. The American view of creativity that became dominant in Anglophone debates on creativity had a built-in individualism, a built-in 'forget the past' and a built-in commercialism.

Amongst the qualities I would want to recognise in creativity – in versions of creativity that could be used in accounts stretching beyond the last seventy years, and beyond America, are qualities such as beauty, insight, craft and dialogic longevity. 'Longevity' is used rather than 'eternity', but either might have been suitable. There are many dangers in thinking of arts as long-lived or 'eternal', or as judging them by how long they are read, seen or heard. The idea of a novel communicating across the ages is one of the contributions that Leavis and Leavis made to literary criticism (Leavis 1948; Leavis and Leavis 1969), and they tied this to the idea of a 'canon' of English literature. The Leavis canon did not seem to recognise or, even worse, seemed to celebrate a powerful idea of class and national dominance. They were sensibly criticised by those wishing to recognise a more diverse tradition (Eagleton 2022) – more diverse *traditions* – and hidden voices or voices heard by hidden groups. Yet longevity is still important, even if there is far more work needed to discover older ignored voices. After all, that is exactly what Mendelssohn did for J. S. Bach.

Alone Together in Childhood

Creativity changes over time, as does solitude. History can be understood through both. Solitude in its various forms is central to human development. When it is said that human beings are essentially social, that is perfectly reasonable, but it is only half the story. Babies are born into a lifelong game of peekaboo. That game, where an adult hides and reappears, to the baby's smiles and giggles, is a metaphor for all of life. Togetherness and intimacy are so important to babies (and to all of us), and they are complemented by separation and solitude. How else can a baby differentiate itself, and learn of its own personhood? Alone and together, this is how human beings grow. Child psychologists such as Bowlby (2005) and Winnicott (2017) describe this vividly, with Winnicott describing even the youngest babies developing 'the capacity to be alone' and experiencing this as a 'paradox' as 'it is the experience of being alone while someone else is present' (Winnicott 2017, p. 243). Although they were hardly new in observing this, Bowlby and Winnicott established the duality in academic literature. 'Alone together' is how we live, whether that is two separate activities (peekaboo) or one. 'We must meet; we must communicate with one another; we must, it would seem, be alone together' (Macmurray 2004, p. 169), as the somewhat lonely communitarian Macmurray said (Stern 2018). It is troubling to be always alone, for most people, but it is troubling also to be always in company without respite. Aloneness can be experienced amongst people – with common practices including reading (a book, a device) or playing, within a busy household. Staring out of the window can achieve the same solitude, or daydreaming. Daydreaming, like sleep dreaming, is a solitary activity. A person who cannot be alone is just as worrying as one who cannot be in company.

Alone together we grow up, with carers and without, with friends and without, with family and without. And just as solitude can be created whilst in company, through reading a book or daydreaming, so can togetherness be created whilst alone. I can have my own company, which is vital. But we can also be in company with distant, dead and fictional characters. In recent research, when young people were given time in school without any allotted tasks, allowed just to think, they often thought about dead people (grandparents were most often mentioned) and other relatives they hadn't seen for a long time. In response to a question about who they thought about, children and young people said, for example, 'I thought about my cousin who I see as a sister and she lives in Brazil', 'My Aunt who previously died', 'I also thought about my Nan [name] who has passed', 'my dad in heavan', 'my ansesters', 'my grandad who has long gone', 'my mums dad died so I thought about him', 'missing my mums unkle because he is dead' (Stern and Shillitoe 2018, p. 15, and see also Stern and Shillitoe 2019). Paradoxically, in company we may achieve solitude by daydreaming, and by daydreaming, we may have the company of the distant and the dead. Reading, of course, can also take us away from people and join us to imagined or fictional people.

Where the Wild Things Are (Sendak 1963) is a fine illustration of a child's life alone and together. In that book – written for children as young as four or five – the hero is a boy who is punished for some misdemeanour by being sent into solitude in his bedroom. There, he enters the world of the Wild Things and his wonderful adventures end in a 'wild rumpus'. Then they stop and he sends them off to bed without their supper. 'And Max the king of all wild things was lonely and wanted to be where someone loved him best of all', Sendak continues. 'Then all around from far away across the world he smelled good things to eat so he gave up being king of where the wild things are'. He went back to 'his very own room where he found his supper waiting for him', 'and it was still hot' (Sendak 1963). Alone but accompanied by the Wild Things, he longs to be together again with his family. This is how we grow up. Although children's books are written by adults, their popularity is determined to a large extent by their speaking children's truths. They voice the barely voiced and speak truth-to-the-powerless. Other accounts of children's growth alone together in children's literature include Catherine Storr's *Marianne Dreams* (Storr 1958, with versions for television – *Escape Into Night* – and for the cinema – *Paperhouse* – and, under its original name, for the opera house). Marianne is forced to be alone, away from her school friends, not as a punishment but because she has a broken leg. Confined to bed and lonely, she discovers that she can 'make' her dreams by drawing pictures with a magical pencil before she sleeps. In her 'constructed' dreams, things don't go quite as she expected, but she does meet a particular boy, who is also ill. Alone and together, she learns when awake that there is a real, ill, boy in the neighbourhood, linked through her governess.

Marianne Dreams is for older children. I read it myself at nine or ten, and remembered it ever since. The dreamed adventures are more grown-up than those in *Where the Wild Things Are*, and Marianne enters her imagined world through her drawing. But both stories tell children the subversive truth that, whatever they think of their family and their friends, there is also access to meaningful solitude when alone. This is itself a creative idea, perhaps accessed (as by Marianne) through conventionally creative tasks like drawing. The subversive character of children's literature has a long history. Alison Lurie wrote *Don't Tell the Grown-Ups* (Lurie 1990) about how fairy stories are subversive, as they tell children about awful, cruel, parents, for example, and it is *parents* who typically tell children about how awful parents are. That is one of the great pleasures of literature, to give people messages and to hide those same messages from others. Nursery rhymes tell of a child in a cradle in a tree when the bough breaks, of mice tails being cut off, of dying of the plague (with a pocket full of posies). A counting book starts 'There were 10 in the bed, and the little one said, "Roll over! Roll over!" So they all rolled over and one fell out' and ends 'There was 1 in the bed, and the little one said, "I'm lonely!"' (Ellwand 2001). Hans Christian Andersen's *Ugly Duckling* (2011, pp. 193–206) is an odd but popular tale of 'ugliness' that is really about not fitting in. You may be ugly by duck standards but you are (or become) handsome by swan standards. If the story were simply about being ugly when young and handsome when older, it would be less likely to have been as popular. (The fictional Lisa Simpson, when reminded of the story by her mother, says, 'so you think I'm *ugly?*', and her mother clumsily replies 'no, you're one of the good-looking ducklings who makes fun of the ugly one, hmm', *The Simpsons*, 4:4.) It is the 'other' story, the one of not fitting in to *these* standards but finding another group that you *do* fit into, that makes the story so popular. Whether the 'other' is another talent or social class or royal lineage, or another sexuality, all of which have been attributed to this tale (Andersen 2005, pp. 329–31; Griswold 2005), a celebration of 'otherness' is this story's subversive message.

Andersen's *Ugly Duckling* (and several of his other stories) can be read as a disguised story of Andersen's sexuality. O'Connor wrote a short story also called *The Ugly Duckling*, starring a gender-ambiguous woman – a 'tomboy' who wears 'masculine' clothes and who rejects the advances of men – and later returns to her 'interior world' and becomes a nun (O'Connor 1957, pp. 57–94). Both ugly ducklings tap into the literary link between loneliness and sexuality (notably Hall 1982, discussed in Chapter 6). Andersen telling subversive stories of his own experience, with or without being aware of it himself, and telling these stories to children is, I think, a fine example of the way in which creative work can influence how we experience and come to terms with (our own and others') solitude and loneliness. *You've Got a Friend in Me* is the theme song to *Toy Story* (1995). That film does indeed supply friendship to children. Imaginary friends are really friendly, even if they are also really imaginary, and can be a 'helpful fantasy to overcome loneliness' (Seiffge-Krenke, in Dimitrijević and Buchholz 2022, p. 175). Lurie, already quoted on children's literature, also wrote about the imaginative world of adults, in *Imaginary Friends* (Lurie 1967). In that novel, a sociologist studying a religious cult joins the group and is deemed divine himself. The wonderfully humorous Lurie had her phrase 'imaginary friend' taken up by the less humorous Richard Dawkins (2006, p. 388) in an atheist polemic.

We find friends in literature, and enemies too. In children's literature there is often a simple division between friend and enemy, good and bad. But even there, there are examples of ambiguity. Solitude can be accompanied by anger, and punitive solitude – of the kind in *Where the Wild Things Are* – is likely to conjure up a wild anger, until it fades, in *Wild Things* style, to something closer to loneliness. A more monstrous ending is given in *Not Now, Bernard* (McKee 1980). A child keeps trying to tell busy grown-ups that there is a monster in the garden, to be told they have no time to talk to him, 'not now, Bernard'. He ends up going into the garden himself, to be eaten by, or perhaps to become, the monster. An unheard child ending up a monster: this sounds like a disturbing pathology of an abusive childhood. And it *is* such a pathology, subversively packaged as a story book to be read by parents and other adults to children. The small exile of being ignored – a colloquial phrase used in the UK is to be 'sent to Coventry', a more geographically explicit form of exile – has a monstrous ending. Unhappy solitude is not always lonely, it can be angry too.

It is hard to know how childhood solitudes have changed through history. Children do not get to write their own histories, or if they do, these are rarely retained. And childhood itself was not always regarded as a significant 'category' of humanity. Ariès (1996) wrote of the *invention* of childhood roughly from the sixteenth to the eighteenth century. There has been criticism of Ariès (e.g. Hendrick 1992), and it was always a Eurocentric viewpoint, but critics still maintain that childhood changes over time and between cultures. The historicity of childhood remains powerful. One of Ariès's main contentions was that in earlier periods, children were merely regarded as 'little adults'. To expect children to do hard physical work as soon as they were able, to leave a child alone – whether working or playing – and unsupervised, to expect children to travel alone for work or to visit people: all of this is more risky and troubling compared to the lives of many children today. But the growth of the more modern kind of childhood was also a process of infantalisation. Young human beings have been 'childed' over recent centuries in many countries, being made increasingly dependent on adults, constantly given adult company and guidance all nominally for the sake of the child, and not for any common purpose of the community. It is the children's literature of recent centuries that 'recovers' the more challenging, dangerous, world of pre-modern childhoods. *Little Red Riding Hood* would today be driven to her grandmother's house (or would arrange delivery of food to her by Amazon), *Hansel and Gretel* would have carers looking into the inspection reports on elderly childcarers living in gingerbread houses and so on. Children's fiction recovers lost solitudes and dangers. But it still warns of real, modern, dangers and the subversive joys of modern solitudes: thank you, Bernard and the Wild Things.

Solitude Themes in History and Geography

If childhoods and childhood solitudes have changed over time, what about adults and adulthood? In a previous publication (Stern 2022b), I presented a history of the art, literature and music of solitude. Rather like Ariès's history of childhood, it had the advantage of simplicity, and its disadvantages, too. So it is worth presenting and unpicking my earlier position here, before moving on to a more complex account in the remainder of this book. In art, literature and music, it was in the Romantic movement that various forms of solitude took centre stage. For example, loneliness was frequently referred to, albeit attributed more to places than to people. There was a growth in the idea of the isolated more-or-less heroic artist. And solitary walks in the countryside became poetic clichés. Romanticism was therefore used as a pivot in solitude arts, and I used it to create a before–during–after model (i.e. Stern 2022b). Before Romanticism, the dominant forms of solitude expressed in the arts were exile (punitive expulsion from a community) and, for the more positive solitudes, religious ecstasies and enstasies. After the Romantic focus on the solitary artist and communing with Nature, the third period of my model described the growth of alienation and its accompanying emotional form of loneliness, the increasing association of loneliness and sexuality, and, more positively, the development of intentional therapeutic solitudes and silences. I hold on to those descriptions in their own right and will reuse many of the examples used in that previous text: Ovid's letters from exile, Wordsworth's daffodils and Hall's well of loneliness, amongst others. However, in writing that account I became increasingly aware of two limitations of the model: one chronological, one geographical.

The chronological problem was precisely the academic's problem with models. It becomes easy to exaggerate distinctive features so that counter-examples become invisible. Preparing Chapter 8 of this volume on individualism and death as expressed in Modernism and Postmodernism, I developed a sense of non-Modernist artists of the Modernist period being ignored – by me and often by other critics – and yet illuminating solitudes more characteristic of other periods. And Postmodernists lived and worked alongside Modernists and those whose work might more easily be ascribed to earlier movements. The very act of being 'unfashionable', in such senses, is a kind of artistic exile or alienation, and that makes these artists particularly interesting to an account of exile and alienation. This is not just about the Romantic 'misunderstood artist', following his (it is usually a 'he') muse and creating art for a posthumous posterity. It is also those persistently unfashionable artists like – for example – Arnold Bennett. Bennett was one of the best-selling artists, in any medium, of the first half of the twentieth century, but he was no Modernist. His were novels of life in provincial England, written for 'ordinary people', and looked down upon by Modernist literary elites, including by Virginia Woolf. (Given his healthy book sales, he might have welcomed the equally unfashionable and well-paid pianist Liberace, who said on hearing elite criticism that he was 'crying all the way to the bank'.) Half a century after his death, Bennett was re-evaluated, and so was Liberace. Bennett's 'old-fashioned' realist novels included vivid accounts of generational division, old age and death, illuminating 'ordinary' loneliness just as finely as Modernists like T. S. Eliot. (Liberace's re-evaluation has more to do with a recognition of the art he made of his sexuality, and his fears of exposure combined with 'hiding in plain sight'.)

There is a similar problem with geography. It is not simply that I am based in the UK and am most familiar with the kind of art recognised by European and Anglophone critical authors. It is also that the big historical periods I referred to – the period of Classical Antiquity, the Renaissance, the Enlightenment, Romanticism, the Age of (alienated) Industry and (European) Empire, Modernism and Postmodernism – all are geographically narrow. In China, do these same periods exist? No. Nor in the Americas, Africa, Australasia. Just Europe. Some periods are more global, but even those are quite different depending on where you are in the world. So a model of the arts of solitude across history is bound to fit one part of the world better than others. I am not beating myself up. Creating a model of how solitudes develop helps highlight important – if not universal – issues and changes. But for this book, I decided to present solitudes more thematically. Each theme might have particular 'centres of gravity', historically and/or geographically, but each is open to outliers, examples from other periods, other places.

The Structure of the Book

A thematic book that is not historically organised and that does not try to be comprehensive? That is a much richer feast than most. And if some authors (Woolf, Larkin, Shakespeare) make an appearance in several chapters, well, that's just the penalty of having a European Anglophone author. Shakespeare often has the last word, and I note that German-based Aleksandar Dimitrijević recently wrote a chapter entitled 'Historical roots of solitude and private self (with continual reference to Shakespeare)' (Dimitrijević and Buchholz 2022, p. 57, title of Chapter 4). And my previous more historically structured account had two positive outcomes. One was a more systematic historical account, the *Bloomsbury Cultural History of Solitude* (currently being written). The other was the generation of themes to be used here. Exile was central to the world of Classical Antiquity, and to the ancient sacred texts of Judaism and Christianity. It helped forge Nordic sagas and much more. The solitudes of exile have been re-expressed ever since. Exiles, refugees and asylum-seekers are constantly with us. Just as one part of the world seems to be at peace with itself, another goes to war, civil or uncivil, and the result of wars or pogroms or persecutions is usually the same: suffering and forced travel, exile and seeking refuge. Whether for economic, legal or military reasons, people are forced to move. And that always has an artistic accompaniment, an explanation, a justification, an interpretation. Through the arts, being homeless or stateless may not be comfortable, but it can be expressed.

Chapter 2 therefore explores the solitudes of exile, whilst Chapter 3 has a more religious theme. Religion is not always welcome at a cultural party, and that puzzles me. One of the best collections of writing about loneliness, edited by Rouner (1998), resulted from a seminar series organised by philosophers and theologians. Those disciplines – to an outsider, so close – rarely come together without arguing, like two unfriendly families at a wedding. But loneliness brought them together on friendly terms. Religious solitude is familiar to many, religious or not: contemplatives, hermits, wandering sages, desert temptations, all are common in different traditions. One of the oddities of religious arts of solitude is, however, the contrast between inward-looking solitudes and outward-looking ones. To be 'outward-looking' is not, in this case, about extroversion or sociability. It is about religious 'ecstasy', to go 'out of one's place' through, for example, prayer or other forms of spiritual exercise, whilst in solitude. A popular drug currently gets called 'ecstasy', and with that, apparently, you can get 'off your head'. Religious ecstasies have a much longer history, but are just as much about – more about – achieving a connection beyond the self.

The obverse of ecstasy is enstasy – a much less well-known word. Enstasy is being *within* yourself, in contrast to being *beyond* yourself. In Hindu traditions, enstasy is an important idea, recommended as a kind of 'steadied thought' or 'steady wisdom' (Zaehner 1992, p. 326). Enstasy is also central to Buddhism, and one of the most common portrayals of the Gautama Buddha is him as enstatic (the *samādhi* Buddha). It would be a neat distinction to make between South/East Asian and West Asian/European religious traditions, to say that the former focus on enstatic solitude and the latter on ecstatic solitude, with these traditions in turn influencing wider cultures in those regions. Neat, but a little too simple. So Chapter 3 recognises both traditions across different cultures. It leads in to one of the European adaptations of enstatic traditions, in Chapter 4's account of the 'solitary artist', especially the Romantic artist as solitary. So much of artistic work is solitary, it can seem strange to identify the *emergence* of the solitary artist in the late eighteenth and early nineteenth centuries in Europe. However, it was indeed a much more common feature of accounts of that period. The artist became the work of art, in a sense. Familiar to performance arts, what happened was that writers, composers and painters had their own lives as part of their art, or at least closely associated with their art. Social isolation – Beethoven's hearing impairment, Hölderlin's mental health problems, De Quincey's drug dependency, for example, contributing to social isolation – seems integrated into their creative endeavours. At least, in popular imagination. (Beethoven's personality sometimes distorts how his music is perceived.)

Ideas of the solitary artist or the influence on art of social isolation is not unique to European Romanticism, even if Romanticism popularised that stereotype. A second Romantic trope with a very long pre-history and plenty of later history is the association of solitude and nature. Chapter 5 has this theme. There is a sense in which nature was 'invented' and honoured by being capitalised as Nature. Yet nature, or Nature, became important precisely as urbanisation and the control of the countryside was being completed. I have lived in towns, in medium-sized cities and in the largest UK city, London. In each location, I realised to my surprise that my sense of what was 'beyond', what 'nature' was, varied. In London, nature could be sought, but that involved a significant intentional journey. In mid-sized cities (in my case, Hull, Oxford, Leicester), nature seemed closer and the weather was more than just a guide to clothing, but a journey – albeit a short one – was still needed to engage more fully. All the cities dominated, with nature apologetic. However, living in a town now, I have a different sense of the urban interrupting a dominant nature. The weather is climate, is part of the agricultural year, of the seasons. I can see cows grazing on a small field from my front window, and can walk into the countryside. All of this 'nature' is human created, long-farmed and managed. It is far from wilderness. Wordsworth and Thoreau were not experiencing wilderness but *Nature*, albeit a clear contrast to the urban (especially the metropolitan) experience, a nature in which the countryside and climate dominated.

Loneliness – along with many other qualities – was attributed to fields, river, hills and other 'natural' features. And that loneliness was a projection or a prediction of the human emotion as it developed in this period. How solitude was sought or loneliness suffered in the countryside was a city-dweller's vision, it seemed. Romantic artists with rural backgrounds or experience of farming were rare. John Clare (1985, 2004) was an exception, as was James Hogg (1996), and they both – as poet and novelist – had a less straightforwardly Romantic view of Nature. Pastoral ideals of nature date back to the ancient world, and are connected to some of the very earliest narratives such as that of the Garden of Eden. In the biblical narratives, the expulsion from the Garden of Eden is not to an urban life, though, but to the hard work of farming. That is also the parallel 'fall' in Marx's and Engels's accounts of the move from 'primitive communism' to a class-based and therefore exploitative social system (Engels 1972; Marx 1976).

Marx's account of human history up to and including capitalism was culturally, socially and politically influential through the later nineteenth and twentieth centuries. He developed earlier uses of the term 'alienation' to describe the human experience of capitalism. Chapter 6 is an exploration of how alienation was artistically described and influenced emotionally. Loneliness, in its nineteenth-century meanings in European culture, might be said to be the emotion of alienation. Yet alienation has a long history before Marx, including as a religious term indicating a separation from God. Chapter 6 therefore also explores this other range of alienation solitudes. Through the nineteenth century, a third strand of alienation came to have a more prominent place in culture, alongside the Marxist and the religious senses. This was the psychological use of alienation to indicate what are now called mental health issues. Those three alienations are associated with different forms of solitude. Alongside these alienations, a distinctively modern form of loneliness was also emerging culturally, particularly in writing. This was a 'three-dimensional' loneliness that included some kind of self-rejection based on guilt or shame (themselves culturally varied), along with the other dimensions of separation/solitude and of a sense of rejection. Amongst the most powerful accounts of this rich form of loneliness are poets such as Dickinson in the nineteenth century and Larkin in the twentieth century. But it is novels of the period that describe lonely and self-rejecting people within a broader social and cultural context. Hall's *Well of Loneliness* (1982) managed on its own to reimagine loneliness of this type as associated with sexuality. Short stories, too, contribute to the character of modern European and North American culture. O'Connor describes the very genre of the short story as essentially lonely (O'Connor 1968), and his arguments have real value, especially if short story authors like Joyce and Yates are considered. Beyond Europe and North America, loneliness had a different history, so this chapter does not attempt a generalised history of the emotion, but rather, a specific account of arts of a time and place.

Similarly narrow is Chapter 7's account of conflict and discord as reflected especially in the novels, theatre and music of the nineteenth and twentieth centuries. The themes of alienation and of conflict are both represented in the artistic movements known as Modernism and Postmodernism, and it is their specific forms of more-or-less utopian individualism and their concern, obsession almost, with death that is the concern of Chapter 8. Modernism acts as a final stage of European colonialism and industrialisation. An odd mixture of celebration of science and industry taken to utopian extremes, and the emptiness of these very achievements, marked much of Modernism. It was an elite cultural development, elite even within the most 'elite' nations, rarely voicing the most exploited victims of industry and empire, but shot through with alienation, anomie and loneliness. The utopianism of Modernism already carried with it a dystopian flavour, and the final stage of Modernism came to be the movement known as Postmodernism, Modernism's graveyard, dystopian and disconnected. Beckett sits at the edge of Modernism, tipping into Postmodernism, and in Beckett we have a solitude for the ages. His one-person plays and monologic novels evoke ancient solitudes, and have much in common with the religious Quietism of the seventeenth century.

It is the relationship of historically and geographically narrow cultural movements to earlier and to distant cultures that 'excuses' my themes in these later chapters. Although it hardly needs saying, all artists will have access to earlier and distant art, so as time marches on, there is more on which to draw, and it becomes harder to be 'new'. The pianist Gould, who could have a solitude book all to himself, was famous for his recordings of Bach. (He rejected live audiences for the recording studio, believing the latter musically 'better'.) At one point (forty-five minutes into the track called 'concert drop-out', disc 3, Gould 1983), he justifies the (quick) pace of some of his performances by saying that, with all the interpretations already available for these pieces, all he could do to be original would be to play faster or slower. Well, faster or slower, my own final chapter, Chapter 9, concludes with an account of how new and old solitudes are being experienced and influenced by artists, writers, composers and performers. As the world has information technologies giving access to arts and audiences unimaginable even a generation or two ago, the opportunities for solitude, silence and loneliness also proliferate.

Easter Eggs

In computer programs, an 'easter egg' is a surprise gift from the programmers to the users. I like to think of books as offering such easter eggs, too. Two small easter eggs that follow Chapter 9 are the bibliography and the index. Underappreciated as they are, bibliographies are far more than checking devices, allowing scholars to follow up the materials quoted. I like to think of them as a quiet party, a gathering of writers who give nothing more than their name, rank and number. Imagine a party with such people present. And, even better (for those who value peace and quiet), imagine such a group when no-one is shouting out their ideas, but merely quietly stating who they are, what their topic is, and where and when they come from. The second easter egg is the index. I could write a book on indexing, except that the best possible title has already been taken: *Index, A History of the* (Duncan 2022). Indices are reimaginings of the whole book, they present topics and people in new ways, allowing the reader to 'see through' the whole book, without having to read the whole book. I always compose my own indices, and see each index as of an equivalent value to any single chapter. So with the easter eggs of the bibliography and the index, the book quietly closes.

2

Solitudes of Exile

I am sent away, and only then do I know what I am worth
Outside my community: will I be all or nothing?

Summary

There is a sense in which all human populations are exiles from earlier homelands, at some point in history, as well as 'exiles' from their birth mothers, and – literally or figuratively – from 'innocent' earlier lives (whether in childhood or in a Garden of Eden). Exile might be experienced as a group, but it is also typically described in artistic forms as isolating and lonely, insofar as it is remembered as an exile. One of the best-known literary exiles is Ovid, relegated from Rome to the edge of the Roman empire, or the edge of the world as Ovid described it. Another exile who is variously portrayed in art, literature and music is Moses, an exile from infancy who never quite returned to his homeland. Along with exile to another country, this chapter explores 'internal' exiles, exile within prisons, hospitals or, even, for children, being sent to one's room, and internal exile generated by colonialism. The philosopher Serres considers exile as necessary as a stimulus to genuine creativity, and he uses music as a model form of expression both of exile and of reconciliation.

Some key artists: Ovid (Publius Ovidius Naso) (43 BCE–17/18 CE), Snorri Sturluson (1179–1241), Shaun Tan (1973-), Albert Camus (1913–1960), Eli Wiesel (1928–2016), Mark Warshawsky (1848–1907), Jerry Siegel (1914–1996) and Joseph Shuster (1914–1992), Alan Sillitoe (1928–2010)

Introduction: We're All Exiles

It seems strange to think of it, but human beings probably emerged in one rather small area of Africa. That means that in every other part of the world, human beings are visitors. No-one is truly indigenous except for a potential group of human beings in Africa – although it is not clear whether current populations are those who have stayed or are returners from other parts of the world. How did the world get populated, prior to fast modern transport? Slowly, and as a result of pushes and pulls. 'Pulls' included the attractions of new places to find food and shelter and security. 'Pushes' included escape from conflict and, central to this chapter, various kinds of exile and rejection from a community. This is not a book of anthropology, so there is no scholarly account of the role of exile in the spread of humanity. However, it clearly did have a role from the earliest times, and is embedded in some of the earliest cultures. By expelling a person or a group, usually as a punishment or sacrifice, the exile is isolated and may be 'decultured': rejected from and with little access to their 'home' culture, and perhaps a stranger to any new cultures they encounter. 'By the rivers of Babylon', sing the Jews expelled from Jerusalem by the Babylonians in the sixth century BCE, 'we sat down [and] wept, when we remembered Zion [i.e. Jerusalem]'. This is a cultural exile, as the Babylonians 'required of us a song'. Exiles being decultured, they cry 'how shall we sing the Lord's song in a strange land' (Psalm 137, 4). Oddly, the narrative about being unable to sing in exile has become one of the best-known songs in all history, from its origin two and a half millennia ago, through Reggae and pop hits of the 1970s, popular in Jewish and Christian religious communities and latterly, especially in Rastafarian communities.

Exile decultures, then, and recultures. Voices of loss and rejection, voices of new homes, memories of paradise lost. Diaspora groups throughout the world – and in a sense, the whole world's population is diaspora, it's just that some people forget and think they've always been there – sing and tell tales and paint pictures of their solitudes. Iceland, a country that is, as an island, physically solitary, was first settled in the ninth century CE by Norse (from what is now Norway) exiled from, and threatened with execution in, their homeland. They picked up slaves from Scotland, and settled in the forbidding island that had been known to only a few daring Norse hunters and fishers. Starting in this way, in relatively recent times (as so many of the world's land masses had long been populated by this time), we have a more vivid relatively unified culture-of-exile in the Icelandic sagas and other poetry from the first four or five centuries of the country's human history. These accounts provide histories of the original exiles, and later accounts from the island of Iceland of families, feuds, further (internal) exiles and returns. A characteristic of the significance of exile is that the sagas generally tell of the remembered exiles of hundreds of years before the telling. *Egil's Saga*, for example, tells of activities between 850 and 1000 CE, but was written (by Egil's descendent Snorri Sturluson) between 1220 and 1240 CE (Smiley 2000, p. 3), and *The Saga of the People of Vatnsdal* tells of activities between 875 and 1000 CE, but was written between 1270 and 1320 CE (Smiley 2000, p. 185). Solitude is not central to the sagas; it is treated as dangerous if inevitable for such people travelling to hunt and to trade, and to escape vengeance or punishment. The exile is 'carried' as a memory of rejection, just as it is carried by earlier exile communities (such as the Jews) and later exile communities (such as African Americans) as defining the *current* existence of those communities. Their solitude is a solitude-in-and-of-community, having a considerable overlap with the individual solitudes of members of those groups (individual Icelanders writing poems of lost ancestors and lost homelands in Norway, individual Jews singing of Babylon, individual African Americans singing the blues). More obviously solitary exiles – Ovid in antiquity, the *Wanderer* of Anglo-Saxon England (Hamer 1970), *Coriolanus* of Shakespeare's account in the seventeenth century or the modern *Superman* (Siegel and Shuster 2006) – overlap in their emotional range, their sense of hurt and rejection, their anger, their (in)ability to come to terms with exile and their struggle with all these emotions. Icelanders retain to this day a sense of individuality and independence, a refusal to bow down to authority, borne of their exilic history. And the 'embeddedness' of their own history is happily reflected in their electing as president in 2016, and again in 2020, Guðni Thorlacius Jóhannesson, an historian of, amongst other things, Icelandic presidents.

Ovid Writes Home

Are we *defined* by our exile – exile from the womb, from the first family, from ancient homelands, from the Garden of Eden, even? Is that what independent adulthood *is*? There are many exiles all through history, the people whose ancestors were exiled and who retain a memory of the exile, and those who are themselves suffering an exile here and now. One of the best-known literary accounts of exile comes from the pen of one of the most privileged of writers. Ovid was a literary superstar in Rome at the height of the Roman empire's powers. He knew and had the support of Emperor Augustus Caesar. Until he didn't. Ovid's writings were often scandalous, and something he wrote seems to have offended the emperor, and he was sent into exile. His exile was a privileged punishment: he was not executed, which would be the more likely punishment for offending the emperor. Ovid's exile was to the edge of the empire, to the city of Tomis, now Constanța in Romania. It was a dangerous journey, and his wife and family remained in Rome. But he had resources in Tomis and his family back in Rome remained comfortable. What is more, Ovid could write of his life of exile, and sent his writings back to Rome where they were published – and remain published to this day, alongside his pre-exile works. The *Black Sea Letters*, letters written with the expectation that they would be published, and *Tristia*, likewise letters to be published, were both written in poetic forms (Ovid 2005). Elegant, erudite, funny and packed with literary allusions, these exilic works are also desperately sad and emotionally complex – more than much of his 'cooler' earlier works. Here is a simple grumpy complaint, from early in his exile: 'If perhaps you're wondering why this letter's drafted / by another's hand, I've been, am, sick, / sick, and at the unmapped world's remotest limits, / scarce certain of my survival. How do you think / I feel, lying here in this godforsaken region, / surrounded by a pack of Danubian Slavs?' (Ovid 2005, p. 44). Or here, telling once again of the difficulty of writing:

> Whoever (if anyone) reads it should ponder beforehand / just where and when it was composed – / he'll make allowance for writings he knows to have been written / in time of exile, in a barbarian world, / and will marvel that in such adversity I could summon / the courage to write – however sadly – at all. / Misfortunes have broken my talent, though even before then / its source had become unproductive, scanty its vein. (Ovid 2005, p. 63)

Ovid lived in exile for the last twenty years of his life and never got the pardon he so often begged for.

Comparing his exile to that of earlier exiles, including heroic exiles like Odysseus (Ulysses), 'though I lack such heroic / stature' (Ovid 2005, p. 7), Ovid has a terrible journey into exile and when he arrives in Tomis finds himself living amongst people he regards as, at best, provincial. The food, the company, the landscape: everything adds to his lamentations, alongside missing his family and his status in Rome. Shame does not seem to trouble him, nor guilt – in part, it seems, because he did not know what the precise cause was of his exile. My own description of loneliness (Stern 2014a, p. 182, 2021a, 2022a, p. 7) gives it three possible dimensions, isolation, rejection and self-rejection. The third dimension – self-rejection – is often evidenced by guilt or shame. Ovid certainly appears to be self-pitying at times, but he does not seem to be lonely in this three-dimensional sense. Depressive perhaps, melancholic in many of the ways described in Burton's *Anatomy* (Burton 2021). (Ovid makes an appearance in Burton's book, of course.) Accidie, too, and anger – if rarely with himself. Ovid's exilic solitude is one of the finest poetic descriptions in any language. It is gradually taking its place in Ovid's oeuvre as distinctive – distinctively personal, emotional and touching. The idea that we only appreciate something once it is lost is central to the appeal of this exilic literature, and Ovid's exile has had an enduring influence on other writers (Ingleheart 2011).

Internal Exiles

Within this chapter on exilic solitude, alongside conventional exiles out of the home country, there will be *internal* exiles. To be sent away from one's country is the basic form of exile, but there are many other ways of being 'sent away'. Perhaps the smallest of exiles of this kind are the ways in which people are pushed out of a group. Children may be punished by being sent to their room. Hardly a punishment for those who enjoy such solitude, as Rufus happily confesses:

> When parents on TV shows punished their kids by ordering them to go to their rooms, I was confused. I loved my room. Being there behind a locked door was a treat. To me a punishment was being ordered to play Yahtzee with my cousin Louis. I puzzled over why solitary confinement was considered the worst punishment in jails. (Rufus 2003, p. xxviii)

Yet the 'small exile' of being sent to a room is still used as a punishment, in homes and in schools. Many schools have separate places to which misbehaving children can be sent. Sometimes, it is just the corner of the classroom, away from other children, sometimes the corridor outside the classroom. And sometimes a separate room. In a chilling piece of newspeak, these rooms, previous called 'exclusion' rooms, have recently been renamed 'inclusion' or 'seclusion' rooms (Barker et al. 2010). The excuse is that by sending children to the 'inclusion' room, they avoid excluding the child altogether from school. However, it is clearly a greater punishment, and more exilic, when the child is put in silent solitary confinement, rather than being sent out of school to be amused in the home or a nearby shopping centre. Home-based 'internal' exiles of children are well represented in children's literature such as *Where the Wild Things Are*

(Sendak 1963), described in Chapter 1, or even *Marianne Dreams* (Storr 1958), a much less punitive exile in which a girl is forced to stay in bed with a broken leg. *The Arrival,* by Shaun Tan (2006), is a picture book, probably for children (but readable by all ages), which has no words but takes the protagonist through arrival in a new and strange city, with odd creatures and alienating bureaucratic and industrial processes all around. It is a superb account of how exile to a new land – perhaps to New York? – might feel to those who have no language suited to and no understanding of the new country. 'What drives so many to leave everything behind and journey alone to a mysterious country, a place without family or friends, where everything is nameless and the future is unknown?', the back cover of the otherwise wordless book says, continuing to say that 'this silent graphic novel is the story of every migrant, every refugee, every displaced person, and a tribute to all those who have made the journey' (Tan 2006, back cover).

> *The Arrival* is a migrant story told as a series of wordless images that might seem to come from a long forgotten time. A man leaves his wife and child in an impoverished town, seeking better prospects in an unknown country on the other side of a vast ocean. He eventually finds himself in a bewildering city of foreign customs, peculiar animals, curious floating objects and indecipherable languages. With nothing more than a suitcase and a handful of currency, the immigrant must find a place to live, food to eat and some kind of gainful employment. He is helped along the way by sympathetic strangers, each carrying their own unspoken history: stories of struggle and survival in a world of incomprehensible violence, upheaval and hope. (http://www.shauntan.net/books/the-arrival.html)

A child sent to their room in a small 'internal' exile might well enjoy reading Tan's haunting account of international exile, and understand the feelings of the protagonist. Yet adults also experience 'internal' alongside 'external' exile, and adult internal exiles are much more fully represented in, and influenced by, art, literature and music. The various forms of imprisonment and incarceration for other reasons (mental health issues, contagious illnesses, 'moral depravity', political opposition, religious or ethnic 'errors' or whatever) are all described both second-hand and first-hand. Wilde's *Ballad of Reading Gaol* (Wilde 1966, pp. 843–60) or Gaddis's *Birdman of Alcatraz* (Gaddis 1955, but see also Babyak 1994), and the even more fictionalised film of the book (Frankenheimer 1962), contributed to prison reform, just as Dickens's novels contributed to the reform of debtors' prisons. *One Flew Over the Cuckoo's Nest* (Forman 1975; Kesey 2002) similarly contributed to the reform of hospitals for those with mental health issues. (Frieda Kahlo's pictures related to her many years of treatment in hospital for her damaged back has had less of a reforming influence, I fear, whatever their intention.) Wilde's poem, Gaddis's somewhat idealised account (and Burt Lancaster's implausibly heroic film portrayal) and Kesey's novel were all *intended* as campaigning tools, as were Dickens's novels. This does not take away from their artistic qualities, any more than it adds to them. But some non-campaigning incarceration art can provide different insights into the solitude of internal exile.

The novels of Dostoevsky (2003) or Kafka (2015), the art of Louis Wain (Beetles 2021) and Richard Dadd (Tromans 2011), the poetry of Clare (2004) or the music composed in Terezin (Terezin Music Memorial Project 1998): all enlighten and, all too often, terrify the reader all the more for not being romanticised or idealised, and not written explicitly with reform in mind. King's short story *Rita Hayworth and the Shawshank Redemption* (King 1982), and the film made of it (Darabont 1994), is less heroic than most prison-based literature, even if it ends up – as the title tells us – with redemption. Solitude themes in such art have much in common with 'external' exile literature such as that of Ovid. The loss of home, the loss of family and friendship networks, for example, along with the unfamiliar surroundings, the noises, the food and the landscape. And the sense of injustice and/or guilt or shame, the pointlessness of a life lived 'away', without work or contribution to (one's own) society. There are also often changes in opportunities for sexual encounters, albeit not in the more 'coy' writers such as Dickens.

Solitude is not only experienced by those incarcerated in solitary confine-ment. Confinement with strangers is as likely to be experienced as lonely or solitudinous as genuinely solitary confinement. (That is not to underplay the pain of solitary confinement, just to say other forms of confinement may be experienced as solitudinous.) There is so much 'cutting off' in confinement, and in some conditions the solitude is a cause as well as an effect of internal exile. The therapist Frieda Fromm-Reichmann describes all mental health issues – all the most challenging ones – as forms of loneliness (Fromm-Reichmann 1959), and she was one of the few therapists – along with Melanie Klein – to consider loneliness a central feature of mental health. There is more on her work in Chapter 9, along with that of the personal construct theorist, clinical psychologist and later psychologist of education, Salmon (2004). Recovery – for Fromm-Reichmann as for Salmon – is described in terms of returning into relationships, of returning to community, as if returning from exile. Schizophrenia is a problem with *personhood* (Salmon 2004, p. 78).

Colonisation as Internal Exile

Internal exiles, in family houses, schools, prisons or hospitals, are as rich sources of art as external ones. There is a sense in which they come together in the experience of being colonised. A colonised country becomes alienated from its own (colonised) population. In the late seventeenth and much of the eighteenth centuries, there were Scottish people who regarded the Protestant monarchy as imposed and the country as taken over by English Protestants. They were known as Jacobites as they supported the Catholic King James II, exiled in 1688, and his son Prince Charles, who would have been King Charles III. A Jacobite song from the eighteenth century says 'this is no' my ain house, / I ken by the biggin' o't' (or 'I can't bide the biggin o'it'), that is, this is not my own house, I know by how it is decorated (or I cannot stand the way it is decorated). A (barely) disguised rebel song, the song is an eloquent description of the home country feeling like a strange and unfamiliar land. The absence of the 'true' monarch created a sense of homelessness or exile for many of those living in Scotland, well represented in Jacobite songs. By the nineteenth century they no longer felt quite as rebellious, but they were well established in the culture and became popular in England too, as part of a Romanticised Victorian history of Scotland. Jacobite songs remain popular today, a folk memory of internal exile, a memory that has become part of Scotland's self-identity.

Other countries that have the 'wrong' rulers, and especially those that have been colonised, often have a persistent exile culture in songs, literature and art. Irish songs and poetry (World Music Network 1999; Yeats 2002), South African arts (the music of, for example, Hugh Masekela https://www.youtube.com/watch?v=I7thMkI3hBo, the plays of Athol Fugard 1999), Finnish nationalist music (of Sibelius): all describe loss and different kinds of solitude, including loneliness and the silencing impact of colonialism or other forms of foreign or illegitimate rule. How do artists respond to silencing? Some by deception, referring to a country as a house, portraying silenced people with great nobility, for example. Some create a nostalgic past, in order to help build a utopian future. And some create protests, direct and dangerous, often distributed through elicit or alternative means of communication. Such 'internal' exile arts may combine with conventional (external) exile arts, as with Irish rebel songs sung in New York as well as in Ireland, or the melancholy musical expression of colonisation and exploitation in West Africa developing into the blues traditions in North America.

What should not be forgotten in this account of the solitary arts of exile is the attempt of so much exilic art to *affirm* existence. The existential significance of such work is itself an attempted recovery from or rebuilding a new life in the midst of exile. An interesting example of this is the work of the Algerian writer Camus. Better known as a French writer, he was born into a 'coloniser' French family in Algeria, and set his most famous works – *The Stranger* (also *The Outsider*, Camus 2012) and *The Plague* (Camus 2001) – in the country of his birth. A remarkably ambiguous position, as 'coloniser' (and apparently broadly supportive of Algeria remaining part of France), he wrote of the poor and oppressed within a colonised country, and became an exile himself in France, precisely as France was taken over by German invaders in 1940. His writing is existentialist in the philosophical sense and also clearly existential in its attempt to affirm – or undermine – existence itself in an alienated world of both internal (colonial) and external exile. Camus provides us with an example of an insider–outsider, a coloniser–colonised, an exile-going-home-into-exile, a rebel-who-opposed-revolution and so much more, in his life and in his richly ambiguous novels, plays and short stories. His view of solitude – in his own voice in a speech in New York – was that of the need for an intellectual- and values-universalism:

> To leave solitude behind we must speak, but we must always speak frankly, and on all occasions never lie and always say everything we know to be true, but we can only speak the truth in a world in which it is defined and founded on values shared by everyone. It isn't Mr Hitler who decides what is true or false. (Camus 2016)

Is Exile Necessary for Creativity?

As it says at the start of this chapter, everyone is an exile at some point in their family history, and new exiles have been created throughout history, the result of conflict, all too often, or punishment or economic pressures. Exile has generated distinctive creative traditions. A writer who describes leaving, breaking away, being forced out of a comfortable position, as *necessary* stimuli to creativity is the French philosopher Serres. He describes such creative people as 'troubadours of knowledge' (Serres 1997), travelling performers forced to keep moving and only enabled by the process of travelling. Oddly, he describes the experience of being left-handed, himself, and of being forced to write right-handedly as a liberating rather than abusive act, and generalises: 'do schoolmasters realize that they only fully taught those they thwarted, or rather, completed, those they forced to cross?' (Serres 1997, p. 7). Serres's promotion of an exilic creativity may betray his own rather privileged exile from France to the United States, but he did – like Camus – live through the Nazi occupation of France in the 1940s, and his experience of war, as a child, influenced all his work. Serres wrote of translation as needed between different ways of living and being (including between science and the arts), and translation is also a description of movement. (Donne wrote sermons on our 'translation' to heaven – described as a library – when we die, Donne 1990, p. 271.) It is our translation out of our comfortable places that, for Serres, makes us able to learn and teach as troubadours: 'I never learned anything unless I left, nor taught someone else without inviting him to leave his nest' (Serres 1997, p. 7).

> No learning can avoid the voyage. Under the supervision of a guide, education pushes one to the outside. Depart: go forth. Leave the womb of your mother, the crib, the shadow cast by your father's house and the landscapes of your childhood. In the wind, in the rain: the outside has no shelters. Your initial ideas only repeat old phrases. Young: old parrot. The voyage of children, that is the naked meaning of the Greek word *pedagogy*. Learning launches wandering.
>
> To break into pieces in order to launch oneself on a road with an uncertain outcome demands such heroism that it is primarily children who are capable of it. But, children must, moreover, be seduced to become engaged in it. (Serres 1997, p. 8)

He concludes:

> Depart. Go out. Allow yourself to be seduced one day. Become many, brave the outside world, split off somewhere else. These are the first three foreign things, the three varieties of alterity, the three initial means of being exposed. For there is no learning without exposure, often dangerous, to the other. I will never again know what I am, where I am, from where I'm from, where I'm going, through where to pass. I am exposed to others, to foreign things. (Serres 1997, p. 8)

Serres does not *quite* say that being exiled is a gift, but he does recommend that we go out, break free, leave, challenge boundaries. This is about migration, therefore, as much as exile. The two are not entirely separate: some pushed out of a community will go willingly. But both have in common the loss of home and the need to come to terms with an alien environment, along with a loss of, or diminished, membership of a (home) group.

> I believe, in my very depths, that belonging causes the evil in the world, by reason of exclusion. Half-breed, I take care of belonging through the intersection of one thousand memberships. (Serres 1997, p. 148)

Arendt links birth (being born, not giving birth) and creativity through the concept of natality (Arendt 1998). The 'newness' of birth, when the baby leaves the mother – is exiled, one might say, from the womb – is echoed in Serres's ideas on creativity. The suffering and loneliness of exile is, for Serres, turned into the creative energy of exile. Serres recognises suffering in exile but it is not the suffering itself that stimulates the arts but the 'newness' of the translation to a different environment. Those who stay at home, those in powerful positions and well-established institutions such as universities and academic disciplines, may pretend creativity, but theirs is a safe and comfortable and essentially unoriginal, uncreative, existence. From a therapeutic perspective, this is related to the creativity of loneliness (as in the work of Moustakas and Moustakas 2004, addressed in Chapter 9). Serres retains an image of the individual exile and the individual creative. His is a continuing solitude, albeit one that is always communicating – the troubadour who keeps on performing, whether or not anyone is listening. 'If you must be going', sings Paloma Faith, 'make your own kind of music, even if nobody else sings along' (https://www.youtube.com/watch?v=1ksjdlA4i9A).

Musical Solutions to Exilic Solitude?

Serres does not simply use musicianship as a metaphor. He writes of music itself as the existential 'solution' to the breaking away, the breaking apart, needed for creative thought. Music 'solves' the mystery of existence: '*Audio musicam ergo sum*' ('I listen to music, therefore I am') (Serres 2022, p. 168).

> What part of me hears music when I listen to it? My body trembles, dances, kicks up its heels, perhaps jumps with joy; music innervates and stretches the muscles, accelerates the pulse, moves the stomach and stimulated the genitals. My intellect counts, unconsciously, admiring the harmonic composition and construction of counterpoint. My hearing, in its delight, floods the whole sensory system with musical waves; inner rhythms and tempos keep time with the same metronome. My feelings move me to tears and fill me with happiness – all these bonds, suddenly global, construct my unity. (Serres 2022, p. 168)

He describes this as an 'ecstatic' experience, and a 'unifying' one, overcoming dualism:

> No part of me is unaffected by the mute ecstasy that listening to music induces. Music seizes me, holds me spell-bound, passes through me, possesses me, makes me all its own, causes some unknown federative and existential function to

operate in me, unifying the integral of what I am like an immense embrace –
this intense ecstasy that is called existence. (Serres 2022, p. 169)

'Music', Serres concludes, 'federates the subjective, body and soul; the objective,
copper, wood, chords, and waves; the cognitive, artistic composition and
aesthetic appreciation; and, finally, the collective, carried away by its rhythms
and charmed by its melodies' (Serres 2022, p. 169).

This brings us back to the ancient Jewish exile, sung in the Psalms. Whereas
many exile groups become the new 'home' group (as Angles and Saxons, and
later Normans, who invaded the country now known as England, became 'the
English'), Jews have retained an exile status, repeatedly moved on. Earlier exiles
are remembered in song (Psalms) and in meals. The Haggadah is the book of
the Seder meal eaten at Pesach (Passover). Each item of food has an important
symbolic value, and each person in the household has a role in the meal.
Haggadah books themselves are illustrated to illuminate the narrative, and are
works of art in their own right. The memory of exile is passed on from generation
to generation, and the possibility of meeting again, next year, in Jerusalem (Zion)
is the eventual recovery or return from exile. The book, the words themselves
and the book as carrier of symbolism, the meal and the communal performance
of the Seder all keep exile and return from exile as central to Jewish life. Such a
communal event seems like an odd feature in an account of solitude. However, it
is the lonely figure of the multiply exiled Moses who stands at the centre of Jewish
life. Described as 'the loneliest and most insulted man in the Bible' (Wiesel in
Rouner 1998, p. 138), he was repeatedly separated and alone, he was never 'home'.
Sent off down the river in a basket as a baby, he was brought up in the Egyptian
court, and this was his first exile. Discovering his true identity, he became a
stranger in his Egyptian home. Killing a man, he became subject to punitive exile.
And leading his people – the Jews he hadn't known he had belonged to – out of
Egypt, out of exile, he died in a cave in sight of but not having reached freedom.

> And so Moses ascended Mount Nebo alone. … The Almighty Himself guided
> him to a cave and God alone took care of his last moment.
>
> Finally, there they were – far from all human beings. Far from their voices. Far
> from their troubles. Far from everything.
>
> Moses, at last, was alone with God.
>
> As God is, always, for eternity … alone. (Wiesel, in Rouner 1998, p. 142)

Repeatedly exiled, a reluctant prophet and leader, Moses was repeatedly ignored
by his own people, and died before he achieved his life's work.

And one might add that Jews had a long future of persecution and exile after Moses. In the late nineteenth century, Mark Warshawsky wrote the Yiddish song, *Oyfn Pripetshik*, which is still taught to and sung by Jewish children. When young children are learning to read Hebrew, the teacher will sometimes dip a wooden or plastic letter in some honey, and let a child taste the honey. This is to show how 'sweet' the letters are – and therefore how sweet it is to learn to read and write. The song is of how two Hebrew letters, *alef* and *kometz*, together make a third, *O*, and how valuable literacy is to an exiled people. *Oyfn Pripetshik* sounds like a lullaby, but it is – like many lullabies – a sad song, a song of exile and of the comfort, in exile, of reading and by implication remembering the words and melody of this song.

Oyfn Pripetshik

A flame burns in the fireplace,
and the room warms up,
as the Rabbi teaches the little children
the alphabet.

So remember, dear children, and see
what you are learning here.
Repeat it again and again:
Alef with Kometz makes 'O'.

Learn, children, with great desire,
and this I say to you:
Whoever among you learns Hebrew most quickly
will receive a gold star.

So remember, dear children, and see
what you are learning here.
Repeat it again and again:
Alef with Kometz makes 'O'.

When you grow older, children,
you will understand
how much in these letters lie tears,
and how much weeping.

As you, my children, suffer in exile,
and work to exhaustion,

may you find your strength in these letters.
Look into them!

So remember, dear children, and see
what you are learning here.
Repeat it again and again:
Alef with Kometz makes 'O'. (Warshawsky, sung for example by Patinkin 1998
and at https://www.youtube.com/watch?v=RWW_ahttpW8)

Remembering and Reinventing Moses

Exile and solitude are well represented by Moses. Whether he was lonely in the
modern, three-dimensional, sense is less clear. On his own? Certainly. Rejected?
Yes. How did his rejection affect him emotionally? That is harder to say. It would
be interesting to explore what guilt or shame Moses might have experienced
(with Sacks claiming that Jewish culture is more dominated by guilt than shame,
Sacks 2021, p. 5) or whether he associated it with his solitude or rejection. Biblical
language does not include the word 'lonely' or straightforward translations of
that word. Like Ovid, a range of emotions is implied, but a modern sense of
loneliness is not easy to discern. So how is Moses portrayed in art, literature and
music? Biblical literature is just one source of course. Of the many later accounts
of Moses it is easy to see two distinct traditions, in the Jewish and the Christian
communities. One distinctive feature of Christian art portraying Jewish figures
from the Bible (including Jesus) is that they are most often portrayed as looking
like white Europeans rather than Middle Eastern Jews. (The rather predictable
exceptions are portrayals of Judas Iscariot and King Herod, who are more often
portrayed as somewhat stereotypically Jewish-looking.) But, other than looking
more or less Jewish, how is Moses portrayed artistically, and what role does
solitude play in these accounts?

Three moments in Moses's life are commonly presented in both Jewish and
Christian arts: Moses as a baby, Moses crossing the Red Sea, and Moses and
the Ten (or more) Commandments. Each is interpreted differently – over time,
and between religions. (A separate account could be made of Islamic narratives
of Moses, as he is recognised as a major prophet in Islam, and this would be
somewhat closer to the Jewish than the Christian portrayals, with a greater
emphasis on exodus in the face of persecution.) Moses as a baby, being saved
from being killed by being put in a basket on a river, to be discovered by an

Egyptian princess who, even though she knows the baby is Jewish (presumably because he was circumcised), adopted the baby as her own. This is a tale often told as a romantic rescue of a future hero. A famous modern telling, in this form, is the Superman story (e.g. Siegel and Shuster 2006). Superman's wise and loving parents, fearing their community's destruction, put the young (to be) Superman into a pod and send him off to be discovered by kindly people (of another 'race') who bring him up as their own. In Superman, as in the biblical Moses, the baby is exiled and comes to miss his home; in both, he reluctantly becomes a hero. An important difference is that Moses eventually turns against his Egyptian host community, whereas Superman fights for 'truth, justice and the *American* way'. Still, exile and missing the lost home community make Moses's babyhood and that of Superman remarkably similar. What tends to be underplayed in many tellings of the Moses story in Christian traditions is the attempted genocide that starts the story, and the shock of an Egyptian princess bringing up a Jewish baby as her own. The common, continuing, history of anti-Semitism, persecutions, pogroms and attempted genocide against Jews is much more familiar to, and therefore central to the retelling of, the story of Moses as a baby in Jewish art. Incidentally, Superman's defence of 'the American way' presumably reflects the authors' histories. Jerry Siegel was born in the United States of Jewish parents who had escaped anti-Semitic persecution in their native Lithuania. Siegel wrote the first Superman stories; they were drawn by his friend, Joseph Shuster, also the son of European Jewish migrants to North America (initially Canada, later the United States). They wrote these first stories in 1938. The image of Superman was apparently based on Douglas Fairbanks Snr, also of Jewish heritage. Being sent across the water in exile from persecution is all too common to this day.

The second scene from Moses's life often portrayed in the arts is his crossing of the Red Sea. In all the accounts, the sea is parted for the Jews escaping from Egypt, but closes again to thwart the Egyptians in pursuit. In more Christian accounts, this is portrayed as the action of Moses as 'superhero'; in more Jewish accounts, it is portrayed as the action of God to protect His chosen people. Neither, though, emphasise solitude or loneliness, so I do not dwell on them here. The third scene is the bringing of the commandments by Moses to his people. Again, more of the accounts of the Christian tradition portray a heroic, stern, Moses bringing just ten simple rules to an unruly community, like a rather overbearing headteacher bringing an undisciplined class to order. In more of the Jewish accounts, there are descriptions of Moses's isolation from (and disappointment with) his own community, feeling like a failing leader (for whom 'it is lonely at the top', perhaps) *and* feeling let down by God, as things are not going so well for the Jews. The commandments, more in Jewish than Christian arts, represent part of a new *covenant* between God and the Jewish people. Moses is the lawgiver, and there are 613 laws, not just ten. So the dangerous solitary encounter with God, where Moses and God both made demands of each other, is the more common Jewish portrayal of this part of the Moses narrative. There is certainly more isolation in Jewish than in most Christian accounts.

Alongside these three incidents in Moses's life, a fourth one, mentioned by Wiesel, is much more prominent in Jewish than Christian arts. This is Moses's encounter with God as Moses is dying. Moses is the only prophet who is said to meet God face-to-face, and he describes Jewish exile as a divine punishment for faithlessness. In this context, Moses dying before his prophesised return to Israel is a perfect example of the 'lonely leader', or a 'lonely death', portrayed, oddly, as Moses in the company of God. The 'lonely' Moses is well portrayed on a Jewish website (at https://www.myjewishlearning.com/article/deuteronomy-33 1-3412-the-death-of-moses/), bowed and walking in the opposite direction to other people, looking downwards and walking hesitantly, in contrast to a rather healthy-looking and heroic dying Moses on a Christian website (at https://www.lookandlearn.com/history-images/M811240/The-Death-of-Moses),   standing upright and firm and looking strongly into the middle distance. It is the former characterisation, the treble solitude, the solitude of exile, the solitude of Moses's separation from his own people and the solitude of facing death (dying in a cave, uncertain of the willingness of the community to do the right thing), that makes this situation so affecting to Wiesel. A lonely life ending in a lonely death, buried 'by God' in a place never found by his people. The end of Deuteronomy, the last of the five books attributed to Moses, is the end of Moses himself.

First and Last Wanderings

In death, people approach what is often called their 'final journey', sent into exile from this life. The exile as wanderer between this life and the next is a well-established theme in the arts, from ancient adventures in the underworld through Dante's compelling wanderings to Friedrich's characters lost in the dour landscapes he imagined. All provide solitudinous accounts of the boundaries between living and dying. *The Wanderer* (e.g. Hamer 1970, pp. 172–83), one of the best-known Anglo-Saxon poems, expresses this well. A 'lone-dweller' who is 'treading the tracks of exile' has been left alone as 'there's no one living' to talk with. The wanderer is a 'friendless singular', whose 'friends were a load' and where 'family only ever a lone' as 'this whole foundation of earth wastes away'. ('Friendless' or 'friendlessness' is a translation of 'freondleasne', which is also translated as 'loneliness'.) Not a great deal is known about this poem or its author. Whether the wanderer in the poem is literally an exile or not, he certainly writes of exile either literally or figuratively. To 'wander' is not the same as to 'walk' or 'travel'. Wandering implies a less purposive travelling, either entirely aimless or in the sense of 'hiking' or walking for the sake of walking without an end-point or destination in mind. (The modern German *Wanderer* is translated in modern English as *hiker*.) *Don Quixote* (Cervantes 2003) is something of a wanderer (and Quixote wanders all-too-briefly into Chapter 9). In the Anglo-Saxon poem, wandering is done alone, as others close to the wanderer are dead or otherwise absent. Is there really 'no one living' to talk with? Perhaps no-one present, at least. But the idea of being 'the last person in the world' is itself a common literary device and, I suspect, a common feeling for people in solitude.

Thoreau writes that 'at night there was never a traveller passed my house, or knocked at my door, more than if I were the first or last man' (Thoreau 2006, p. 141), even though he was at Walden Pond just a walk away from his mother's house. Back in the seventeenth century, Góngora's *The Solitudes* (Góngora 2011) has the form of a classical quest, but the solitude experienced in 'nature' is itself the implied quest, and is at many points as careful a study of nature (and personhood experienced in nature) as that of Thoreau. (More on him in Chapter 8.) In the twentieth century, Sillitoe writes of *The Loneliness of the Long-Distance Runner*:

> I've just come up out of the sunken lane, kneed and elbowed, thumped and bramble-scratched, and the race is two-thirds over, and a voice is going like a wireless in my mind saying that when you've had enough of feeling good like the first man on earth of a frosty morning, and you've known how it is to be taken bad like the last man on earth on a summer's afternoon, then you get at last to being like the only man on earth and don't give a bogger about either good or bad, but just trot on with your slippers slapping the good dry soil that at least would never do you a bad turn. (Sillitoe 1958, p. 42)

The ability to feel wholly isolated, even not of this world, whilst wandering is a feature of travelling because a journey, especially one that is unclear in its precise route or destination (or whose route and purpose is not currently in mind), gives a person an experience of the liminal, the in-between, neither wholly *here* nor wholly *there*. Depending on who is experiencing this liminality, there may be a sense of being between life and death, human life and merging with nature, a human and a non-human world, home and 'nowhere'. In Sillitoe's novel, this is experienced as an escape, a largely positive experience. The protagonist is being punished, restricted to a borstal (a residential school for young offenders), so he was psychologically escaping, in his running. Only when he became conscious of the competitive elements of his situation (his school was competing with a more 'respectable' school, and his headteacher was relying on him to win) did he leave the solitudinous liminality of running, to return to a world populated by people, people willing to exploit him.

The physicality of running is central to Sillitoe's novel, and physicality plays a role in many modern exile narratives, with the character 'Indian' running free at the end of *One Flew Over the Cuckoo's Nest* (Forman 1975; Kesey 2002), and relentless work gangs central to *One Day in the Life of Ivan Denisovich* (Solzhenitsyn 1963) or *Cool Hand Luke* (Pearce 1965; Rosenberg 1967). External exiles are 'exercised' by their travels and the work needed to survive beyond the comforts of home. It is the hard agricultural work and the pain of childbirth that Adam and Eve were said to be given as punishments, as exiles from the Garden of Eden. Both internal and external exiles seem to be accompanied by awareness of one's physicality. Being 'out of place' is a stimulus for being aware of one's body, and a lack of – or limited experience of – human contact may have a similar effect. The solitary exile may become conscious of treading the tracks of exile, the physicality of 'treading' being stronger than 'walking'. By the rivers of Babylon, 'we sat down', and this exile is remembered in the eating of bitter herbs at Pesach. Conscious of one's body may be both an expression of the pain of exile and, in artistic representations, a symbolic projection of that suffering. It may also be both an expression and symbol of the reality of escape, a positive feeling. The rich ambiguity of exile is, like the rich ambiguity of solitude, well represented in the arts. It is a song that expresses the inability to sing, in exile. There are similar ambiguities in the long tradition of solitudinous 'escape from the self' and 'comfort in oneself', the topic of the next chapter.

3

Ecstasy and Enstasy, Successful and Failed

Comfy with myself, alone: a steadied wisdom is all that I need
Or shall I find an escape, a way to reach the beyond?

Summary

The solitary experiences of ecstasy, or going 'out of oneself', and enstasy, being comfortable 'within oneself', have been central to religious practices throughout history. Both illustrate how a person can find solitude even in company, and both are illustrated by the arts and, almost as much, by the ways in which artists isolate themselves in order to focus on their arts. Religious solitudes such as St Anthony and Julian of Norwich, and in a different way Blake, are good examples of how withdrawal may be intended precisely to be able to contribute socially, politically and/or culturally. Some other solitudes, such as those of Hölderlin, Gould, Lowry, Wittgenstein, Woolf, Larkin and Burton, are perhaps more like *failed* ecstasies or enstasies, albeit no less interesting or creative for that. Dürer seems able to create images of both successful and failed ecstasy or enstasy.

Some key artists: Percy Grainger (1882–1961), Julian of Norwich (1343–1416), Friedrich Hölderlin (1770–1843), William Blake (1757–1827), Glenn Gould (1932–1982), L. S. Lowry (1887–1976), Virginia Woolf (1882–1941), Samuel Beckett (1906–1989), Philip Larkin (1922–1985), Albrecht Dürer (1471–1528), Robert Burton (1577–1640)

Introduction: Definitions

Ecstasy and enstasy are words that were first popularised in religious contexts. Religion is still an important context for them, and yet the terms and what they refer to have stretched well beyond religions, making them significant for many arts, ancient to modern. Both terms are associated with solitude and silence, usually in positive senses. And although the two words are opposite in their meanings, there is a way of thinking of them as remarkably similar, especially when seen through a solitudinous lens. This chapter therefore explores the arts of ecstasy and enstasy. Sometimes, attempts at ecstasy or enstasy fail, and artists describe and create failure as well as success. (Eco 2011 writes eloquently on how ugliness can make for beautiful art: art does not restrict itself to the good and the beautiful; the bad and the ugly, the failing and the inadequate, are all there.) From pictures of St Antony's ecstatic visions to the trance music of modern clubs, selfhood is escaped (or is it achieved?) artistically, in all periods of history.

First, the terms 'ecstasy' and 'enstasy' should be described. Etymologically, the terms are quite straightforward. 'Stasis' is one's place, so ec-stasy is to go out of one's place, to leave the self, as it were, or, in terms related to the modern drug known as 'ecsatsy', to 'get off your head'. Being 'ecstatic' has come to mean 'overwhelming happiness or joyful excitement' (SOED), but that meaning is not a theme of this chapter. At least, not a central theme: joy may be an *outcome* of ecstasy, but it is not central to the chapter. It is the 'leaving oneself' (e.g. in religious and/or drug-induced senses) that is more of a focus. 'Enstasy', meanwhile, is a much less well-known word and is not – at the time of writing – in most major English language dictionaries, despite its use in various texts over many decades. To have en-stasy is to be within your place, to be in the self. In that sense, as I say, it is the opposite of ecstasy. I came across the word myself in a translation of the Bhagavad-Gītā (Zaehner 1992, pp. 143, 149, 151), one of the central sacred texts of what is called Hinduism. Since then, I have also heard it used as a description of a type of yoga – itself derived from (or an active part of) Hindu practice – and of particular portrayals of the Buddha (the Gautama Buddha) as 'samādhi' or 'enstatic'. In modern Greek, enstatic (ενστατικός) is used more widely, roughly meaning solitudinous or inward-looking: its use is loose, rather like 'ecstatic' is loosely used in English to mean 'happy'. In this chapter, both ecstasy and enstasy are used in the slightly narrower senses of leaving oneself or being within oneself.

Exemplifying Ecstasy and Enstasy

How have artists, writers and musicians portrayed ecstasy and enstasy? This history of enstasies and ecstasies stretches far beyond narrowly religious contexts, although some may be captured by the modern phrase 'spiritual but not religious'. But first accounts are in the sacred texts of Judaism, Christianity, Hinduism and Buddhism, along with artistic and musical interpretations of those texts. The arts come into their own in more mystical tradition of these religions, and I should add Sufi Islam to the list, as the poetry and music of that tradition is strikingly both ecstatic and enstatic (Rumi 1995). There are religious portrayals of failed ecstasies or enstasies, but failure is more commonly portrayed outside religious arts.

Let us start with a song. The Jewish and Christian *Song of Songs*, also known as the *Song of Solomon*, is one of the oddest biblical texts. It does not seem to mention God or, indeed, anything particularly religious. It appears at first reading to be an erotic love song, and its apparent 'rudeness' makes it an especially popular 'discovery' for adolescents. And yet it was chosen for inclusion in scripture. Advice from an authoritative ancient rabbi, Akiva, tells readers that they must not read or sing it with a 'trilling' voice, in order to avoid any hint of eroticism: 'He who trills his voice in the chanting of the Song of Songs in the banquet halls and makes it a secular song has no share in the world to come' (Bowker 1997, p. 914). Most religious commentaries on the Song of Songs say that it describes humanity's relationship with God. To understand the song is to understand how we can reach beyond ourselves to be 'in touch with' God, with an emphasis on 'touch' or, rather, with all the senses. Sight, taste, smell, sound and touch: all are referenced in this most *sensual* (in both senses of that word) of texts. Ellen Davis refers to the Song of Songs as expressing 'the ecstasy of intimacy' (Davis 2019, p. 360). An intimacy, a *sense* of God, can be achieved, and this *Song of Songs* describes that experience. Why is that a good example of *solitary* ecstasy? Well, the song does not talk of 'humanity' experiencing ecstasy but an individual person. Judaism is a very 'we' religion: almost all prayers are written to be said as 'we' and 'us', not 'I' and 'me'. (The prayer used by Christians beginning 'Our Father ...' is in this same tradition.) So a whole book of the Bible that has 'me', 'you', 'I', 'my', 'he', 'him' throughout is clearly much less communal and more solitudinous even if 'I' also represents humanity. And a personal encounter with a god, like a personal encounter with nature, is generally portrayed as solitudinous if no other *people* are involved.

Ecstasy is an individual achievement, even if experienced in company. Or perhaps I should say ecstasy is – in the language of the *Song of Songs* – an achievement of intimacy beyond the self, in this case with God. That in turn reminds us of the difficulty of pinning solitude down. Are you in solitude only if not in the company of other people? What about other animals? Many people describe going on a solitary walk in the company of dogs. Is a shepherd in solitude, accompanied by sheep and perhaps a dog too? Did the 'birdman of Alcatraz', Robert Stroud (mentioned in Chapter 2), have company when in solitary confinement with his canaries? And if there is a god or gods, present everywhere, are we ever in solitude? What about non-animal living things or landscapes with or without living inhabitants? Wordsworth describes the 'bliss of solitude' stimulated by the memory of a solitudinous encounter with daffodils. Solitude involves a variety of disengagements, 'perceptual, cognitive, emotional, actional' (Koch 1994, p. 52), but disengagement from *what*? In most accounts of solitude, it is, understandably, human disengagement. Or to be more precise, disengagement from *living* human beings, as solitude is often used of those wandering through graveyards. What about those who are alive but sleeping? Kafka describes his nocturnal solitude whilst the rest of the household sleeps.

> Franz Kafka [was] waiting impatiently for his parents and sisters to go to bed so that he could have the dining room table for writing, writing that ran away into the night, every night for most of his adult life. Only in that solitary silence could he relax and breathe, only there could he write through and write beyond the ever-present anxiety. And for that writing, 'one can never be alone enough … there can never be enough silence around one … even night is not night enough'. (Koch 1994, p. 2, ellipses in original)

There is no clear boundary between solitude and the absence of solitude, although the ambiguity of the term makes it more, not less, interesting. And the intimate ecstasy of the *Song of Songs* is as good an example of ecstatic solitude as any. The sensuality of the poetry reminds us of how solitude can make us more aware of the sheer physicality of existence. In Chapter 2, the solitude of the runner was a theme, and ecstatic solitude is often of a similar kind.

Before leaving the Song of Songs, it is worth considering how it has been interpreted by artists since biblical times. The Australian composer Percy Grainger composed a piece known as *Love Verses from the Song of Solomon* (Gardiner 1996). Only seventeen when he composed this, Grainger was opposed to institutional religion and may have chosen the text specifically because of its lack of mention of God or other explicitly religious themes, in addition to its vibrant sensuality. Grainger was someone who thought of sensuality as important to musical performance. An odd illustration of this was his habit, as a concert pianist, of running to the concert venue and running onto the stage, sweating and out of breath, to give energy to the performance and to project the physicality of performance to the audience. The *Love Verses* are sensual and yet rather contemplative, suited to the spiritual or transcendent (i.e. ecstatic) if not religious origin of the verses. Marc Chagall, a near-contemporary of Grainger, painted a series of *Song of Songs* paintings (Chagall 2007). These add horses and birds to an ostensibly human pair of lovers, a rich and full landscape that is only solitudinous in being sufficiently fantastical and anti-realist to be primarily of the imagination rather than describing 'real' lovers – and horses and birds. An earlier artistic interpretation by Egon Tschirch (https://www.youtube.com/watch?v=wjuDj5zDNMI) may have influenced Chagall. A later one by Dalí (https://www.thedaliuniverse.com/en/song-songs-solomon-illustrated-book) is – surprisingly for that artist – somewhat more literal, if still describing human lovers. A biblical print from the seventeenth century is captioned *King Solomon composing the Song of Songs in ecstasy* (https://www.lookandlearn.com/history-images/M595471/King-Solomon-composing-the-Song-of-Songs-in-ecstasy), with the king sitting alone on a chair almost surrounded by curtains but visited by an angel or muse with the text in her hand.

Alone in the Desert

Solitudinous visits by angels, communion with God (as described of Moses in Chapter 2) or other sacred or divine beings became a staple of Christian arts, especially following the solitudinous experiences of the Desert Fathers. Once Christianity was becoming an established religion in the Roman Empire, a tradition arose of Christians seeking solitude away from cities and towns. In the Middle East, this meant going into the desert. The first of these Desert Fathers (and there were also some less-well-known Desert Mothers), or at least the first to become famous for it, was the man who came to be known as St Anthony, and also Anthony the Great, the Anchorite, the hermit. Living in the late third and early fourth centuries of the common era, his experiences were eloquently described in a hagiography by Athanasius (1980), who lived in the fourth century during which Emperor Constantine finally made Christianity the empire's official religion. Hagiographies have come to be thought of as unduly generous and complimentary, but originally the term simply meant a biography of a saint, and it was Athanasius who established the genre. Describing Anthony's early life as a somewhat solitary and perhaps 'ill-fitting' young man, it was as a young adult that he retreated to the desert, living in a cave. He was not the only person retreating to the desert, but his experience was hugely influential, and introduced a whole tradition of solitary religiosity to Christianity, both in solitary retreats and in closed isolated communities, that is, monasteries and convents.

Anthony lived for twenty years in his cave – a cave-like ruined fort, apparently, but more often described as a cave. Followers brought him food, lowered into the cave on a rope. Occasionally he was persuaded out of this place, for example, to settle a religious dispute. And later he set up communities living a strictly disciplined religious life, these becoming known as monasteries. Clearly then, Anthony's life was full of engagement with others, mixed with intense and harsh solitude. It is the solitude that provides the most striking examples of his ecstatic religious experiences. Anthony is said to have been 'tempted' in his solitude. To be tempted was well-established in Christianity, as in all religious traditions. Jesus is said to have been tempted by the devil during his own desert retreat. A temptation is a rather weak word today, making us think of eating a fattening pudding. (I am tempted to say that this would have led to an alternative tradition of the Dessert Fathers, but that would not be fitting.) The meaning of 'temptation' in ancient texts, however, is closer to a 'test': it was not just a sinful opportunity, but a real test of one's moral strength. Anthony described being visited by many kinds of monstrous creatures. His temptations were truly horrifying, in Athanasius's account. It is a narrative of ecstatic horrors, escaping from human solitude to be in the company of demons. It is also an account of religious devotion expressed through spiritual exercises – also ecstatic experiences attempting to be in communion with God. Athanasius says the demonic visitations may have come at the behest of the devil, or God might have sent them to test Anthony.

The temptations have been portrayed vividly by artists in recent centuries. Best known are the rather genteel and domestic account by Murillo, a baroque painter in mid-seventeenth-century Spain, and the much more shocking account in the late fifteenth century by Michelangelo (https://kimbellart.org/col lection/ap-200901). In Michelangelo's painting, completed when the artist was just twelve or thirteen years old and based on a previous print by Schongauer, a serene elderly looking Anthony floats in mid-air (having 'escaped' his solitary cave) whilst sharp-toothed-and-clawed demons tear at him. Murillo's painting is more of 'visions' (http://www.hispalis.net/turismo_y_cultura/monumentos/catedral/san_antonio.phtml), whilst in a comfortable-looking room, an image similar to that of Dickens dreaming up his characters portrayed by Buss in 1875 (https://www.charlesdickenspage.com/buss.html). Renaissance ecstasy seemed to have more 'bite'. The writing of Anthony's life by Athanasius has a surprisingly empathetic description of the solitudinous tests. This may have been helped by Athanasius's own conflict-filled life as a bishop sent into exile himself by four different Roman emperors, albeit, unlike Ovid, returning each time. So his Life of Anthony may, like many biographies, have also been something of an autobiography. (It may simply be that biographers choose people to write about who echo something of their own life.) And, like his subject, Athanasius was sainted after death. MacCulloch (2013) refers to Anthony's retreat, and that of the other Desert Fathers and Mothers, as a 'radical act of tax-dodging' (MacCulloch 2013, p. 38), promoted to almost-martyrdom by Athanasius as the imperial persecution of Christians (resulting in actual martyrdom) had ended by Anthony's time. I have yet to see artistic portrayals of Anthony as tax-dodger, though.

Nowhere to Go, but All Shall Be Well

Someone with a major role in Christianity who was *not* made a saint (for a reason I will give later in this account) is Julian of Norwich. St Anthony was known as an 'anchorite'. This was a term used to refer to someone 'anchored' to a single place to achieve solitude for religious reasons. The practice of living as an anchorite or anchoress became popular in England from the thirteenth century, a thousand years after Anthony's retreat (Georgianna 1981, p. 36). Another of Anthony's descriptions was as a 'hermit', but hermits are not always restricted to a single space. In thirteenth-century England, there were fewer places to live as a wandering hermit, if you wanted to maintain solitude. Almost everywhere in England was, by then, within half a day's walk from a town or village. So one could visit a hermit for lunch, and still be home for tea. This made an eremitic life less attractive. (In later centuries, it became fashionable to host a hermit on one's large country estate, but that was more of a hermit-as-exhibit, or in Campbell's phrase 'ornamental gnome', than the earlier practice, however sincerely the hermit's religious wish for solitude, Campbell 2013.) So from the thirteenth century, many churches across England had a stone-built room added to the side of the church as an anchorhold. (Beverley, the town where I currently live, had one on both the churches in the town.) Before entering an anchorhold, which was a commitment for the rest of one's life, the anchorite or anchoress was given the sacraments of the dying, as they would henceforth be, as it were, 'dead to the world'. However, food and other basic services could be obtained, and some might have a servant in an adjoining room able to come and go and not themselves locked in.

The most famous English inhabitant of an anchorhold, and one of the most important English authors of the medieval period, was Julian of Norwich. Ill and believing she was close to death, Julian (the name of the saint to whom her church was dedicated, not her own given name – which remains unknown) had a series of religious visions. She applied for and became an anchoress, but only after she had, as a much younger woman, already wished to be ill to the point of death:

> I quite sincerely wanted to be ill to the point of dying, so that I might receive the last rites of Holy Church, in the belief – shared by my friends – that I was in fact dying. … I wanted to undergo all those spiritual and physical sufferings I should have were I really dying, and to know, moreover, the terror and assaults of the demons – everything, except death itself! My intention was that I should be wholly cleansed thereby through the mercy of God, and that thereafter, because of that illness, I might live more worthily of him. Perhaps too I might even die a better death, for I was longing to be with my God. (Julian of Norwich 1966, pp. 63–4)

As well as such elements of autobiography, she wrote of her visions, becoming the first known English-language authoress. One of her first visions was of seeing the world as a whole.

> And he [i.e. God] showed me more, a little thing, the size of a hazelnut, on the palm of my hand, round like a ball. I looked at it thoughtfully and wondered, 'What is this?' And the answer came, 'It is all that is made.' I marvelled that it continued to exist and did not suddenly disintegrate; it was so small. And again my mind supplied the answer, 'It exists, both now and for ever, because God loves it.' In short, everything owes its existence to the love of God. (Julian of Norwich 1966, p. 68)

(In a comparable account, from what is known as the Hindu tradition, Krishna's mother Yashoda hears that the boy Krishna has been eating mud, but when she looks in his mouth, she sees the whole universe, and this vision is well represented in art, http://www.harekrsna.de/artikel/krishnas-mouth.htm.) Julian's most famous statement, often translated as 'all shall be well, and all shall be well, and all manner of thing shall be well', comes from her account of sin:

> I did not see *sin*. I believe it has no substance or real existence. It can only be known by the pain it causes. This pain is something, as I see it, which lasts but a while. It purges us and makes us know ourselves, so that we ask for mercy. The passion of our Lord is our comfort against all this – for such is his blessed

will. Because of his tender love for all those who are to be saved our good Lord comforts us at once and sweetly, as if to say, 'It is true that sin is the cause of all this pain; but it is all going to be all right; it is all going to be all right; everything is going to be all right.' These words were said most tenderly, with never a hint of blame either to me or to any of those to be saved. (Julian of Norwich 1966, p. 104, with a different translation of the key phrase used here.)

Surviving more than forty years as an anchoress, even in her isolation, Julian became one of the most famous religious sages of the late fourteenth and early fifteenth centuries. Julian wrote two accounts of her visions, a shorter and a longer version, and talked with visitors, and seems to have corresponded, too. And yet her isolation was itself a powerful symbol of her piety and simplicity.

There were guides written for those in anchorholds, the most famous of which was the *Anchrene Wisse*, the wisdom of the anchorhold (Savage and Watson 1991), written by a (male) priest for women in anchorholds. This advised anchoresses to live simply but to avoid punishing themselves too much:

Let no one belt herself with any kind of belt next to the body, except with her confessor's leave, nor wear any iron or hair, or hedgehog-skins; let her not beat herself with them, nor with a leaded scourge, with holly or briars, nor draw blood from herself without her confessor's leave; let her not sting herself with nettles anywhere, nor beat herself in front, nor cut herself, nor impose on herself too many severe disciplines to quench temptations at one time ... [as] I would rather that you well endure harsh words than harsh hairclothes. (Savage and Watson 1991, p. 202)

In a revealing account of life in anchorholds, the advice continued to recommend to anchoresses that they might own farm animals and might trade from their anchorholds, but should avoid taking an active role in local disputes.

My dear sisters, unless need drives you and your director advises it, you must not have any animal except a cat. An anchoress who has animals seems more like a housewife than Martha was; she cannot easily be Mary, Martha's sister, with peace in her heart. For then she has to think of the cow's food, of the herdsman's hire; to flatter the bailiff, curse him when he impounds it, and pay the damages anyway. It is a hateful thing, Christ knows, when people in a town complain about an anchoress' animals. Now then, if anyone has to have one, see that it does not bother or harm anyone, and that her thought is in no way fastened on it. An anchoress ought to have nothing which draws her heart outward. (Savage and Watson 1991, p. 201)

Such is life, for the generally well-off anchoresses and anchorites. Or, should I say, such is death, as life is said to have ended for them. (Most did, in fact, live out their lives in anchorholds, although some were able and willing to leave.) A (post-)modern book on Julian suggests we might all benefit from being part-time anchoresses or anchorites:

> Perhaps in postmodernity there must, in addition to those who are fully enclosed, also be 'part-time' anchoresses and anchorites, those whose lives and duties are so focused as to make times and spaces for withdrawal from routine and willingness to stand at an angle to the contemporary symbolic in openness to the divine. Perhaps there are many who are invited to be anchoresses and anchorites of the heart. (Jantzen 2000, p. xxiii)

Julian's visions included more optimistic views of the world than one might expect from someone who was ill and thought she was dying. If 'all shall be well', as quoted above, then what about hell? She looked into hell and saw that no-one was there. God in his grace would not put someone there, and 'hell' is no more than the experience of sin (Julian of Norwich 1966, p. 123). Hell is not talked about much in the modern world, other than as a much weaker term: 'I've had a hellish week at work' is unlikely to imply anything from Dante. There is an odd asymmetry in today's often delicate culture. Amongst self-declared Christians, far more believe in the existence of heaven than believe in the existence of hell. This is not just about where they or their loved ones will go, or have gone, but the very existence of the place of torment. Julian's theology is an interesting solution to a modern religious challenge: there *is* a hell, but it is unpopulated. A theologian, who was also a nun, told me that this was why Julian had never been declared a saint. For all her suffering, and for all her huge influence on her contemporary world and her continuing influence ever since, Julian said that hell was empty. How could the church continue to maintain discipline without this ultimate threat of going to hell? (In the 1980s, UK education minister John Patten said that school discipline would be improved if more children were persuaded of the risk of going to hell, Macleod 1992: why would churches give up their persuasive powers if even education ministers thought them so useful?)

Readers of Julian's books are often struck by their kindness, care and humanity. To live such a life, a life beset by illness and one led bricked up on the side of a church for more than forty years, and to live it so humanely, is as impressive today as it seems to have been in her own day. Solitude has rarely had such an eloquent advocate, although little of Julian's writing is itself about solitude. It focuses instead on her understanding of Jesus, of the Trinity, the father, son and holy spirit. These solitudinous experiences of communion with the sacred and divine were – well, were they solitudinous? Julian's creativity (creative in the sense of the ability to write original theology, not the ability to 'make things up') seems to have been hugely enhanced by her existence as an anchoress. Her poetic writing communicates directly with modern audiences. An earlier religious figure, also suffering from illness early in life, yet living into old age, was Hildegard of Bingen (2001). Hildegard was a poet and composer, and also a scientist and medical writer as well as being a theologian, and from her thirties was an abbess who set up convents across what is now called Germany. A far more 'social' figure than Julian, Hildegard nevertheless attributes her inspiration to the visions she had from childhood onwards. She describes these specifically as not being heard or seen with her ears and eyes, but internally. Her solitude is less physical or spatial than that of Julian, but just as perceptually and emotionally withdrawn. And Hildegard, even more productively than Julian, was generously creative out of her religious visions.

Hölderlin Alone

Solitude and ecstasy are paired in these two medieval women. Such religious ecstasies have a continuous history from biblical times to the present day. In more recent times, having visions or hearing voices is more likely to be attributed to illness – mental or physical – but even in these times, attempts are made to differentiate the more or less substantively and/or religiously founded voices and visions from those that might be regarded as evidence of illness. Julian's own description of illness and visions itself blurs the distinction, of course. Also at the boundary of ecstasy and illness was Hölderlin, whose poetry, although not primarily conventionally religious, does describe an attempt to break through isolation, to become ecstatically one with the world. Repeatedly failing in attempts to become one, he describes the temptation and suffering implied by this attempt in the two-line poem *The Root of All Evil*, written in 1799:

The Root of All Evil
Being at one is god-like and good, but human, too human, the mania

Which insists there is only the One, one country, one truth and one way.

(Hölderlin 1990, p. 139, with an alternative translation provided by Behrmann 2020, p. 38)

As an undergraduate in Tübingen, Hölderlin studied with and was a good friend of the philosophers Hegel and Schelling. There followed an impressive literary career whilst his friends progressed their even more impressive careers in academic philosophy. Hölderlin's paid work was less secure, working as a tutor as well as earning money from his poetry. Schiller, writer of the play *William Tell* (Schiller 1988) and the *Ode to Joy* used by Beethoven in his ninth symphony, was an advisor to and sponsor of Hölderlin. If not quite flourishing, Hölderlin's writing was hugely influential, including on the philosophy of his friends. But as he was finishing his major poetic novel, *Hyperion* (Hölderlin 1990), itself an exploration of the tension between solitude and oneness with the world described as his great work of 'lost oneness' (Guignon 2004, p. 53), he gradually seemed to sink further into himself and further away from the rest of humanity.

Diagnosed as ill, with the diagnosis roughly corresponding to what would today be called schizophrenia, after several years he could no longer live independently, and was given a room in the house of a carpenter who had admired Hölderlin's poetry. The poet lived there for thirty-six years. In occasional lucid periods he would write short poems and letters. Befriended by the much younger poet Waiblinger, it was Waiblinger who wrote the first biography of Hölderlin (Waiblinger 2018). Some more recent commentators have made the second, 'quiet', half of Hölderlin's life into a Romantic dénouement of his earlier poetry, a meaningful silence that gives added significance to the earlier work. This is beautifully expressed by Steiner, in his account of language and silence.

> Hölderlin's silence has been read not as a negation of his poetry but as, in some sense, its unfolding and its sovereign logic. The gathering strength of stillness within and between the lines of the poems have been felt as a primary element of their genius. As empty space is so expressly a part of modern painting and sculpture, as the silent intervals are so integral to a composition by Webern, so the void places in Hölderlin's poems, particularly in the late fragments, seem indispensable to the completion of the poetic act. His posthumous life in a shell of quiet, similar to that of Nietzsche, stands for the word's surpassing of itself, for its realization not in another medium but in that which is its echoing antithesis and defining negation, silence. (Steiner 1967, pp. 47–8)

Eloquent as this description is, it sits uncomfortably with Wäblinger's account of a troubled poet balancing the real and unreal, with fragments of insight only occasionally breaking through. Hölderlin's 'madness' (the word used by Wäblinger) is described in a sensitive and empathetic way – and all the more terrifying for that care. 'He held a particular fascination for the pantheistic

One and All inscribed in giant Greek letters on the wall above my work desk' (Waiblinger 2018, p. 50), although it was a little earlier, in his late twenties, that he wrote *The Root of All Evil*. 'I once discovered amongst his papers a terrifying phrase replete with mystery', Waiblinger says: 'After honouring the renown of a list of Greek heroes and the beauty of the realm of gods, he says: "Now for the first time I understand humankind, because I dwell far from it and in solitude"' (Waiblinger 2018, p. 58).

In *Hyperion*, Hölderlin wrote of a child as 'wholly what it is' as 'the child is peace; it has not yet come to be at odds with itself' (quoted in Guignon 2004, p. 53). (The poet Larkin, 150 years later, similarly describes the easy solitude of childhood – when solitude simply 'lay at hand' – being lost in adulthood, as described in Chapter 8, and Larkin 1988, pp. 56–7.) Hölderlin himself seemed to become increasingly at odds with himself, and increasingly troubled by the solitude he had long sought. Krell says that 'when the German poet Hölderlin was twenty-five, he wrote to Schiller, who at that time was a kind of foster-father to him: "I am living a very solitary life, and I believe it is good for me"' (Krell, in Jones 2019, p. 24). However, this was not to last, as his long-sought solitude became a painful and lonely isolation. Krell continues:

> Six incredibly creative years later, he was less sure. He wrote to his friend Christian Landauer: 'Tell me, this being solitary – is it a blessing or a curse? My nature determines me to it, and the more purposefully I choose my state with a view to finding out who I am, the more irresistibly I am forced back into it again and again – this being lonely.' (Krell, in Jones 2019, p. 24, quoting Hölderlin 2009, p. 197)

The second half of his life, Hölderlin struggled with unhealthy solitude, with the experience of sought-and-found 'being at one', a solitude that, when found, is a lonely place. His host family looked after him well, but his birth family and friends either drifted away or pre-deceased him. With a spirituality that had more in common with Ancient Greek religion than the Christianity of his undergraduate theology studies, Hölderlin pushed solitude to the centre of his art. In *Hyperion* he found his 'hermit' alter ego, a 'god-like and good' figure at risk of being 'only the One'. The love of Hyperion's life dies before they can be together and Hyperion becomes a hermit 'at one' with nature. But Hyperion's distance from humanity is much less successfully negotiated by Hölderlin. Understanding humanity and the world only by being at a distance from it, he ended up with a failing understanding yet still at a distance from humanity.

Blake and Troubling Ecstasies

The Romantic artist-suffering-in-an-attic became a cliché of nineteenth-century European culture, but Hölderlin lived his troubles too disturbingly for the cliché. Another major Romantic figure who pushed against Romantic clichés and who had a far from conventional spirituality was William Blake. Blake (2000), in his art (the poetry and pictures combined together into a single art), gives us ecstatic visions, sacred and terrifying, separately and together, a 'radical self-alienation', as Altizer (2009, pp. 34–5) describes it. The humans ecstatically reconfigured as god-like, in Blake's art, are as disturbing as Hölderlin's, and Blake's determined individualism made for as distinctive a contribution to Romantic ideas of solitude and ecstasy as that of Hölderlin. Individual 'wholeness', with a divine connection, is often portrayed with less terror than his German contemporary's visions. Blake describes himself as frequently having visions that inspired his work (Ackroyd 1996, passim). At a personal level, though Blake may have been considered argumentative and at times 'mad' (Altizer 2009, p. 33), he remained well able to look after himself and was married for forty-five years until his death. His works are good representatives of ecstatic religious art. As Altizer describes it, this is particularly an erotic ecstasy:

> The penultimate plate of Jerusalem depicts the apocalyptic union of Satan and Jerusalem, one that is perhaps the most erotic in all of Blake's art, as the body of Jehovah or Satan ecstatically penetrates the body of Jerusalem, a penetration realizing an absolute apocalypse, and an absolute apocalypse occurring here and now. If we have ever been given a Christian Tantric art, this is surely its purest expression, and one truly reversing the Augustinian foundation of Western Christianity. (Altizer 2009, p. 36)

An artist closer to Hölderlin in terms of his difficulty living independently, who also portrayed an ecstatic visionary view of life, was Richard Dadd. His obsessively detailed portrayals of supernatural beings often in pastoral scenes were mostly produced during his more than four decades in the 'criminal' wing of Bethlem hospital and then Broadmoor (Tromans 2011). He had killed his father, thinking him the devil, and might now be diagnosed with paranoid schizophrenia. Dadd's art was considered a form of therapy in the hospitals in which he lived. Living a solitudinous life, in the sense of focusing on his paintings whilst in hospital and having few relationships, as far as we can tell, whilst there, his isolation is transferred to his paintings. Although much is happening in most of the art, one of the striking features of them is that the people and supernatural beings (mostly fairies) usually have oddly staring eyes, rarely purposefully staring *at* something. In the twentieth century, another artist with a diagnosis related to what would now be called schizophrenia was portraying wide-eyed staring figures in his paintings. Louis Wain had been a popular illustrator and artist, famous for anthropomorphised cats (Beetles 2021). Later in life, he was overwhelmed by illness, and his humorous cat paintings became more strange, with staring eyes and surrounded by abstract backgrounds. Wain's personal isolation at his stage of his life, though reflected in his paintings, does not provide such a vivid portrayal of ecstatic solitude as did the art of Blake or Dadd, or the poetry of Hölderlin. Instead, a different form of ecstatic solitude, also prefigured in the early nineteenth century, became more popular through the twentieth century. That was drug-induced ecstatic visionary art. From Thomas De Quincey's essay *Confessions of an Opium-Eater* (De Quincy 2013) through the works of Wilkie Collins, Edgar Allan Poe, Charles Baudelaire and Arthur Conan Doyle, and on to twentieth-century figures such as Jean Cocteau, William Burroughs or Aldous Huxley: all described opiate-induced ecstatic experiences in their arts. De Quincey's contemporary Coleridge had already written *Kubla Khan* (Coleridge 1994, pp. 229–31) out of an opium-induced dream vision before De Quincey wrote his *Confessions* (De Quincey 2013), and in different ways, each of these artists describes ecstatic solitudes (or solitudinous ecstasies) associated with drugs. However, notwithstanding my own account of people using drugs or suffering from conditions that might be diagnosed as schizophrenia, there are many artists of ecstatic solitude without any such associations. Blake, perhaps, of those I have listed, along with St Anthony, and Julian of Norwich – who was ill but not (as far as we know) with any mental health or drug-induced difficulties. In the twentieth century, such a singular and surreal (Surrealist) artist as Dalí was quoted as dismissing the need to take drugs as 'the drug is *me*'.

Enstasies Successful and Failed

Ecstatic solitudes in art are accompanied by an overlapping tradition of enstatic solitudes. Enstasy is vividly described and explained in the ancient *Bhagavad-Gītā* (Zaehner 1969), part of the epic *Mahabharata*, the central text of what is known as Hinduism. In the *Bhagavad-Gītā*, the human hero, Arjuna, leads an army about to go into battle. The divine hero, Krishna, accompanies him. Arjuna says he cannot go to war against people who include members of his own family and his teachers, people he respects. Krishna responds, telling Arjuna he must fight and to do that he must become enstatic, a man of steadied thought. Withdraw into yourself, Krishna says, 'and when he draws in on every side / His senses from their proper objects, / As a tortoise might its limbs, / Firm-established is the wisdom of such a man' (Zaehner 1992, p. 326). Avoid striving after external things. In modern language, sports coaches recommend 'getting into the zone', to withdraw into yourself, avoiding external distractions. What will be, will be, and you must simply do what your own job is. Enstasy is needed for those entering a battle (literal or figurative), or for those needing to prepare for other major events. To be enstatic is to be comfortable within oneself. Enstatic yoga is familiar to many who practice yoga. But this gives an impression, at least in Europe and North America, of contemplative, quiet, spiritual practice, wearing comfortable clothing in an ashram or gym. It doesn't seem like an eve-of-war practice. Yet that is how it was promoted in the *Bhagavad-Gītā*.

Gandhi read the *Gītā* every day. An interviewer asked Gandhi about this, as 'at the end of the Gita Krishna recommends violence'. Gandhi responded: 'I do not think so. I am also fighting. I should not be fighting effectively if I were fighting violently' (Beckerlegge 2001, p. 307). This bridges the war-like and contemplative versions of yogic enstasy: the person of steadied thought is as it were ready for anything. And ready for nothing. Enstasy is a non-striving condition, not a 'psyching yourself up' for something – whether war or sport or anything else. Whereas ecstasy might be described as going beyond, as dynamic, enstasy is staying still. They are opposites. And yet they also have something in common, a solitudinous character. Ecstasy is so often achieved in solitude, with the escape from oneself not to connect with other people (which might be called 'dialogue', as in Buber's 'reaching out to' and 'touching' another person whilst 'remaining on one's own side of the relationship' Buber 2002a, p. xiv), but to connect with, for example, the sacred or divine, those who have already died, nature or the world as a whole. Connection to anything might be described as dialogic, but then solitude would be in danger of losing its meaning. Or dialogue could, instead, be 'allowed' in solitude. One form of ecstasy little discussed so far is erotic ecstasy. That is not necessarily solitudinous, but in the account by Anderson (2008), dance in its Modernist forms – of Isadora Duncan and of H.D. – is ecstatic and erotic, drawing on ancient rituals and avoiding the masculine fantasies of male Modernists such as Lawrence. It is a connection made by the body and is dialogic in the sense of physical engagement beyond the self in order to achieve ecstasy. Enstasy, however, is not dialogic, as that would imply a 'striving', yet it can also achieve a solitudinous oneness with the world. In the *Bhagavad-Gītā*, this is made clear. Withdrawal into oneself can achieve a nothingness that is a oneness with all (with the number zero coming out of this Indian culture, a number that means nothing but that when added to another number, increases it, Ifrah 1998), an enstasy that is therefore also an ecstasy.

> The athlete of the spirit 'sees the self in all being standing, all beings in the self: the same [Brahman] in everything he sees'. By detaching himself from all things he becomes Brahman, he sees 'self in self', he sees himself solely and simply as immortal, eternal, static, beyond time, One: but 'contact' with Brahman as other than himself transforms the vision from one of completely static en-stasy into one of all-comprehending ec-stasy: the cosmos flows into him, and he flows into the cosmos: the unity remains, but there is boundless diversity too. (Zaehner 1969, p. 233)

How is enstasy represented in the arts? Alongside the broad set of traditions known as Hinduism are the distinct traditions known as Buddhism. Gautama Buddha is often portrayed in an enstatic pose. There are many enstatic or *samādhi* Buddha statues and paintings. In these, the most famous of which is in Anuradhapura in Sri Lanka, the Buddha sits cross-legged with his hands upturned in his lap and his eyes half-closed. There are different Buddhist accounts of what 'state' the Buddha is in, in this statue, but an enstatic state is the most common. Within Buddhism and the more Buddhistic elements of Hinduism, life involves suffering resulting from striving for things. To withdraw into oneself without striving is a way of not suffering, therefore. In religious settings, the arts of enstasy include statues and paintings of Arjuna and Krishna, and of the Gautama Buddha. There are also abstract *samādhi* mandala paintings. Both Hindu and Buddhist chants and musical interpretations of, and support for, enstasy are widely available. The streaming service Spotify, for example, had at the time of writing a playlist named *The Path of Samadhi: Hindu Meditation Music*.

Within religious traditions, the arts are not simply portrayals of religious topics. They form parts of practices, whether forms of worship or meditation, ways of reaching yogic 'levels', ways and objects of contemplation and meditation. This has been as true of Jewish and Christian traditions as Hindu and Buddhist traditions. But arts have developed beyond narrowly religious settings even within the broad religious cultures. So enstatic arts, just like ecstatic arts, are widespread and stretch well beyond their origin stories. Much non-religious yoga music has many of the characteristics of more authentically enstatic music. And the art of musical performance is filled with techniques to relax into the performance without striving. Scales and exercises are used to practice technique without an attempt at 'expressive' (or dialogic) performance. The pianist Glenn Gould was known for practicing with the radio and/or television on in the background so that he could not hear his own playing (Ostwald 1997, p. 274), and his was a withdrawal often referred to as 'ecstatic' yet closer perhaps to enstasy. 'Solitude was for Glenn a cherished state of existence' (Ostwald 1997, p. 230).

> Solitude reduced the tensions he felt in the presence of other people and allowed him to focus exclusively on himself – his thoughts, feelings, music, and artistic aspirations. He often said that only under conditions of solitude was he able to experience ecstasy. (Ostwald 1997, p. 230)

Gould himself said that solitude was 'the prerequisite for ecstatic experience, especially the experience most valued by the post-Wagnerian artist – the condition of heroism' as 'one can't feel oneself heroic without having first been cast off by the world, or perhaps by having done the casting-off oneself' (Gould, quoted by Ostwald 1997, p. 267). Gould's solitude may, however, have exacerbated his hypochondria, yet 'he claimed that "isolation is the indispensable component of human happiness ... for every hour you spend in the company of other human beings, you need x number of hours alone"' (Ostwald 1997, p. 231, quoting Gould). The critic Said referred to Gould's 'ecstasy' as referring to 'John Donne's sense of standing outside of' (Said 2008, p. 196), a sense of 'not belonging to one's own time and place' (Said 2008, p. 197), yet he said Gould fell into a striving, a 'hunger for control' that was 'unappeasable' and that therefore led to 'loneliness' and to 'his health deteriorating and his body abused beyond resistance as a result' (Said 2008, p. 227). This is as much a (failed) enstasy, with striving continuing despite the separation and solitude, as a (failed) ecstasy, I would suggest. Yet at times the separation or withdrawal – including a withdrawal from all public performance, as well as the withdrawal from *listening*, at times, when he practiced – helped Gould focus on the physicality of the movements required to play the music. A withdrawal from music (musical performance to an audience and even from listening to his own music) in order to generate music is surely a kind of enstatic withdrawal. And if Gould could be said to have failed, ultimately, in his attempts at ecstasy or enstasy, in the meantime he did live a life of remarkable musical achievement.

Attempts at ecstasy can be successful, but forms of what may be called mental illness can be described as 'failed' ecstasies. The same might be said of enstasy. A 'failed' withdrawal into oneself could be described in terms of mental illness or disability, or could be described more simply in terms of loneliness, as with

Said's description of Gould. An artist like Lowry describes his art as coming from his loneliness. 'Had I not been lonely', Lowry said, 'none of my works would have happened' (formerly available at http://www.thelowry.com/ls-lowry/his-life-and-work/). His isolation or separation from other people is well expressed in his pictures. People are separated by an isolating white space. (Lowry is unusual in making white a colour of choice for portraying harsh, oppressive, social and psychological conditions.) There is rarely a relationship between the people portrayed. *Three Men and a Cat* is a good example. All three men stand apart, in a row, one facing the viewer and staring forward, one turned sideways but with his head turned to face the viewer and one turned away from the other two facing out to the right of the picture. The third man is holding what looks like a dog lead, but the lead loops out of the picture: the man is connected only to something unseen. The pale background separates the figures further. A cat walks left across the picture, with its head turned towards the men, none of whom seem to notice it. This picture was used in a research project where children aged seven or eight were asked to fill in 'thought bubbles' attached to each of the four characters. 'What were each of these characters thinking?', each child was asked. Their imagined thoughts were fascinating. All the children recognised the separation of the characters, and most described this in terms of rejection, suggesting they may have had an argument. The man on the left is interestingly described by Andrew (aged seven) as thinking 'Why am I all alone on the street?', notwithstanding the others in the picture, and he says of the man in the centre 'I ges we have fallen out'. He continues the theme, saying of the man on the right, 'Why did we fall out?' Cary (aged eight) suggests the left-hand man is thinking 'I am worried', whilst the man in the middle is thinking 'I am lost', and the one on the right 'I am fed up'. It is the cat that stimulates more active thoughts, and is given the critical viewpoint of the viewer of the picture. 'Why aren't those people talking' (Tanya, aged eight), or 'I have to listen to this every day' (Annie, aged seven), whilst for Cary (aged eight) the cat is thinking 'I need company', or for Amina (aged seven), 'I wish i found my mum so I can be with my mum all day' (all quoted from Stern 2014a, p. 158). The characters are on their own, then, but uncomfortably so. This is – I suggest – a vision of failed enstasy.

A Solipsistic Risk

Although not an artist, the 'failed enstasy' category might be applied to the early career period of Wittgenstein. In his *Tractatus*, he describes a confident solipsistic philosophy, describing it in his preface as the 'final solution' to all philosophy.

> The *truth* of the thoughts that are here communicated seems to me unassailable and definitive. I therefore believe myself to have found, on all essential points, the final solution [*endgültig gelöst* not the term *Englösung* used from 1941 to refer to the answer to the 'Jewish question'] of the problems. And if I am not mistaken in this belief, then the second thing in which the value of this work consists is that it shows how little is achieved when these problems are solved. (Wittgenstein 1961, p. 4)

The philosophy is immensely impressive and very influential, so it can hardly be said to have 'failed' in a conventional sense. However, there are two senses in which it can be seen as a model of failed enstasy. One is related to the scope of the philosophy, the sense in which, as Wittgenstein says, 'how little is achieved'. The origins of professional philosophy in Europe were in Greek traditions of philosophy as a guide to living well. By the early twentieth century, Wittgenstein represented a technical vision of philosophy as providing limited solutions to a limited range of questions. Philosophy seemed to have turned in on itself and withdrawn – quite explicitly – from all of ethics, aesthetics and religion. 'The world is all that is the case', and 'the world is the totality of facts, not of things' (Wittgenstein 1961, p. 5), and there is nothing meaningful to say on questions of value.

> The sense of the world must lie outside the world. In the world everything is as it is, and everything happens as it does happen: *in* it no value exists – and if it did exist, it would have no value.
>
> If there is any value that does have value, it must lie outside the whole sphere of what happens and is the case. For all that happens and is the case is accidental.
>
> What makes it non-accidental cannot lie *within* the world, since if it did it would itself be accidental.
>
> It must lie outside the world.
>
> So too it is impossible for there to be propositions of ethics.
>
> Propositions can express nothing that is higher.
>
> It is clear that ethics cannot be put into words.
>
> Ethics is transcendental.
>
> (Ethics and aesthetics are one and the same.)
>
> (Wittgenstein 1961, p. 71)

On the rest, Wittgenstein concludes, silence: 'What we cannot speak about we must pass over in silence' (Wittgenstein 1961, p. 74). There is much to be said about Wittgenstein's silence. He certainly valued matters of ethics, aesthetics and religion, so there is a good argument for Wittgenstein's silence being rich and significant, with Rée saying 'as far as he was concerned the fact that ethical and religious attitudes fall outside the limits of articulate thought was not their weakness but their glory' (Rée 2019, p. 8). But Wittgenstein's – or philosophy's – determined solipsism ('what the solipsist *means* is quite correct', Wittgenstein 1961, p. 57) and withdrawal from ethics can still be called an enstasy of a kind. It 'failed' to address many of the issues philosophy and humanity as a whole have considered vital. Kagge interprets the silence as a withdrawal from the trivial:

> It was the chatter that Wittgenstein overheard in the decadent bourgeois salons of Vienna at the start of the 1900s which motivated him to draw such conclusions. Wittgenstein believed that the empty babble of his fellow countrymen threatened the very meaning of life. I tend to agree with him. It is frighteningly easy to dispose of time. (Kagge 2017, p. 91)

Beyond Failed Enstasy

A second 'failure' of Wittgenstein's early philosophy comes directly from Wittgenstein. Withdrawing, himself, from philosophy (having 'solved' it), he became a schoolteacher and later designed a house for his sister. Eventually drawn back into professional philosophy, he came with new ideas on what philosophers might do and say. The more-than-a-suggestion of the later philosophy was that the earlier philosophy had not, after all, been philosophy's final solution. There was more to be done. His work was carried on mostly in discussion with other people, in a more dialogic form, in contrast to the *Tractatus* which had been set out like a mathematical proof.

Is Woolf's a failed enstasy, deepening into suicidal depression – both in the novels and in her own life – or an occasionally successful enstasy? Two elegant descriptions of something like enstasy are given in *The Years*:

> She threw herself on the ground, and looked over the billowing land that went rising and falling, away and away, until somewhere far off it reached the sea. Uncultivated, uninhabited, existing by itself, for itself, without towns or houses it looked from this height. Dark wedges of shadow, bright breadths of light lay side by side. Then, as she watched, light moved and dark moved; light and shadow went travelling over the hills and over the valleys. A deep murmur sang in her

ears – the land itself, singing to itself, a chorus, alone. She lay there listening. She was happy, completely. Time had ceased. (Woolf 2000b, p. 255)

And again:

He drew himself back. No more speech-making for me, he thought. He had his glass in his hand still. It was still half full of pale yellow liquid. The bubbles had ceased to rise. The wine was clear and still. Stillness and solitude, he thought to himself; silence and solitude … that's the only element in which the mind is free now.

Silence and solitude, he repeated; silence and solitude. His eyes half closed themselves. He was tired; he was dazed; people talked; people talked. He would detach himself, generalise himself, imagine that he was lying in a great space on a blue plain with hills on the rim of the horizon. (Woolf 2000b, p. 391, with ellipses in original)

Woolf's descriptions are almost Buddhistic.

Where else – where in the arts – in the mid-twentieth century are enstasies (failed or successful) to be found? Two examples here, both of which will return in later chapters. One is the poetry of Larkin, the other the novels and plays of Beckett. Larkin is one of the greatest writers on solitude and loneliness, Beckett one of the most powerful authors on quietist alienation. Both, however, also give insight into the attempt to be comfortably alone, when that attempt *fails*. In *Best Society* (Larkin 1988, pp. 56–7), Larkin bemoans the fact that we are all expected to be sociable, to the extent that all virtues are social. This is something I found myself, with a struggle (described earlier in this chapter) to discover an appropriate 'virtue word' for being good at solitude. 'Enstasy' was the word I found, but that was and is all too rarely used. Larkin wants solitude, and his title references Milton's 'solitude is sometimes best society' (Milton 1980, p. 311), and this poem is further analysed in Chapter 8. In another poem, *Vers de Societé*, the narrator gets an invitation to a party and imagines various offensive ways of saying 'no', before writing a polite 'yes'. It is the inability to achieve a good – a *virtuous* – solitude that makes these poems examples of failed enstasy.

Perhaps even better examples of failed enstasy are provided by Beckett in the *Trilogy* novels (Beckett 2009a, 2010a, 2010b). The protagonists suffer, they are unsuccessful and are barely alive. Both striving and not really caring, Beckett's characters are not peaceful. To an extent, the failure of enstasy is mitigated by the humour of the characters and their situations. The characters themselves laugh at their circumstances, and it is no coincidence that some of Beckett's favourite actors in his play were comedians and comic actors – such as Bert Lahr, the vaudeville comic and cowardly lion in the *Wizard of Oz* film, who premiered in Beckett's *Waiting for Godot* (Beckett 2010b). In Chapter 8, Beckett appears as a *reductio ad absurdum* of Modernism, laughing off the utopian absurdities of the post-Holocaust world, and he also provides a fine account of an attempt – albeit a failed attempt – to achieve 'quiet'. Failure generated one of Beckett's most quoted lines:

Ever tried. Ever failed. Never mind. Try again. Fail again. Fail better. (Beckett 2009b, p. 81)

Failure, then, rather than a calm acceptance, was clearly on Beckett's mind. Through the ages there have been other failed enstasies, and failed ecstasies.

Where does Dürer's *Melancolia I* (https://www.metmuseum.org/art/collect ion/search/336228) fit? An angel-figure sits, looking melancholy. Artists' and writers' tools surround the angel, but are being ignored. The angel is doing nothing, in a room full of things to do. There is a putti, a small angelic child, sitting in the background, also looking bored. Both ignore the other, and both appear to be intensely alone – like the Lowry figures. A dog lies curled on the floor, perhaps asleep, and also ignored. The angel stares into the middle distance, perhaps looking for, but not finding, inspiration, holding a compass in her hand, but doing nothing with it. Is this a picture of depressive melancholia as an emotional state, or a deeper commentary on the limitations of scientific intellectual struggle? Dürer drew more ecstatic pictures, notably the engraving of *St Jerome in His Study* (https://www.metmuseum.org/art/collection/sea rch/336229). So I would like to suggest *Melancolia I* is a picture of a more worldly condition. Despite the angel-figure being central, she is firmly placed amongst worldly implements. And rather than being lost *within* such intellectual pursuits, she appears to be failing to be so lost. Hence, I suggest, a failed enstasy rather than ecstasy.

A century after Dürer, Burton's *Anatomy of Melancholy* (2021) provides a fuller account of the various relationships between melancholy and solitude, with much on religion too. Religion and solitude may both cause or mitigate melancholy, he says, as may the arts. Taking us from the time Shakespeare was writing through to admirers as diverse as Keats and Beckett, it seems that ecstasy and enstasy were equally hard to find and prone to failure. Burton's own life was a model for his studies of melancholy, with his book a most 'confessional' book of troubles, and the withdrawal ('void of sorrow and void of fear') into a discomforting (failed?) somewhat suicidal enstasy.

When I go musing all alone
Thinking of diverse things fore-known,
When I guild Castles in the air,
Void of sorrow and void of fear,
Pleasing myself with phantasms sweet,
Methinks the time runs very fleet.
All my joys to this are folly,
Naught so sweet as melancholy.
… All my griefs to this are jolly,
Naught so sad as melancholy.
… None so sour as melancholy
… None so damn'd as Melancholy.
… Naught so harsh as Melancholy.
Naught so fierce as Melancholy.
… None so divine as Melancholy.

My pain, past cure, another Hell,
I may not in this torment dwell,
Now desperate I hate my life,
Lend me a halter or a knife.
All my briefs to this are jolly,
Naught so damn'd as Melancholy.

(Burton 2021, pp. 13–15)

For Burton, solitude can be a comfort or a problem. 'Cousin-german to Idleness, and a concomitant cause, which goes hand in hand with it, is *nimia solitudo*, too much solitariness', he says, with such 'enforced solitariness … commonly seen in Students, Monks, Friars, Anchorites, that by their order and course of life, must abandon all company, society of other men, and betake themselves to a private cell' (Burton 2021, p. 243). In contrast, 'voluntary solitariness is that which is familiar with Melancholy, and gently brings on like a Siren, a shoeing-horn, or some Sphinx to this irrevocable gulf' (Burton 2021, p. 244). The end of his book is often quoted as advice against all forms of solitude, but the text is worth quoting in full, as it seems, instead, that he is advising against the problematic forms of solitude (with idleness), having written so much, earlier in the book, about the positive forms of solitude:

I can say no more, or give better advice to such as are in any way distressed in this kind, than what I have given and said. Only take this for a corollary and conclusion, as thou tenderest thine own welfare in this, and all other melancholy, thy good health of body and mind, observe this short precept, give not way to solitariness and idleness. *Be not solitary, be not idle.* (Burton 2021, p. 1081)

Melancholy is inevitably described as something of a failure, even if at times 'sweet' or 'divine', and modern melancholies such as depression are seen as to be cured. This started with Burton. Currently, there are artistic approaches to 'cure' that replicate some earlier religious practices – often separated from their systematic religious context. A fashion for 'mindfulness' through colouring (such as Farrarons 2015) echoes mandala art of earlier centuries; writing prayers and wishes on paper in the shape of a leaf and hanging it on a prayer tree (as at https://www.pinterest.com/dixonumc/prayer-tree-ideas/) echoes many earlier prayer practices. Enstasy and ecstasy through art, even in such watered-down forms, remind us of a long tradition. The idea that artists are themselves representatives of solitude, prefigured in Dürer's disguised self-portrait, perhaps, or Shakespeare's Prospero, came into its own in the Romantic era. The artist *as* solitary is the theme of the following chapter.

4

The Artist as Solitary

My identity as a creative artist will hardly survive
If I am just a worker making things for the public

Summary

In the early nineteenth century, musicians such as Beethoven helped create the idea of the solitary artist, with the artist and the art together in the public's mind. This was part of the creation of a social and economic system in which artists could be financially independent, but it also involved a move to more self-regarding, sometimes 'heroic', solitary artists such as Percy Bysshe Shelley, along with the portrayals of solitude by Wordsworth or Coleridge. Mary Shelley's *Frankenstein* is a novel that speaks not only to the idea of the solitary artist but also to some of the trauma implied by this role. Even more troubling are artist-solitaries such as the poet Clare and the artist Friedrich. Novelists from Defoe through the Brontës and on to George Eliot and Awad developed new ways of describing solitude, and poets from Philips to Dickinson and Sarton saw more loneliness in their own artistic products.

Some key artists: Ludwig van Beethoven (1770–1827), Franz Liszt (1811–1886), Niccolò Paganini (1782–1840), William Wordsworth (1770–1850), Samuel Taylor Coleridge (1772–1834), Percy Bysshe Shelley (1792–1822), Mary Shelley (1797–1851), John Clare (1793–1864), Caspar David Friedrich (1774–1840), Daniel Defoe (1660–1731), Charlotte Brontë (1816–1855), Emily Brontë (1818–1848), George Eliot (1819–1880), Katherine Philips (1631/2–1664), Emily Dickinson (1830–1886), May Sarton (1912–1995), Mona Awad (1978–)

Introduction: Commercial Art

The early nineteenth-century image of the artist-as-solitary is – a little ironically – in large part a creation of changes in *social* conditions. Forms of patronage that had continued through much of the eighteenth century was by the end of the century in decline. Patronage had been from the church, royalty and aristocracy, with newer forms of support from civic and entrepreneurial sources. But there was also an increase in individualised commercialisation in both publishing and performance. This led to the emergence of the apparently 'self-made' artist. Rather than being salaried (or more commonly 'pensioned') by patrons, freelance artists were able to become famous and wealthy, whilst others suffered starvation in garrets. The self-created and ego-driven Romantic artist emerged as 'celebrities' in their own time, but also in the art and in the modes of performance. The image of the solitary artist was not invented by Romanticism, but it reached a peak then, and the image is still with us in modern artist-celebrity culture. (The artist David Hockney writes of how, aged eleven, he decided he wanted to be an artist and assumed this would mean working in a job painting Christmas cards or drawing posters, with painting for galleries only possible as a hobby, Hockney and Holzwarth 2021, pp. 6–7.) This chapter will centre on some of the significant European Romantic artist-solitaries, but will also work outwards from that, historically and geographically.

Solo Musicians

Starting with musicians, as it was in music that the commercial, artistic and personal changes of the Romantic period seemed to be most evident, with the figure of Beethoven looming large. Indeed, 'looming' is one of the qualities that particularly suit Beethoven. Recent comparators like Mozart – born just fourteen years earlier – had strikingly different careers. Although Mozart, after an early life as a child prodigy, tried to make his own way in the world selling publishing rights and performing to paying audiences, his was still a career mostly based on patronage. Beethoven, by reputation difficult to get on with and less prone to flatter patrons, developed a much more independent career. Moving from the virtuosic classical style of Mozart and of Haydn (the teacher he shared with Mozart), Beethoven moved towards a much more introspective style, less easy to understand and more for the 'serious' music lover than the general public. By the time he came to write his third symphony, initially dedicated to Napoleon as a revolutionary hero (rather than as a potential patron, aristocratic or not), he was going profoundly deaf and increasingly disillusioned by Napoleon's change to an imperial political dictatorship. The third symphony was being written at around the same time as his *Heiligenstadt Testament* (http://w3.rz-berlin.mpg.de/cmp/beethoven_heiligenstadt.html). In that letter to his brothers, he talked of his suicidal feelings resulting from his worsening hearing loss – troubling for anyone in their early thirties, a greater tragedy for a performer of music. Politically disillusioned, facing personal isolation, the third symphony was much larger and longer than previous classical pieces, more emotionally explicit, a grand piece by any standards and even more so in its own time. Beethoven's personal, social and political isolation, his breaking free from some earlier patrons, ended with one of the greatest of the early Romantic works of art.

The more isolated Beethoven became, the more personal his art – the more it rejected conventions and performance traditions. Larger orchestras, bigger sounds from pianos that had extended ranges and the power to fill concert halls as solo instruments, Beethoven's solitude was apparently freeing. Later in his life and even more profoundly deaf, his late piano sonatas and string quartets were thought by many at the time to be unplayable, unmusical and pointless, yet these have ensured his later reputation as a genius. Such pieces, like many of his mid- to late-period compositions, are indeed hard to perform, often 'unsympathetically' scored (unsympathetic to the performer, that is), and they do almost transcend musical forms. They would be avant-garde, in whichever garde one could imagine. Such a distinctive combination of personal circumstances and artistic skills, the Beethoven figure – a bad-tempered, isolated, glowering, looming artist, breaking with convention and making no concessions to performers or audiences, and much more – this became a cliché of the solitary Romantic artist. There were plenty of distinctive and isolated composers before Beethoven. Mozart suffered more from poverty, J. S. Bach had as much of a reputation for being bad-tempered, for example. But Beethoven's situation was much more loudly announced in his music. Fate bangs on the door, in the fifth symphony; music gradually emerges as if the volume is being turned up from silence, in the ninth symphony. The suffering artist and the art of suffering, the solitude and the solos, are entwined. And he *taught* us aloneness through his music. The pianist Biss describes how 'Beethoven provides this incredible guide to being alone'.

He was alone for most of his life for various reasons, circumstances, and to do with his personality as well. But most of all, in the latter part of his life, he was functionally deaf, which I think is maybe the most profound form of isolation a person can experience. And in writing this extraordinary music that he did, he showed us how to be alone, and reminded us that there is an incredible power and possibility in aloneness and isolation. I don't think he wrote this music in spite of being alone, but because he was alone. (Biss 2020)

In piano performance, the 'lineage' of a performer's teachers is of significance. One of Beethoven's most famous piano pupils was Carl Czerny, although Czerny is best known today for writing 'exercises', repetitive and melodically or harmonically uninteresting, the bane of many young pianists' lives. However, Czerny himself taught the young Franz Liszt. Liszt went on to have many pupils who were active until the middle of the twentieth century. Their pupils in turn have been active much more recently. Contemporary pianists can therefore claim to be fourth-generation pupils of Beethoven, connected in a line of solitudinous performers. But it is Liszt, of the second generation, who is of most interest here. (Liszt could be described as 'first generation', as he played for Beethoven as a child prodigy: Beethoven was apparently impressed, but did not actively advise or teach the youngster.) Liszt extended the repertoire of the piano as composer, as arranger and as a great virtuoso. His arrangements, of everything from Schubert songs to extracts from Wagner operas, were part of his attempt to show how the piano could 'replace' all other forms of instrumentation. Even Beethoven symphonies were remade into solo pieces for the piano. In his hands, the piano became the prime solo instrument, replacing orchestras and choirs alike. It was a modern mechanical, mass-produced, instrument that could replace many people's work with that of a single performer (described in Chapter 6). This was the spinning jenny of the musical world. (The spinning jenny was one of the great inventions early in the Industrial Revolution that mechanised cotton spinning and led to mass unemployment of hand-spinners.) Liszt popularised the piano as a 'replacer' and helped make it the model 'bourgeois domestic instrument', as described by the sociologist Weber (1978, p. 382, originally published in 1921).

Making the piano into the great individualist instrument of the nineteenth and much of the twentieth century, Liszt also created the career of the superstar charismatic solo performer. In these ways he finished the job started by Beethoven, of being a solitary Romantic artist. He could reasonably be called the first 'pop star', someone whose sexual charisma as much as his barnstorming performances drew people to concerts across Europe. 'The early works are vulgar and great', says Rosen, and established his performing style, whilst 'the late works are admirable and minor' (Rosen 1995, p. 474). Solo piano concerts in large halls were established by Liszt. 'The concert is – myself' (Liszt, quoted in Sennett 1978, p. 199). Solitary musical star, always on tour, Liszt's influence on performance is at least as important as his influence as a composer.

> Liszt was the great philistine musician. Right-thinking music lovers looked with horror on what they considered his charlatanry. He was indeed a charlatan, and he knew it, and sometimes laughed at it. He was also a composer and pianist of the utmost refinement and originality. It is, unfortunately, useless to try to separate the great musician from the charlatan: each one needed the other in order to exist. (Rosen 1995, p. 510)

This was an intentional performativity, and was well described by a critic, Jules Laurens, who met Liszt in 1844 and asked him to play his piano arrangement of a Bach prelude and fugue for organ. Liszt ask how Laurens wanted him to play it, to which Laurens said 'the way it ought to be played'. Liszt responded:

> 'Here it is, to start with, as the author must have understood it, played it himself, or intended it to be played.'
>
> And Liszt played. And it was admirable, the perfection itself of the classical style exactly in conformity with the original.
>
> 'Here it is a second time, as I feel it, with a slightly more picturesque movement, a more modern style and the effects demanded by an improved instrument.' And it was, with these nuances, different … but no less admirable.
>
> 'Finally, a third time, here it is the way I would play it for the public – to astonish, as a charlatan.' And, lighting a cigar which passed at moments from between his lips to his fingers, executing with his ten fingers the part written for the organ pedals, and indulging in other *tours de force* and prestidigitation, he was prodigious, incredible, fabulous, and received gratefully with enthusiasm. (Eigeldinger, quoted in Rosen 1995, pp. 510–11, with ellipses in original)

His contemporary, Chopin, was rather more influential as a composer. Rather than being quite the pop star (although he was impressive enough as a virtuoso performer), Chopin's influence on solitudinous art was greatest in his short and relatively easy pieces played in parlours around the world by domestic, amateur, pianists who would never play in large concert halls. Chopin was the equivalent of a television star, welcome in parlours and living rooms, in contrast to Liszt as the film star. But Chopin fulfilled a different Romantic stereotype, living as an exile from his native Poland in the then – as now – fashionable Paris, with fashionable friends such as his partner Georges Sand, and dying young of tuberculosis.

A third early nineteenth-century solo performer-composer was the violinist Paganini. Liszt, Paganini's friend (to the extent that Paganini had friends), vividly describes him in an obituary. So self-involved as a musician, he says, Paganini was lost in his own unhappy largely friendless world, unable to have relationships with individual people, but only with audiences. 'He is unlike them', as Sennett described Paganini and his audiences, 'as are all charismatic figures', and also, he continues, 'he is ... permanently isolated from anyone he arouses' (Sennett 1978, p. 202). Liszt wrote Paganini's obituary:

> This man, who created so much enthusiasm, could make no friends among his fellowmen. No one guessed what was going on in his heart; his own richly blessed life never made another happy. ... Paganini's god ... was never any other than his own gloomy, sad 'I.' (Sennett 1978, p. 202, ellipses in original)

A sad, perhaps lonely, end for one of the modern world's great celebrity performers.

The Poetics of Solitude

The poetry of Romanticism is full of solitary artist descriptions, notably those of Wordsworth. Unlike the socially isolated Beethoven, the emotionally 'apart' Paganini or the deeply troubled Hölderlin, Wordsworth was more connected, conventionally, and financially secure. He nevertheless frequently wrote of solitude and its joys, with much of this writing more or less explicitly autobiographical. Brought up and living throughout his life in rural communities, his walks in the countryside were not 'escapes to Nature' from dour urban life, a distinct theme of much nineteenth-century art (addressed in more detail in Chapter 5), but Wordsworth did use his solitary walks as central to his poetic self-image as emotional contemplative. The poetry as autobiography that emerged from this process was filled with solitude. Wordsworth's most famous poems – *Daffodils*, the most famous with the general public, and *Prelude*, the most popular with critics – have solitude at their core. As a scholar of loneliness, I find it frustrating how often *Daffodils* (Wordsworth 1994, p. 187) is described as being about loneliness (as, e.g., in Batsleer and Duggan 2021, p. 37). The end of the poem is its culmination, and that concerns the 'bliss of solitude'. Wandering 'lonely as a cloud', as the narrator does at the start of the poem, does not seem to refer to loneliness in the more modern emotional sense. I have suggested elsewhere (Stern 2014a, p. 83) that to modern ears, it would make more sense to start the poem 'Alone I wandered, as a cloud'. Aloneness is appropriate for a cloud, and the lack of attention or attachment is being referenced, rather than an emotional loneliness. Wordsworth was using 'lonely' as many writers did at that time, of places and objects that are simply *apart*, with lonely clouds and also yew trees, streams and primroses (Wordsworth 1994, pp. 25, 241, 455), amongst others. Seeing classes in schools and universities where teachers/tutors and students alike struggle with an exploration of the emotional state of clouds, as part of their analysis of the poem, is an experience that regularly annoys me.

It is in *Prelude* that Wordsworth completes an extended analysis of solitude. 'Though I had learnt betimes to stand unpropped', he tells us, 'Yet could I only cleave to solitude / In lonely places', that is, whilst alone. This was because other people distracted him: 'if a throng was near / That way I leaned by nature'. He describes himself as social and as enjoying 'idleness and joy' in society. In an odd way, he finds solitude just as sociable, and certainly not 'lonely' in the modern sense. Quoting Milton, as Larkin did a century and a half later, he describes 'solitude / More active ever than "best society"' (Wordsworth 1994, pp. 632–752). Milton's original refers to the idea that 'solitude sometimes is best society'. Perhaps Wordsworth read a limitation in Milton's phrase, as though solitude might sometimes *not* be best society. Wordsworth explains how solitude is social *and* congenial: 'Society made sweet as solitude / By silent inobtrusive sympathies'. Do we need to be conventionally sociable in order to enjoy solitude as best society? The contrast between Wordsworth and Larkin might suggest this, as Larkin – in his antisocial poetic self-image – seemed to quote Milton ironically, finding, with difficulty, no more than a solitary vice when in solitude, whilst Wordsworth thought Milton had underestimated solitude's sociability.

Helping create an emotionally satisfying solitude was one of Wordsworth's many contributions to the idea of the solitary artist. His was not the terrible aloneness of Coleridge's *Ancient Mariner* (Coleridge 1994, pp. 81–100), even though the two poets published their poems in the same book. Wordsworth used the term 'lonely' in a way that was conventional for his time: many poets used the term of places, precisely as Wordsworth did. Lonely heaths, seas, hills, ice-floes. 'I'm sinking in the lonesome sea' cries the 'little sailor' of his betrayal by the ship's captain (Carter Family 1935, https://www.youtube.com/watch?v=uQLLRQNaVxg). The places are 'lonely' because a person might be alone there. Of course poetic descriptions of places may also involve emotional projection, but the actual uses do not – to me – suggest modern emotional loneliness. John Clare uses loneliness of places in this way, of thickets, glens, lakes, tempests, shores, deserts and fields (Clare 2004, pp. 20, 208, 212, 265, 285,

327, 390 respectively). I will return to Clare on nature in Chapter 5. Here, it is his poetically articulated solitude as an artist that is considered, and in this he does *not* use the term 'lonely'. Writing *I Am* (Clare 2004, p. 361) whilst in an asylum, it seems to be a bridge from Descartes's *cogito* (I think therefore I am) of the seventeenth century all the way through to twentieth-century existentialists and the life-death prevarications of Beckett, via Dickinson's grave *Because I could not stop for Death* (Dickinson 1970, p. 350).

I Am

I am: yet what I am none cares or knows,
My friends forsake me like a memory lost;
I am the self-consumer of my woes,
They rise and vanish in oblivious host,
Like shades in love and death's oblivion lost;
And yet I am! and live with shadows tost

Into the nothingness of scorn and noise,
Into the living sea of waking dreams,
Where there is neither sense of life nor joys,
But the vast shipwreck of my life's esteems;
And e'en the dearest – that I loved the best –
Are strange – nay, rather stranger than the rest.

I long for scenes where man has never trod;
A place where woman never smil'd or wept;
There to abide with my creator, God,
And sleep as I in childhood sweetly slept:
Untroubling and untroubled where I lie;
The grass below – above the vaulted sky.

(Clare 2004, p. 361)

This poem expresses Clare's rejection, being forsaken, but also a wish to be apart, a longing for scenes where man has never trod. He asserts 'I am' in a Cartesian sense and yet, like Descartes, he is conscious that this may be no more than a dream. Descartes 'escapes' his fear of living in an illusory world by invoking God (who would not deceive him) (Descartes 1912, p. 27 and passim). Clare also invokes God, albeit with less certainty than Descartes had, as God is not 'proven' but 'longed for'. And for Clare, being with God is also associated with death, the sleep beneath the 'vaulted sky'. He is scorned and disconnected from 'life and joys', including from his sweet sleep as a child. A life described as dreams yet wishing for sleep is a picture of an older form of alienation, a word used to refer to conditions also described as 'madness' or mental health issues. A letter written in 1860 by the aging Clare expresses this existential alienation even more vividly. 'Dear Sir', he writes, 'I am in a Madhouse & quite forget your Name or who you are you must excuse me for I have nothing to communicate or tell of & why I am shut up I dont know I have nothing to say so I conclude yours respectfully John Clare' (Clare 1985, p. 683).

Painting Alone

Wordsworth and Clare manage to project two models of the artist in solitude, one a rich and sociable solitude, the other an alienated solitude close to death. Other artists might be placed along the spectrum from Wordsworth to Clare. Yet it would be wrong to see either poet as simply 'positive' or 'negative' in their portrayals of solitude. Wordsworth was sympathetic to the alienated solitudes of loss and of poverty, and Clare describes – as Larkin did – the easy solitude of childhood. Closer to Wordsworth, perhaps, were poets like Keats or the earlier proto-Romantic *Robinson Crusoe* (Defoe 2001). Closer to Clare, perhaps, the poet Hölderlin and the artist Caspar David Friedrich. It was Friedrich who created the most vivid images of solitude in nature (addressed in Chapter 5) and of the solitary artist (in his pictures and his life). The solitary human figures in a landscape are as much an autobiography as Rembrandt's self-portraits. A few have more than one person in the landscape, but most have only one. In almost every case, the figure stands with their back to the viewer, less the object to be seen and more the subject viewing the landscape, a representative of humanity or, rather, a representative of a singular person, like the artist, viewing the world alone. Nearly all the singular people in the pictures are men, but one is a woman, Friedrich's then wife Caroline Bommer. That picture, *Woman Before the Rising Sun – Woman Before the Setting Sun* (Wolf 2003, p. 51) (the title given by puzzled owners, and not by Friedrich), is in lighter tones with more colours, as was characteristic of the paintings completed during the marriage and the birth of his three children. The solitude of the figure in Friedrich's paintings is in part a way of contrasting the small stature of humanity with the grandeur of Nature. The artist, like the figure in the painting, stands in awe. (Such awe-before-Nature is a theme of Chapter 5.) It is the artist's solitude and Friedrich's reputation – increasing throughout his life – as the 'most solitary of the solitary' (Schmitz 2012, p. 39) that concern us here.

Friedrich as a solitary artist is evident even in his more optimistic and colourful paintings. *Chalk Cliffs on Rügen* was apparently painted to celebrate his marriage (Grave 2017, p. 217). A grand landscape with the people in the landscape rather small and all with their backs to the viewer. Friedrich's wife is in a bright red dress, looking down and to the right, positioned at the lower left of the picture. Someone looking like Friedrich himself is at the far right of the picture, looking ahead and not at his wife. In the large space between the newly married couple is an older-looking man crouched down and pointing, as though noticing an insect or small plant in the grass. So the couple are separated, with another person between them, and are not looking at each other. Friedrich is the only figure observing the landscape – Friedrich the figure in the painting, and Friedrich the painter of the picture in which, characteristically, people are dwarfed by the landscape. The artist sees the world, others merely scrabble in the undergrowth. This may be an optimistic picture by Friedrich's standards, but it is hardly optimistic as a portrait of newlyweds.

In *Woman Before the Rising Sun – Woman Before the Setting Sun*, Caroline is again in a red dress, facing away. Unusually, the figure is relatively large compared to the landscape and she stands centrally, blocking part of the landscape, rather than to the side, allowing the viewer to share the figure's view. Caroline's arms are held away from her body, almost cruciform. The sun lights the picture, but Caroline's position with her arms apart makes even that ambiguous. A seven-year-old child taking part in a research project (reported in Stern 2014a, p. 159), asked to write the thoughts of the figure in the picture, suggested 'Am I lighting the sun?' Another child aged seven, picking up on Friedrich's (and her own?) death-obsession, along with, perhaps, a child's view of arms away from the body as an imitation of flight, wrote, 'Sun rise to the sky may I travele by and die and may fly'. When children aged seven recognise the morbidity of Friedrich's most optimistic of paintings, it is clear that such optimism is only relative. (It also suggests that the sun may be setting, rather than rising.) The solitary artist, worrying about death even during better times, is also well represented by another of Friedrich's 'couple' portraits. The woman, again in red, stands next to a man with her hand on his shoulder, in *Man and Woman Contemplating the Moon*. The 'weeping' trees, and the view of the moon (itself a common symbol of death), leave the artist lost in his own solitude. For an artist so concerned with landscapes, Friedrich's position as solitary artist is not primarily stimulated by walks or work in the countryside (as it was for Wordsworth or Clare) but by *inner* visions. Recommending that as an artist you should 'close your bodily eye so that you may see your picture first with the spiritual eye … so that [the picture] may react upon others from the outside inwards' (quoted in Vaughan 1980, p. 68). His later art becomes even darker, emotionally and literally, with 'Seashore in Moonlight' (Grave 2017, pp. 254–5), for example, being a picture of dark-sailed ships on a dark sea under a dark sky.

Possessive and Personal Individualism

Describing the artist as solitary, so central to the arts of the early nineteenth century, can refer to artists and to their art of solitude as quiet and peaceful, or as dangerous and violent. A century earlier, Defoe was a religious and political and economic challenger, a trader who ended up bankrupt, a journalist who acted as a political agitator and government spy. Yet in his novel *Robinson Crusoe*, he also created a 'spiritual autobiography', as it was called (Starr 1965), of a man shipwrecked on a desert island. The novel has been reinterpreted to suit every age, and in the Romantic period it was read as a novel of romantic heroism, Crusoe creating his own world, the author's 'inner visions' as vivid as those of Friedrich. Defoe's trading activities and political engagement were revisited later in the nineteenth century, with Marx calling out the individualist illusions of classical capitalist economics and liberal philosophy as 'Robinsonades', or what later became known as 'possessive individualism' (Macpherson 1962).

> The individual and isolated hunter and fisherman, with whom Smith and Ricardo begin, belongs among the unimaginative conceits of the eighteenth-century Robinsonades, … [as does] Rousseau's *contrat social* … . This is the semblance, the merely aesthetic semblance, of the Robinsonades, great and small. (Marx 1973, p. 83)

Prawer describes how, for Marx, 'the loneliness of Robinson Crusoe becomes a symbol for social alienation in the "civil society" of the nineteenth century', suggesting that 'literature may thus be "prophetic", even if in most cases the prophecy could be clearly recognized only by hindsight' (Prawer 1978, pp. 275–6). By the early nineteenth century, the archetypical religious and political challenger-artist was Percy Bysshe Shelley, even if Byron ran him a close second. An atheist when that was dangerous (as Defoe's nonconformist Christianity was dangerous in his time), and a political campaigner and radical, he ended his life at twenty-nine as an exile in Greece. His poem *Ozymandias* describes a crumbling statue to a once great leader, ending 'look on my Works, ye Mighty, and despair!' (Shelley 2017, p. 153), before describing the wreckage. This is inevitably seen as much about Shelley's own works – his fame and arrogance – as about Ozymandias, and Shelley's awareness of how they (and his reputation) may be lost in times to come. The mortality of the poet and of the poems is a solitary sadness of all artists.

It is another Shelley, though, who creates a different model of solitude, albeit, again, one in which the creator and created are both condemned to solitude. Mary Shelley's reputation was for many years overshadowed by that of her husband (whose posthumous reputation she did a lot to maintain), and by that of their friend Byron. The popularity of her first novel, *Frankenstein*, has also overshadowed her other writing, with the film of the novel (Whale 1931) in turn overshadowing the novel. More recently, her stature and the range of work have been better appreciated. But Frankenstein, the scientist of the novel, and the Creature, whom he creates, are both important examples of solitary artists in their own right. Frankenstein is creative as a scientist precisely as wanting to create a being out of body parts. The arrogance of science, but also its astonishing power, drives Frankenstein to a dangerous alienation from all his colleagues. Shelley's father, the anarchist individualist William Godwin, was perhaps being referenced by the still teenage Shelley. (Some critics see the Creature as itself a misunderstood adolescent.) But the idea that creation requires separation from society, and is itself dangerous and has its own life independent of the artist, is an important theme in early-nineteenth-century culture. The artist is required to separate and be obsessed, but for Shelley this is not a positive or heroic situation, as it is for so many of her contemporaries including her husband. A more communitarian view of society than that of her father or of many of her friends and contemporaries, Shelley was providing a warning far more current than the future-oriented *Ozymandias*.

The Creature in *Frankenstein* is also a kind of solitudinous artist in his own right. A clever, swift-footed, multilinguist, in contrast to the Monster of Whale's film, the Creature is a figure prone to inhabiting lonely places. Whether or not the Creature is a misunderstood adolescent, an alter-ego of the author, he is certainly not understood by his creator 'father', he doesn't know what to do with his intelligence and skills, he has no intimates, no 'mother' (as Shelley had no mother at the time of writing the novel, her mother having died a few days after Shelley was born), no partner. He is a social misfit who, thinking this will be his lifelong fate, decides to kill himself on the icy, lonely, wastes of the Arctic. 'I shunned the face of man', he says, and 'all sound of joy or complacency was torture to me; solitude was my only consolation – deep, dark, deathlike solitude' (Shelley 1999, p. 70). A representative of humanity, as much as of adolescence, alienated from 'the creator' – also the phrase used of God – in an increasingly atheist culture, notably in Shelley's own household, with scientific thinking challenging some religious confidence. The Creature was not described as 'lonely' in the novel, but his surroundings were. As with the poetry of Wordsworth and Clare, 'lonely' had yet to make the transition to the name of an emotion. But, in contrast to the older poets, Shelley's Creature could easily have loneliness in the modern sense attributed to him. The solitude both of the creator, Frankenstein, and of the Creature contributes to the model of artist-as-solitary. The author, Shelley, is less of a model, in opposing individualism and promoting communitarian social reform. But her grief at the death soon after birth of her first child, a daughter, is yet another dimension of alienation to add to the complex life of the artist. Plato said that teachers, and by implication writers more generally, taught in order to achieve a kind of immortality (Plato 1997, pp. 490–1, from *Symposium*) – a kind of immortality that women could achieve through giving birth to children. Shelley did, later, give birth to a child who survived, but that was after she wrote the book that has indeed given her a kind of immortality.

Novel Ways of Being Alone

Women's experiences of the solitary artist were, unsurprisingly, affected by different pressures and expectations than the experience of men. Almost a generation younger than Shelley, who was herself a generation younger than Beethoven, Hölderlin or Wordsworth, came Charlotte, Emily and Anne Brontë. In the very centre of the nineteenth century, yet often continuing a gothic style that *Frankenstein* exemplified, the novels of the Brontës, as well as their lives, added to the image of creative solitude. *Jane Eyre* (Brontë 2006) is structured as an intimate and solitary, deeply personal and emotional, first-person account – a 'spiritual autobiography' more intimate but no less solitudinous than *Robinson Crusoe*. Like Crusoe, and unlike Frankenstein or the Creature, *Jane Eyre* has a reasonably happy ending, resolved back into a communal, happy, household. The same cannot be said of Emily Brontë's *Wuthering Heights* (Brontë 2003). The harsh solitudes and alienated togethernesses of the novel are left, by the end of the novel, as a Dantesque posthumous world more vividly populated by the dead than by the living. The Brontës lived most of their lives in their father's parsonage, relatively isolated socially and further alienated by the lifestyle of their brother Branwell, addicted to alcohol and opium. Branwell may have been a kind of model for Heathcliff, but his was hardly a hero's life (like Byron's or Percy Bysshe Shelley's). Solitude was not heroic but tragic, in these novels.

Far more domestic, but with a far greater influence on literary culture, the novels of Eliot show us a different solitary artist – Eliot as a radically independent thinker, and her characters who live oddly disconnected lives yet, like Shelley, in a society that was or could be a 'solution' to alienation. Her philosophical depth, drawing on Spinoza (whose *Ethics* she translated, Spinoza 2020) and J. S. Mill, amongst many others, made her art echo well beyond its quiet rural, or occasionally urban, contexts. The quiet life that is remarkable: this is a different kind of solitary artist-figure, far from the grand heroic 'celebrity' of P. B. Shelley, and closer to the domestic solitudes, staring out of the windows, of Austen's characters such as Fanny Price (Lau 2004). Eliot's was an embodied sense of art, sensuous in the Romantic sense. Her poem *Stradivarius* sings the praises of 'that plain white-aproned man' called 'dull' and 'a machine' by his contemporaries, who yet created the violin that when played lifts your soul. Stradivarius was as much the artist as the composer and the performer, with his quiet life, an 'eloquent silence at the chasm abrupt / Where knowledge ceases' (Eliot 1878, p. 213). The challenge for the artist, a challenge distinctively present in the nineteenth century, is to escape from oneself. In *Middlemarch*, Eliot gives this challenge to Dorothea, who finds it difficult to understand the 'otherness' of Mr Casaubon. She finds it hard to 'conceive with that distinctness which is no longer reflection but feeling – an idea wrought back to the directness of sense, like the solidity of objects – that he had an equivalent centre of self, whence the lights and shadows must always fall with a certain difference' (Eliot 1965, p. 243). Such self-transcendence (as also noted by the editor, Harvey, in Eliot 1965, p. 15) expresses Eliot's sense of the social having primacy over the individual, but also, I suggest, Eliot's own attempt at – and most would say, successful achievement of – self-transcendence as *artist*.

Lonesome Voices

A decade younger than Eliot, a more solitudinous artist still, one of the strongest voices of artist-solitude, Dickinson wrote poetry of such power, her domestic quietude is still speaking loudly today. Loneliness is gaining its emotional voice in Dickinson's poems, half a century after Wordsworth's not so lonely cloud. Or is it *lonesomeness*? She perhaps suggests both, as she asks herself whether loneliness is the 'maker' of the soul or its 'seal' (Dickinson 1970, p. 379). Yet there is an argument that American culture generated lonesomeness which was a distinct emotion, a poignant and less painful variation on loneliness experienced – in music, poetry and novels – by wanderers (Huckleberry Finn, Twain 2001), cowboys (in the songs of Hank Williams and many others) and by Dickinson (1970).

> 'Lonesomeness' American born and bred, as I shall argue, has proven a regrettably ignored but demonstrable locus of personal and cultural religious-like meaning. The lonesomeness examined in this essay is the 'lonesomeness' which in usage signals an evolved, culture-specific, subjective feeling-state whose interesting complexity students of American culture have yet to "see" or to grasp sufficiently. (Lewis 2009, p. xv)

In an account that complements the idea of the artist-as-solitary, Lewis talks of how 'lonesomeness can function as a kind of unbidden gift of spiritual self-therapy' (Lewis 2009, p. xxi), and although lonesomeness 'presupposes depressive loneliness as a ground, … it lifts those who experience it, in what feels like a gift, above mere loneliness for a transitory, savoury, nearly-but-probably-not-quite epiphanic moment in the old sense of that term as descriptive of a moment of illuminating revelation' (Lewis 2009, p. 16). Dickinson is one of Lewis's key writers, and he notes her account of 'another Loneliness' which can make its bearer 'richer than could be revealed / By mortal number' (Lewis 2009, p. 33, quoting Dickinson 1970, p. 507). This is an example of a loneliness (a *lonesomeness*, for Lewis) that is not the deprivation of relation but 'a richness of feeling *and* perception akin to Otto's encounter with "the Wholly Other"' (Lewis 2009, p. 33). This matches some other models of the solitary artist – seeking solitude to 'discover' the Other, and suffering somewhat in the attempt. However, Lewis also recognises in Dickinson the 'depressive loneliness' that 'can be devastating' (Lewis 2009, p. 33), but that is not a form of the distinctive American lonesome tradition.

Although I am not convinced that 'lonesomeness' is so distinctive and separable from loneliness, or distinctively American, Lewis does describe well some of the artist-solitudes that had developed in Europe early in the nineteenth century and were extended into American culture through the nineteenth and well into the twentieth century. Dickinson does describe a range of lonelinesses, and she is at times very much developing a more modern sense of loneliness, layered with separation, rejection and self-blame. She was writing her life into her poems, looking ever deeper inwards, and sensuous in a way that – as with Eliot – disguises an intellectual rigour, and she was more than this, a modern innovator, outside her time and place. Dickinson's own life, like that of many of her contemporaries, became a centrepiece of her art. Not a wandering exile like Percy Bysshe Shelley, but more like the earlier 'locked away' poets, Clare or Hölderlin. However, although Dickinson may have been described as fearful of wide social contact, perhaps in modern terms agoraphobia or prone to panic in social situations, her life seems to have been more within her control, and less disconnected from 'reality', than those other poets.

Seeking Solitude

Exploring some of the artists-as-solitary, we should recognise those well outside the nineteenth century who nevertheless exemplify many of the same ideas. As well as Defoe, whose *Robinson Crusoe* became a Romantic trope, even if it was later reinterpreted in other ways, there are two poets of solitude that I would like to mention. One is the seventeenth-century poet Katherine Philips, the other the twentieth-century poet and novelist May Sarton. Philips's short thirty-three-year life was remarkable for her achievements as a poet and translator. Her most famous poem – in part famous because of a popular musical setting by Purcell – was a translation. *O! Solitude, my sweetest choice*, the poem begins (Philips 1710, p. 210–225, with the poem entitled *La Solitude de St. Amant. Englished*). It continues with solitude as a place to meet nature, for trees, mountains, water-fowl, streams, adders, owls, spiders, snails, sea, sand and deserts. In solitude, the narrator also meets human-made 'ruin'd castle walls', and sacred and divine beings, demi-gods, Jove, Nayads, nymphs, witches, tritons and Neptune. Central to the poem is the chance in solitude to meet absent people: the carcass of a person who hanged himself for a love that did him wrong, drowned men, those who finish their lives by throwing themselves off mountains and, most of all, Bernieres, the narrator's own lost lover. 'O! how I Solitude adore / … For thy sake I in love am grown / With what thy fancy does pursue; / But when I think upon my own, / I hate it for that reason too. / Because it needs must hinder me / From seeing, and from serving thee'. The narrator learns 'Apollo's lore' (i.e. the art of poetry) in and through solitude. Rarely has solitude been described as so busy at the same time as being so haunted by suicidal thoughts over lost love.

Apollo's lore is itself a poetic description of the art of poetry, and the poet learns poetry in solitude, contemplating nature, the divine and sacred, lost or dead people and solitude itself. Like Wordsworth, solitude is *chosen*, but unlike

Wordsworth or Milton before him, it can hardly be described as 'best society'. It has more in common with Hölderlin's terrifying visions (and his classical allusions), or Dante's *Inferno* (2005). The author of the poem translated by Philips, Saint-Amant, wrote it in French. His authorship is of additional interest as the lost lover is given a male name, so it was presented originally as a male poet's love of (somewhat suicidal) solitude for the absence of his male lover. And Philips, who left the male name in her translation, was herself thought of as the great poet of female friendship and perhaps female–female eroticism (Andreadis 1989). It may be a little anachronistic to apply terms like gay or lesbian to seventeenth-century culture. But the sensuality of Saint Amant's and Philips's poem is vivid, even amongst all the classicism and ambiguity. And this example of the artist as solitary, in a landscape that might have been painted by Friedrich, makes a fine pre-Romantic example of the Romantic idea of artist-as-solitary.

A quite different example of artist-as-solitary is the twentieth-century novelist, poet and diarist May Sarton. One of her best known works is *Journal of a Solitude* (Sarton 1973), but she wrote often about solitude and described her own preference for – and need for – solitude. A difficult and ornery personality, as she describes herself and as others describe her, solitude enabled her to live well.

> I am here alone for the first time in weeks, to take up my 'real' life again at last. That is what is strange – that friends, even passionate love, are not my real life unless there is time alone in which to explore and to discover what is happening or has happened. Without the interruptions, nourishing and maddening, this life would become arid. Yet I taste it fully only when I am alone here and 'the house and I resume old conversations'. (Sarton 1973, p. 11)

Like Philips, she wrote of female–female love, and though much more openly erotic, unsurprisingly for the time in which she wrote, she rejected being categorised as a 'lesbian writer'. Sarton's solitude is that of an artist, and it is also of a gardener, a (not very good) neighbour, a walker. 'Alone one is never lonely: the spirit adventures, walking / In a quiet garden, in a cool house, abiding single there' (Sarton 1974). Exhausted by company, she says she is rarely lonely, only occasionally when tired (Sarton 1974): after rest and her own company, she recovers her 'wholeness' in solitude.

> For a long time now, every meeting with another human being has been a collision. I feel too much, sense too much, am exhausted by the reverberations after even the simplest conversation. But the deep collision is and has been with my unregenerate, tormenting, and tormented self. I have written every poem,

every novel, for the same purpose – to find out what I think, to know where I stand. (Sarton 1973, p. 12)

When it comes to her art, Sarton makes an interesting distinction. If she were imprisoned in solitary confinement, not thinking anyone would read what she wrote, she says she would write poetry rather than novels, 'because the poem is primarily a dialogue with the self and the novel a dialogue with others' (Sarton 1973, p. 41). 'Solitude', she says, 'is the salt of personhood … [as i]t brings out the authentic flavor of every experience' (Sarton 1974). Seeking or exploiting solitude in order to be in dialogue is a common feature of solitude, well-described by the philosopher Taylor:

> The impulse behind the life of the hermit, or to take a case more familiar to our culture, the solitary artist … might [be] see[n] … as aspiring to a certain kind of dialogicality. In the case of the hermit, the interlocutor is God. In the case of the solitary artist, the work itself is addressed to a future audience, perhaps still to be created by the work itself. The very form of a work of art shows its character as addressed. (Taylor 1991, pp. 34–5)

For Taylor, this means that 'the making and sustaining of our identity, in the absence of a heroic effort to break out of ordinary existence, remains dialogical throughout our lives' (Taylor 1991, p. 35).

Being a person who values solitude, who is an artist, is not the same as being an artist-as-solitary. Sarton is both, having written into her poetry and her journals and novels complex accounts of her creative solitude. Engaging with nature is important. But so is trying to understand those who do not value – or are fearful of – solitude. Why be scared, she says, of a man who describes his fear of being alone, what is it you fear, being on your own? 'That, suddenly alone, he would discover that he bored himself, or that there was, quite simply, no self there to meet?' (Sarton 1974). The obverse of an artistic love of solitude is perhaps an unartistic dislike of solitude. We can contrast monks and prisoners. Both are given cells and therefore given *themselves* for company: 'a reward for a good person, a punishment for a bad person' (William of St-Thierry, in Webb 2007, p. 71). Would it be appropriate also to say that the creative can create in solitude, whilst the uncreative will realise their *lack* of creativity in solitude? The 'good' and 'bad' person, in the example of the cell: can they be replaced with 'creative' and 'uncreative'? For academic writers, this may be the case. In extensive conversations about research, in several universities, I found that many saw the need for a *space* for doing research (such as an office unshared with colleagues) and they also needed *time* for doing research (Stern 2014b). However, some if given space and time move to saying they need additional *skills*. The impression given is that a minority of the academics were – as Sarton might put it – fearful of the creativity they think they may lack if finally given solitude (i.e. space and time). My own belief is that this is the situation (for this minority of people), and that solitude on its own may be regarded by the 'uncreative' as a punishment rather than as a reward.

Solitary Selves

The idea of the artist-as-solitary is exemplified by Sarton, well outside the nineteenth-century heyday of the idea. Solitary artists keep returning, as in this description of a 'creative writing' student who, without creative writing, 'would be dead … [o]r at least seriously, seriously maimed … [e]motionally broken by loneliness … [m]y lifeless body hanging from my broken light fixture until the smell of my rot alerts the pervert down the hall' (Awad 2019, p. 248). The protagonist's tutor realises the protagonist may be about to spend Christmas alone:

'So what are your plans for the holidays?'

Think of a lie, think of a lie. Lie lie lie.

'I –'

But she's looking at me as if she already knows. Can see me twirling ramen with a warped fork in front of illegally downloaded television that keeps freezing due to a bad connection. Watering a sad rosemary bush I've strung with Christmas lights.

'I hope you're not planning on spending it *alone*? Are you?'

The way she says *alone* makes it sound like a cave. Like some hideous, dark cave whose oozing walls are teeming with all the unpleasant things of this world, and I am crawling willingly, brazenly, into this awful space of my own free will. Shoveling the vermin I find scuttling across the floor into my mouth for sustenance.

I tell her, no, of course not. Not *alone*. But her smile says how easily she has punctured my sad girl lie. (Awad 2019, p. 240)

The examples given in this chapter are far from a single model of solitude. Some, like Sarton, see solitude as a primary way of living; others, like Friedrich and Clare (and more recently, Awad), seem to drive others away. Towards the other end of the spectrum are more collaborative and socially engaged artists like Shelley, Defoe or Wordsworth, who recognise the creative value of solitude, without it being their main way of living. What seemed to bring out the artist-as-solitary in the nineteenth century was not simply a result of the *personalities* of the artists. It was more, I suggest, part of a broader social change that enabled artists to work more independently, which created a 'profession' of independent commercial artist, untied to patrons. Touring artist superstars like Liszt or even Dickens built on reputations of the 'mad, bad and dangerous to know' independent artists from earlier in the nineteenth century. But each was solitary in a distinctive way.

These solitary artists became a model for 'selfhood', a model of the creative self that continues to the current day through some therapeutic, rather than commercial, uses of creative arts. As Taylor describes it, 'artistic creation becomes the paradigm mode in which people can come to self-definition' (Taylor 1991, p. 62):

> The artist becomes in some way the paradigm case of the human being, as agent of original self-definition. Since about 1800, there has been a tendency to heroize the artist, to see in his or her life the essence of the human condition, and to venerate him or her as a seer, the creator of cultural values.

> But of course, along with this has gone a new understanding of art. No longer defined mainly by imitation, by *mimēsis* of reality, art is understood now more in terms of creation. These two ideas go together. If we become ourselves by expressing what we're about, and if what we become is by hypothesis original, not based on the pre-existing, then what we express is not an imitation of the pre-existing either, but a new creation. We think of the imagination as creative. (Taylor 1991, p. 62)

The 'self' is a 'created self' and art therefore becomes central to 'selfhood'. 'My self-discovery passes through a creation, the making of something original and new', he continues, as 'I forge a new artistic language – new way of painting, new metre or form of poetry, new way of writing a novel – and through this and this alone I become what I have it in me to be' (Taylor 1991, p. 62). To be a 'whole' self is to be creative, as Schiller describes in his *Letters on the Aesthetic Education of Man* (Schiller 1967), combining our physical and our moral selves through 'play' or *art*.

One of the themes common to artists-as-solitaries and frequently mentioned in this chapter is that of nature. Or, as it tended to be known in the nineteenth century, Nature. That deserves a distinct account, though, as solitude in nature has a tradition going back to the ancients and forward to the present day.

5

Alone in Nature

Away from people, closer to my surroundings which, if natural,
Give me a sense of being embodied and of the earth.

Summary

To be alone in nature is explored in the arts of all ages, but it reached a high point precisely as industrialisation and urbanisation in Europe and North America made 'nature' less accessible and familiar. Solitary birds, in the music of Vaughan Williams or the poetry of Meredith, P. B. Shelley, Hopkins or Keats, are complemented by the failed flight of Icarus, portrayed by Brueghel, Auden and William Carlos Williams. Gould's solitudinous Canadian Trilogy is in the tradition of Thoreau, Muir and later writers such as Shepherd. Composers such as Cage and John Luther Adams provide musical explorations of solitude in nature. Most portrayals of solitude in nature are broadly positive, yet almost all also carry a sadness or nostalgia for what is or will soon be lost.

Some key artists: Ralph Vaughan Williams (1872–1958), George Meredith (1828–1909), Percy Bysshe Shelley (1792–1822), Gerard Manley Hopkins (1844–1889), John Keats (1795–1821), Pieter Brueghel the Elder (1525/1530–1569), W. H. Auden (1907–1973), William Carlos Williams (1883–1963), Glenn Gould (1932–1982), Henry David Thoreau (1817–1862), Nan Shepherd (1893–1981), John Muir (1838–1914), John Luther Adams (1953–), John Cage (1912–1992)

Introduction: Where Are You, Solitude?

Where are solitude, silence and loneliness? They can be experienced anywhere, from caves and cells to wide open spaces. The arts of solitude are often *placed*, though, whether places are used as metaphors (Clare's lonely thicket, Clare

2004, p. 20) or as stimuli (Sarton's garden, Sarton 1974) or as depressants (Ovid's Tomis, Ovid 2005) or as the material of the art itself (John Luther Adams's Alaskan soundscapes, Adams 2020). Nature is often used in such ways, and exploring aloneness in nature provides a distinctive set of insights for artists and audiences alike. One of the reasons for this is that arts are very often 'consumed' in domestic and urban settings (homes, galleries, concert halls), so art of or in nature is typically *transcendent*, taking the audience to another place. Nature also informs solitude by highlighting a person's embodiment, the sensuality of personhood. Although art is 'at a distance' from reality, involving imagined and represented versions of the world (copies or 'mimetic' representations, in much of the history of art, Auerbach 2003, and then even more distant, as Taylor 1991, p. 62, says, quoted at the end of Chapter 4), those presentations/representations may in themselves bring a person closer in touch with the embodied world. This chapter has an overlap with the previous chapter, as it would be possible to use many of the examples – of artists and of their art – in both chapters. Some will indeed make a second appearance here. But there is plenty of nature to go around, so I will try to introduce variety.

For the Birds

I will start with music, and the idea of birdsong as song. For as long as people have made music, one of their inspirations has been birdsong. Tuneful, varied, attractive (to other birds, in the first instance), and playful, birdsong is an easy starting point in nature. As represented in art, birdsong is most often solitary, too. There are dawn choruses, in nature and in composed music, but the more common representation is as a single voice. Vaughan Williams's *Lark, Ascending* (from 1914) is written for violin and piano, later for violin and orchestra. Often voted the UK's favourite piece of classical music, it is an emotional, pastoral, piece that wears its folk-song affinities on its sleeve whilst being a surprisingly radical piece in mixing its modalities (avoiding much conventional classical harmony) and at times avoiding bar lines and conventional rhythmical consistency. Conventional rhythm and harmony are of course unfamiliar to larks, too, which is one of the attractions of the piece. The lark – played by the violin – ascends into the sky and the music moves heavenwards in both senses. It is often requested at funerals, suited for its contemplative atmosphere as well as its final ascent. Vaughan Williams, like many of his musical contemporaries, drew on folk music as a way of being in touch with nature.

True folk music is produced only by farmers and shepherds; only this can guarantee its mythical status, its down-to-earth contrast with sophisticated urban music. Folk music, in fact, is not art but nature. The composer who turns to folk material is like the landscape artist who paints out of doors: they both reject the artificial for the natural; they start not with what is invented but with what is given by reality. (Rosen 1995, p. 410)

Folk music also establishes a sense of place and of nationhood. Bartok's Hungarian and Czech folk songs, Sibelius's Finnish music or Albéniz's Spanish music: all, like that of Vaughan Williams, speak of their respective nationalisms. (The ambiguities of such nationalisms, and the mixtures of, for example, Gypsy music, Arabic music and other cross-national traditions, make for a more interesting and complex picture.)

Vaughan Williams's solitary lark, and solo violin, seemed at odds with the Modernism of many contemporaries. Whereas Bartok could be regarded as modern or even Modernist in his percussive use of the piano, Vaughan Williams's pastoralism was seen as conservative and backward-looking, belonging to the 'cow pat school' (according to Lutyens, see Rayborn 2016, p. 111). Although the *Lark, Ascending* was original in many ways, it did precisely look back to the poem of the same name by George Meredith, written in 1881 (https://allpoetry. com/The-Lark-Ascending), several decades before Vaughan Williams's musical versions. Meredith's *Lark* is, like the solo violin, a solitary bird. It rises and falls, chirrups and whistles, a 'press of hurried notes'. The sixty-four lines of the first stanza continue without a full stop, it is 'An ecstasy to music turn'd'. A solitary lark yet has an audience, and 'every face to watch him rais'd / Puts on the light of children prais'd'. Ascending to heaven, yet it 'is love of earth that he instils', the song managing, even in its solitude, to 'link / All hearers in the song they drink'. The transcendence is achieved as 'their soul in me, or mine, / Through self-forgetfulness divine, / In them'. The lark finally soars 'to silence', although whether the lark stops singing or is no longer heard is left unclear. After the silence, though, 'the fancy sings'. The solitary bird leaves its human audience 'fancying', just as Wordsworth recalls the daffodils in what therefore becomes 'the bliss of solitude'. It is the lark that is the true artist, its song natural and sincere. Nature sings, and people themselves become, like children, more honest. There is no sense of the lark singing to or for another lark, let alone to or for people. Percy Bysshe Shelley, himself an expert in solitude, wrote of the skylark's 'unpremeditated art' (Shelley 2017, p. 435). But whereas Meredith hymns the lark itself, P. B. Shelley asks to be taught by the lark: 'Teach me half the gladness / That thy brain must know; / Such harmonious madness / From my lips would flow, / The world should listen then, as I am listening now' (Shelley 2017, p. 437). It is P. B. Shelley's turn back to himself that suggests to me his is a use of nature to illustrate the solitude – the harmonious madness – of the artist (and therefore a bigger place in Chapter 4), with Meredith's lark-imitation making the solitary lark the centre of attention (and therefore a bigger place here in Chapter 5).

It is tempting to stay with birds, which have their own more or less solitary characters: a crow in a crowd, it is said, is a rook; a rook on its own is a crow. Gerald Manley Hopkins wrote of a solitary kestrel in *The Windhover* (https:// poets.org/poem/windhover), an astonishing evocation of flight, not song, 'In his ecstasy!' This bird is Hopkins's chevalier, and is an ecstatic metaphor also of Jesus, whilst remaining ornithologically authentic. Instead of staying with Hopkins's kestrel, I would like to contrast the ascent of Meredith's lark with the fall of the all-too-human Icarus. The ancient tale of Icarus is often told. It is a story of a man who, with his father, attempted to imitate the birds and, like so many tales of human technological hubris to come (including Shelley's Creature), ended with his death as the wax wings melted as he flew too close to the sun. The account that is my starting point here is the oddly haunting painting of the story in the mid-sixteenth century by Pieter Brueghel the Elder, from the Musées Royaux des Beaux-Arts in Brussels (https://www.fine-arts-mus eum.be/fr/la-collection/pieter-i-bruegel-la-chute-d-icare?letter=b&artist=brue gel-brueghel-pieter-i). His painting is of a pastoral scene, a farming scene by the coast. A ploughman concentrates on his plough in the foreground, and a ship sails nearby on the sea. All is quiet and peaceful. Only by concentrating do you notice a tiny figure making a splash further offshore. Icarus falls and this is *so* insignificant: it is a double-hubris, thinking he could imitate the bird, and thinking that his fall meant anything to the landscape. It is the quiet, worked, landscape that dominates the viewer's attention, as it dominates the attention of the ploughman and of those sailing the ship. In Auden's poem of this and other Brueghel paintings, *Musée des Beaux Arts* (http://english.emory.edu/classes/ paintings&poems/auden.html), people turn away from suffering, not in shock or embarrassment but in a 'leisurely' way, as they turn to their work. Icarus falls, alone, and falls *ignored*, even by those who have seen or heard his fall. The landscape – nature – has become the whole universe, to which a single person's suffering is insignificant. It has become Spinoza's 'God or Nature' (Spinoza 1955, p. 188), or 'God, i.e. Nature' (Spinoza 2000, p. 226).

William Carlos Williams's *Landscape with the Fall of Icarus* (Williams 1976, p. 212) stresses the field's representation of 'the whole pageantry // of the year' which 'was / awake tingling' whilst Icarus's 'unnoticed' splash led to 'Icarus drowning' (http://english.emory.edu/classes/paintings&poems/williams.html). The sensuousness of the scene, 'sweating in the sun' that also melted Icarus's wax wings, is emphasised. It is the opposite of Wordsworth's *Daffodils*. Instead of being alone in one's thoughts until an apparently insignificant set of daffodils catches the attention of the narrator, to be recalled later in the bliss of solitude, the farmer is fully *attentive* and aware even of his sweatiness, and his attention is therefore *not* drawn to the apparently insignificant fall of Icarus. What Williams, Breughel and Wordsworth have in common (in these works of art) is a lesser care for humanity, with *nature*, the landscape, being more than, and other than, humanity, leaving people 'alone' in the world. Icarus tells us clearly, in all the art in which he is portrayed, that human beings cannot be other creatures, at least not without suffering the consequences. Kafka tells the tale in *Metamorphosis* (Kafka 1961, pp. 7–63) of a man waking up as an insect, instantly alienated from his family. Ovid's *Metamorphoses* (2004) of two millennia earlier is more varied and yet people transforming into other creatures is still painful and alienating. Change itself, the changeability of the embodied human being, is presented in exaggerated form in such tales.

The last of the birds in this account is the nightingale, at least until an albatross makes its usual badly-timed appearance. Ornithologically similar to a skylark in having a varied song with many more notes than the songs of other bird species, the nightingale is also usually poetised alone. As its name suggests, the nightingale sings at night. Keats's *Ode to a Nightingale* (Keats 1956, p. 209) is one of the best-known of all English poems. It is understandably about the poet as well as the bird, but enough of the bird is there to allow this to be an art of nature. The nightingale is introduced singing 'of summer', interrupting the narrator's thoughts of his own death. And yet thoughts of death reappear with the narrator wishing to disappear, to 'fade away into the forest dim'. The forgetfulness longed for by the narrator is not needed by the nightingale who doesn't know of human suffering. Instead of using alcohol to escape, Keats will use the 'viewless wings of Poesy' to join the nightingale, and the bird could sing as he eases into death, 'pouring forth' its soul 'In such an ecstasy!' Finally, the bird simply flies away, leaving the tired poet wondering whether he heard the nightingale's song or just dreamt it. Keats seeks a solitude with such creatures, in a romanticised Nature beyond an urban city: 'O Solitude! If I must with thee dwell, / Let it not be among the jumbled heap / Of murky buildings; climb with me to steep, – / Nature's observatory' (Keats 1956, p. 36).

Unromantic Nature

An anti-Romantic version of Keats's ode is Dickinson's *I heard a Fly buzz – when I died –* (Dickinson 1970, pp. 223–4). The narrator's breaths are 'gathering hard' as death approaches. She has completed her worldly business, having 'Signed away / What portion of me be / Assignable'. And then the fly appears, with a 'stumbling Buzz'. The narrator dies as 'the Windows failed – and then / I could not see to see – '. The solitary fly is just that, a fly. There is no great metaphor carried by the fly. It is not ascending heavenwards or carrying a soul or ecstatically singing. Having a 'Stumbling buzz' as the narrator dies, the fly is not even elegant at the moment of death. Nature is there, just buzzing on. Making poetry of the unpoetic, Dickinson is perhaps the first Modernist poet of solitary nature. Unromantic solitary nature has many practitioners. Sarton's 'solitary doe at dusk' of 1992 (Sarton 2014, p. 16) is not leaping off ecstatically but 'Stamping and huffing', albeit 'In the luscious field'. And the doe is there only to inspire the *in*sight of a man blinded by AIDS-related illnesses. In *Difficult Scene* of 1946 (https://www.poetryfoundation.org/poetrymagazine/bro wse?contentId=24439), Sarton depersonalises the landscape, it 'does not speak, / Exists, is simply there'. The 'thereness' of nature is described in Glenn Gould's *Solitude Trilogy* (Gould 2003). Gould is best known as a pianist, particularly as a performer of Bach. Gradually withdrawing from public performance in concert halls, he believed that the stage performance was less perfect than could be achieved in a studio, and the audience distracted and interrupted his performance. (He was in that sense the opposite of Liszt, the virtuoso who lived for such live performances, or at least understood that as his strength.) Other great pianists, such as Horowitz, withdrew from concert performance for several years, but they usually – and Horowitz did – explain this in terms of stage-fright. Gould continued recording and also composing. He also made the *Solitude Trilogy* (2003), a production that defies categorisation. It is a set of radio documentaries (and there is a film version), each an hour long: *The Idea of the North* (1967), *The Latecomers* (1969) and *The Quiet in the Land* (1977). Each set in Canada, the first in the Arctic North, the second by the sea in Newfoundland, the third in an isolated Mennonite community in Manitoba. Sophisticated radio and film documentaries were nothing new, but Gould's layering of simultaneous voices – which he described as 'contrapuntal' – and his careful use of ambient sounds as well as musical pieces all gave the impression that each of these pieces was also a musical composition, a kind of opera. As a pianist, Gould's playing of Bach is renowned for its ability to separate voices and yet set each against the other in contrapuntal playing of the greatest skill. So his voicing, in the *Trilogy*, is easy to hear in the same way.

Gould's personal affinity for solitude – he lived alone most of his life, as well as withdrawing from live audiences – was well-suited to the solitude of the far reaches of Canada, even though he always lived in Toronto. Recording the voices of those living in, and travelling to, these isolated places, Gould produced what he said was as autobiographical a piece as he was prepared to create. What is the *idea* of the North? You will, in the North, be up against yourself. The landscape itself presents you with yourself. It is set against the urban South of Canada. Nature can be harsh but it is also neutral. Gould has little in these pieces on the indigenous population of the Canadian North, East and West in their own words. That is a striking omission. What it leaves is a picture of *travellers* to these places, rather than those who have lived there for centuries. For Gould it is a 'desert island' of the land, people thrown together almost by accident, and thrown against the landscape to 'meet themselves'. The First Peoples, Inuit and Métis people (referred to in the programme by an older person) are described as either people to be helped or as victims of being 'helped', as stereotyped (as hunters and artists) and as victims of racism. The landscape impresses and it is both frightening and attractive, bringing people together as well as isolating them.

Living alone and together, in a 'frontier' region that has been lived in for centuries, the landscape is said to invite and encourage eccentricity. The ambiguity of a solitary life that is also intensely communal is even more evident in the second programme, based in fishing communities, and more again in the third programme set in a Mennonite community. There is solitude throughout the *Trilogy*, but it is not a straightforward solitude. Gould himself withdrew from concerts and replaced this with intensive work in a studio with collaborators, and seemed in need of (some) company entirely on his own terms. His solitude is closer to self-determination or individualism than it is to complete separation. And that suits his view of nature in the *Trilogy*, too. Whilst celebrating 'the old ways' of fishing or worshipping, this is an anti-Romantic account. In *The Latecomers*, one voice contrasts the way of treating the land in Newfoundland to the way of treating the land in settled agrarian communities. Mining and oil extraction are described as 'raping' the land.

Gould's *Trilogy* is not quite the opera he might have hoped for, nor an entirely new art-form. But it works. The 'ostinato', the lower, continuous, sound somewhat in the background, is the sound of trains in the first part, the sea in the second part and choir rehearsals and a sermon in the third. Pieces with so many voices, bearing comparison with Bakhtin's *heteroglossia* (Bakhtin 1981, p. 263), may seem odd ways to represent solitude, but Gould's greatest renown came from his playing of J. S. Bach. Bach managed to write complex contrapuntal music intended for solo performance. The keyboard pieces played on the piano by Gould, and also pieces for solo violin and solo cello, are now central to the repertoires of each of these instruments. Violins and cellos are primarily single-voiced instruments, so Bach's ability to write contrapuntal music for solitary cellists and violinists is especially remarkable. Yet Gould doesn't refer to his *Trilogy* as Bachian but as Thoreauvian. And it is an apt comparison, as the forms and degrees of solitude described in *Trilogy* are indeed rather similar to Thoreau's Walden Pond (Thoreau 2006). They are also similar in defying easy categorisation. *Walden Pond* is an early work of environmental science; it is a journal of an extended camping trip; it is a work of philosophy; it is a contemplative piece of nature-art.

Thoreau's Pond Life

Notwithstanding his attraction to solitude, Gould was only prepared to travel as far North as the trains would take him. (The people he recorded had travelled much further North, by plane and boat.) Thoreau too was keen on solitude in nature but found the 'wilderness' of New Hampshire much less congenial than Walden Pond, a wooded area within a short walk of Concord, Massachusetts – close enough for Thoreau to visit his mother's home most Sundays. His description of the position makes it seem rather more remote than it was:

> My nearest neighbor is a mile distant, and no house is visible from any place but the hill-tops within half a mile of my own. I have my horizon bounded by woods all to myself; a distant view of the railroad where it touches the pond on the one hand, and of the fence which skirts the woodland road on the other. But for the most part it is as solitary where I live as on the prairies. It is as much Asia or Africa as New England. I have, as it were, my own sun and moon and stars, and a little world all to myself. (Thoreau 2006, pp. 140–1)

The pond and the wood around it remain to this day, now a tourist destination. The railway line running by the wood is still there, and the sounds of the trains providing Gould's ostinato might have provided one for Thoreau, too. How is solitude in nature described by Thoreau? A first point to make is the absence of loneliness, or at least the Romantic loneliness of place and nature. A close and, in this sense, unpoetic observation of nature meant that Thoreau refused to anthropomorphise the environment. Plants and non-human animals never suffer from loneliness: they continue blissfully unaware of and therefore never suffering from that emotion. And Thoreau? No. He describes getting close to it once: 'I have never felt lonesome, or in the least oppressed by a sense of solitude, but once, and that was a few weeks after I came to the woods, when, for an hour, I doubted if the near neighborhood of man was not essential to a serene and healthy life' (Thoreau 2006, p. 142). He experienced, briefly, that 'to be alone was something unpleasant' (Thoreau 2006, p. 142). But he soon recovered, and was 'cured' by his experience of nature itself, insisting that – unlike so many earlier poets – nature was not a lonely place.

> In the midst of a gentle rain while these thoughts prevailed, I was suddenly sensible of such sweet and beneficent society in Nature, the very pattering of the drops, and in every sound and sight around my house, an infinite and unaccountable friendliness all at once like an atmosphere sustaining me, as made the fancied advantages of human neighborhood insignificant, and I have never thought of them since. Every little pine needle expanded and swelled with sympathy and befriended me. I was so distinctly made aware of the presence of something kindred to me, even in scenes which we are accustomed to call wild and dreary, and also that the nearest of blood to me and humanity was not a person nor a villager, that I thought no place could ever be strange to me again. (Thoreau 2006, p. 142)

As well as finding company in nature, he avoided loneliness through experiencing company with himself: 'I am conscious of the presence and criticism of a part of me, which, as it were, is not a part of me, but spectator, sharing no experience, but taking note of it; that is no more I than it is you' (Thoreau 2006, p. 146). He appreciates the irony that 'this doubleness may easily make us poor neighbors and friends sometimes' (Thoreau 2006, p. 146). So he enjoys the 'company' of solitude:

> I love to be alone. I never found the companion that was so companionable as solitude. We are for the most part more lonely when we go abroad among men than when we stay in our chambers. (Thoreau 2006, p. 146)

He says that he is 'no more lonely than the loon in the pond that laughs so loud, or than Walden Pond itself' (Thoreau 2006, p. 148). 'What company has that lonely lake, I pray?', he continues, acknowledging then rejecting the Romantic idea of a 'lonely place', 'yet it has not the blue devils, but the blue angels in it, in the azure tint of its waters' (Thoreau 2006, p. 148). And along with the 'company' of the pond, he enjoys some human company, when balanced with solitude: 'I had three chairs in my house; one for solitude, two for friendship, three for society' (Thoreau 2006, p. 151). His meetings with passing farmers and traders make for good conversation. And he could be perfectly sociable. There are some similarities to Gould in his personality, at least from what can be read from their autobiographical and other more personal writings. Enjoying both solitude and company, company is generally enjoyed very much on the author's terms, and the author soon returns to a restorative solitude.

Nature, in *Walden*, is far more than a backdrop for Thoreau's philosophy. The detail of his descriptions of plants, animals or ice on the pond, of weather: all are respected and given their own identities and relationships. It is an ecology, unlike the individual skylark or nightingale, buck or fly. Nature as ecology was not original to Thoreau, but was built on the earlier work of Humboldt, who was at the centre of Romantic intellectual life. According to Wulf, 'America's most revered nature writer, Henry David Thoreau, found in Humboldt's books an answer to his dilemma on how to be a poet *and* a naturalist' (Wulf 2015, pp. 5–6). The scientist Humboldt influenced his friend Goethe and many other writers of the period and throughout the nineteenth century, and a number of ecological writers (with or without acknowledgement) in the twentieth century. Accounts of nature that were most affected by Humboldt's work as a naturalist are less anthropomorphic and more respectful of the interconnectedness of the natural world, independent of humanity. Darwin, Thoreau's contemporary, made the point even more clearly, in his comparison of human selective breeding and the way in which nature is developed through 'natural' selection. It is the absence of a 'selector' in nature that shocked the political and religious authorities of Darwin's time. But Thoreau was doing similar work across the pond, describing the complex interrelationships observable in nature with no sign of a divine planner. Nature is so busy, or so tranquil, so noisy or quiet, so competitive or collaborative, Thoreau could see it all, as a consequence of his withdrawal to the slightly isolated hut. House-dwelling in human company distracts us from such an awareness.

The Living Mountain

Neither Romantic nor anti-Romantic, Thoreau is not even easy to describe as a realist or as a scientist, as he cannot help but introduce thoughtful philosophical interpretations stimulated by his observations. It took Thoreau far longer to write *Walden* than the eighteen months he spent living there, but the experience was clearly formative and flavoured all his subsequent work. He was not an individualist, and yet at times, he says, he felt he was the first or the last man in the world, albeit without the survivalist hard work implied by such a situation. Thoreau's nature allows for a comfortable and comforting solitude. Recuperative and inspiring, nature can demonstrate what solitude without loneliness can feel like, as the non-human elements live and die together without the intensity of human social and cultural expectations, and in particular without the moral responsibility of Adam and Eve after the Fall. A companion piece to Thoreau's, similarly hard to categorise and similarly temporary as a solitude experience, is Nan Shepherd's *The Living Mountain* (Shepherd 2011). Shepherd was a novelist and taught in a teacher training college in Aberdeen. For much of her adult life, she spent weekends and holidays walking and camping in the Cairngorms. It was this experience that is described in *The Living Mountain*. Like Thoreau, she was usually alone, but occasionally met other walkers and describes companions positively. Yet solitude in the mountains remains the dominant image. By describing the mountain as 'living', let alone the plants and animals living on the mountain, Shepherd always has 'living' company, just rarely of the human kind. And the *livingness* of the mountain is vital to her narrative. Men, she says, tend to see mountains as objects to be 'conquered'. Mountaineers are victorious when they reach a mountain's summit, and then go on to 'battle' with another mountain. In contrast, Shepherd was living *with*, in or on the mountain, coming to appreciate and understand it, returning repeatedly in different weather conditions and different growing seasons.

> The talking tribe, I find, want sensation from the mountain. ... Beginners, not unnaturally, do the same – I did myself. They want the startling view, the horrid pinnacle – sips of beer and tea instead of milk. Yet often the mountain gives itself most completely when I have no destination, when I reach nowhere in particular, but have gone out merely to be with the mountain as one visits a friend with no intention but to be with him. (Shepherd 2011, p. 15)

Shepherd's solitude in nature is not heroic, as Gould's was (at least in his own mind), and Shepherd would have been appalled, if not surprised, by Gould's reference to Canadians 'raping' the landscape. (This is not to say Gould approved himself: he was appalled by aggression, finding even performing in a concert hall too 'aggressive'.) Hers was a quiet if not silent experience. 'As I stand there in the silence, I become aware that the silence is not complete ... [as w]ater is speaking' (Shepherd 2011, p. 22).

Having disciplined mind and body to quiescence, I must discipline them also to activity. The senses must be used. For the ear, the most vital thing that can be listened to here is silence. To bend the ear to silence is to discover how seldom it is there. Always something moves. When the air is quite still, there is always running water; and up here that is a sound one can hardly lose, though on many stony parts of the plateau one is above the watercourses. (Shepherd 2011, p. 96)

Even when silence is present, it is not a mere absence:

Now and then comes an hour when the silence is all but absolute, and listening to it one slips out of time. Such a silence is not a mere negation of sound. It is like a new element, and if water is still sounding with a low far-off murmur, it is no more than the last edge of an element we are leaving, as the last edge of land hangs on the mariner's horizon. (Shepherd 2011, p. 96)

The Cairngorms are dour, glowering, misty and bare-looking mountains, not the scenic snowy peaks beloved by mountaineers and downhill skiers. Yet Shepherd found them companionable, and her readers quickly understand this. Many would describe a mountain as *covered*, or not, with vegetation and *inhabited* by animals, but Shepherd takes the mountain as a whole system, an ecology in Humboldt's sense, and it is the Cairngorms that she describes – a whole set of linked mountains, rivers, lochs and vegetation. Even the weather is part of the mountains. Walking, writing notes, eating, setting up camp – often just a shelter by bushes – the author enjoys the sensuousness of the experience. Feeling and presence: the nature writer Robert Macfarlane who writes the preface to the current edition of Shepherd's book helpfully compares her work to that of Merleau-Ponty. Shepherd, like Thoreau, wears her philosophy lightly or, more suited to their contexts, *lives out* her philosophy as she lives out in the mountain. Well, she doesn't live continuously in the mountain: she is a temporary visitor, albeit a regular one. Some of the people she meets are more permanent residents, but Shepherd doesn't wish to be one. She ends her book with a pilgrimage metaphor, and a description of what I might call *enstasy*:

I believe that I now understand in some small measure why the Buddhist goes on pilgrimage to a mountain. The journey is itself part of the technique by which the god is sought. It is a journey into Being; for as I penetrate more deeply into the mountain's life, I penetrate also into my own. For an hour I am beyond desire. It is not ecstasy, that leap out of the self that makes man like a god. I am not out of myself, but in myself. I am. To know Being, this is the final grace accorded from the mountain. (Shepherd 2011, p. 108)

Muir Wanderings

One of the most famous nature-writers who *did* live for many years in wilderness environments was Scottish, like Shepherd, but lived as an adult in North America. John Muir was an author and campaigner, someone who was said to have *taught* Americans their own wild landscapes, and who was the main influence on the creation of America's national parks. 'John of the Mountains' was more like the stereotype of a mountain-dweller than the close-to-town Thoreau or the weekender Shepherd. Yet Thoreau remains a hero to Muir. Muir's influences, along with Thoreau and Emerson, included intense biblical study from early childhood. Muir's 'wildness' was controlled and university-educated, albeit dropping out of university after four years, saying 'I was only leaving one University for another, the Wisconsin University for the University of the Wilderness' (Muir 2017, p. 123). He walked thousands of miles (one text of many publications was entitled *A Thousand Mile Walk*, Muir 2017, p. xxx), travelling across the United States and Canada, and spending much of his time in California. A oneness with nature was spiritually rich, almost a theology in its own right.

> We should think about John Muir as the inventor of a new American religion. …
> I think he is a religious prophet, and a lot of people in this country have followed him or followed those ideas. (Williams, in Muir 2017, p. xiii, quoting Donald Worster)

'Nature is holy', Williams says of Muir, and 'all the world seems a church and the mountains alters' (Muir, quoted by Williams, in Muir 2017, p. xiv). Muir's 'voice [is] often rhapsodic and, at times, ecstatic', as (quoting Muir) 'everybody needs beauty as well as bread, places to play in and pray in, where Nature may heal and cheer and give strength to body and soul alike' (Williams, in Muir 2017, p. xv). Solitude in wild places gave Muir his quasi-religious, or actually religious, sense of creation and wholeness. A deeper ecology, in that sense, than Thoreau described of the more 'managed' environment at Walden Pond. But Muir was consciously developing his nature-solitude from Thoreau's writings, and also those of the more explicitly transcendentalist Emerson.

So much nature-writing goes back to Thoreau (as Thoreau's goes back to Humboldt), Thoreau's fingerprints are on such writing up to recent years, including Macfarlane's work (e.g. Macfarlane and Morris 2017, for children), and that of those living in (human) solitude with or, more rarely, *as* non-human animals (Birkhead 2012; Foster 2016; Lindén 2018; Wohlleben 2017). The 'deeper' the ecology, the more often Muir is an influence alongside Thoreau. The philosopher who established deep ecology as a current philosophical system is Arne Naess. He lived much of his later life in a hut in the Norwegian mountains, after giving up his impressive academic career whilst still able to enjoy mountaineering. His ecology builds on the work of Rachel Carson (1962), as well as Muir, but also Spinoza. The holism of Spinoza, and his understanding of self-realisation as only possible in harmony with the world as a whole, was important to deep ecology as a political, campaigning, movement, as well as its somewhat religious character. It is Spinoza's definition of joy as a transition from lesser to greater perfection – which Naess paraphrases as 'integrity' or 'wholeness' (Naess 2008, p. 128) – that gives Naess's (human) solitude within and of nature a philosophical significance.

> Joy is linked intrinsically to an increase in many things: perfection, power and virtue, freedom and rationality, activeness, the degree to which we are the cause of our own actions, and the degree to which our actions are understandable by reference to ourselves. … An increase in power is an increase in the ability to carry out what we sincerely strive to do. Power does not presuppose that we coerce other people; a tyrant may be less powerful than some poor soul sitting in prison. (Naess 2008, p. 128)

Solitude within nature is generally needed in order to achieve a 'higher' oneness, rather than a separation, therefore. Separation is only needed, more or less temporarily, from the distractions that other people bring. Thoreau, Muir, Macfarlane and Naess are not anti-humanists. All recognised and valued human beings. But all might reasonably be called post-humanists. Solitude as post- not anti-human is a significant theme.

Music from Alaska

A musician influenced directly by Gould's *Trilogy*, rather than his conventional musical compositions and performances, is John Luther Adams. Adams – no relation of the better-known composer John Adams – lived first in US cities and felt caught between active social engagement and a wish for solitude, before moving to the 'wilds' of Alaska. 'I've steered an uneasy course between the Scylla of solitude and the Charybdis of politics', he says, 'between my desire to help change the world and my impulse to escape it' (Adams 2020, p. 9). 'The vessel in which I navigate these turbulent waters is music' (Adams 2020, p. 9), with the music drawing from his many years living in a remote house in Alaska, in what he calls a 'shared solitude' with the neighbours spread out through the area, 'a ragtag and sometimes rowdy crew of musicians, poets, fishermen, and other kindred spirits' (Adams 2020, p. 1).

> Those years in the woods were essential for me, as an artist and as a man. In our shared solitude, I found a sense of community that I doubt I could've found in any other place. And the visions of music and of the world that emerged in that cabin have sustained me ever since. (Adams 2020, p. 76)

'Ever since encountering the film version of Glenn Gould's *The Idea of North*', he says, 'I'd dreamed of traveling in northern Canada and Alaska' (Adams 2020, p. 17).

> Running away from the cities and the suburbs. Running away from academia, and from the competitive world of 'the music business.' Coming here to this cabin in the boreal forest, I imagine that I'm running away from everything. But I'm actually running *to* everything. (Adams 2020, p. 1)

Adams's composing is hugely influenced by his experience of nature in Alaska. Although the music is more conventionally 'musical' than Gould's pieces, it also often used ambient sounds of nature. These were sometimes recorded in situ, and sometimes reproduced by instruments. And whereas Gould disliked the discomforts of the wilderness, and made little attempt to understand the knowledge and experience of indigenous peoples, Adams lived more closely with 'wild' nature, and came to know indigenous communities well. This is evident in his music as well as his writing, and he recognised those occasions when his solitude in the wild was *not* good. 'So there I was – heartsick, a little frightened by the fierce cold, and feeling utterly alone', he says of one occasion lost in the wood in winter: 'Suddenly, my isolation no longer seemed so splendid ... [as i]t was more like solitary confinement' (Adams 2020, p. 80). An early, pre-Alaskan, piece was an interpretation of birdsongs (*songbirdsongs*, Adams 2012). He wrote of the sea in *Become Ocean* (Adams 2014), of the air in *Sila: The Breath of the World* (Adams 2022) and of travels amongst spirits in the indigenous-influenced *Inuksuit* (Adams 2013). These are not romanticised interpretations of solitude in nature but immersive experiences. Of *Become Ocean*, Adams writes:

> Then is this music about the sea? Yes. Well, in a way ... But what I really hope is that this music is an ocean of its own, an expansive sea of sound that just may carry the listener away into an oceanic state of mind. (Adams 2020, pp. 5–6)

The music of Adams is described by him as at times ecstatic, and he draws on indigenous spirituality to explain and demonstrate this.

> The strange power of noise can open doorways to the ecstatic. Musical traditions throughout the world have explored this power for centuries. I knew it from my years as a rock drummer. But my most profound experiences of this have come through the all-night drumming, chanting, and dancing of the Iñupiat and Yup'ik peoples. The rapid reiteration of loud, acoustically complex sounds alters our consciousness. In this state, as my Native friends might say, we can travel to and from the spirit world. (Adams 2020, p. 99)

Is solitude in nature really *solitude*, if it is so intensely engaged with plants, animals, the wind, water, mountains and landscapes? The arts of such solitudes tell us yes, and no. As Adams says of one of his own compositions, even the artists may answer both yes and no.

> I imagined each musician and each individual listener as a singular figure in a vast landscape. I thought I was composing a piece about solitude. It was only when I heard the first performances of *Inuksuit* that I realized it's all about *community*. (Adams 2020, p. 122; emphasis in the original)

There are themes of individual self-realisation (Stern and Wałejko 2020), expressed indirectly through individual birds and bears. There are individual trekkers, campers and hunters. And there is the often-repeated oddity of separation from people allowing a 'oneness with the world'. That oneness is itself the heart of the 'no' response to 'is this really solitude?'

Being of the world, at one with all of nature, is often described in religious or spiritual terms. But it is also a recognition of the artist's simple embodiment. This doubling is well expressed in Coleridge's *Rime of the Ancient Mariner*. The mariner kills an albatross and is forced to wear it like a cross around his neck. His fellow sailors all die and he is left to take the ship home (with some ghostly help): 'this soul hath been / Alone on a wide wide sea: / So lonely 'twas, that God himself / Scarce seemed there to be' (Coleridge 1994, p. 100). It sinks close to home and he is rescued by a hermit. His lesson learned, to love 'All things both great and small' (Coleridge 1994, p. 100), he retells his tale to educate others. The solitary, Christ-like, albatross, the solitary sailor, the hermit-rescuer: all are solitary nature representations. The moral is more holistic (and more Humboldt-tinged, if more 'emotional' than Humboldt's writing): all creatures living together in nature. 'The new love of nature', as Taylor describes it, is 'associated with the cult of sensibility … [that] captures both the centrality of feeling and its link to the sense that our moral sources are within us, in an inner nature which marks what is significant for us' (Taylor 1989, p. 302). This is sourced in such creative artists, and is itself also a tale of the creative arts:

> Rather like Coleridge's Ancient Mariner, the spiritual or creative traveller may return transformed from the journey bearing some kind of 'message' which will often have an ineffable quality, calling for symbolic or metaphoric expression beyond the limitations of the verbal or the narrowly cognitive … [one that] accepts the plurality of modes of meaning-making and embraces the individual narrative. (McCarthy, in Craft et al. 2001, p. 129)

UnCaged

A final piece of music. Almost. Huxley said that 'from pure sensation to the intuition of beauty, from pleasure and pain to love and the mystical ecstasy and death – all the things that are fundamental, all the things that, to the human spirit, are most profoundly significant, can only be experienced, not expressed', and 'the rest is always and everywhere silence' (Huxley 1950, p. 19). He continued:

> After silence that which comes nearest to expressing the inexpressible is music. (And, significantly, silence is an integral part of all good music) (Huxley 1950, p. 19)

MacCulloch describes the same in the history of the Christian religion, in which, he says, 'silence is allied to wordlessness, and wordlessness is allied to music … [which] plays the role of mediator between silence and words, because it stretches between and melts into either polarity … [and therefore] traces the border between sound and silence … [making it] one of the great sustainers of spiritual exploration' (MacCulloch 2013, p. 231). A magisterial survey of the uses of silence in music is provided by Losseff and Doctor (2007), but what remains the most famous piece of music demonstrating this rich ambiguity is the one by John Cage. Cage's *4'33"* of 1952 is one of the best-known classical compositions of the second half of the twentieth century. It consists of four minutes and thirty-three seconds of a pianist playing no notes. This would give it a well-deserved position in Chapter 8 on postmodernism. But it equally deserves mention in this chapter, as a consequence of a special performance of the piece. Cage's book, *Silence* (Cage 2009), gives a vivid account of his trip into a wood. (Cage was a keen collector of mushrooms, alongside his musical enthusiasms.) There, he stands still and conducts a version of his silent piece. The animals of the wood perform the piece – as audience members, with their shuffles and sniffs, perform the concert-hall version of the piece – in three distinct movements.

> I have spent many pleasant hours in the woods conducting performances of my silent piece, transcriptions, that is, for an audience of myself, since they were much longer than the popular length which I have had published. At one performance, I passed the first movement by attempting the identification of a mushroom which remained successfully unidentified. The second movement was extremely dramatic, beginning with the sounds of a buck and a doe leaping up to within ten feet of my rocky podium. The expressivity of this movement was not only dramatic but unusually sad from my point of view, for the animals were frightened simply because I was a human being. However, they left hesitatingly and fittingly within the structure of the work. The third movement was a return to the theme of the first, but with all those profound, so-well-known alterations of world feeling associated by German tradition with the A-B-A. (Cage 2009, p. 276)

The idea that nature is a work of art is hardly new, and even the conceit of the sounds of nature being a representation of silence is well-established. Kierkegaard wrote, a century before Cage, of the mysterious silence of and in nature, in which nature 'is in a mysterious and thus in turn silent harmony with the silence' (Kierkegaard 2000, p. 335, quoted in Chapter 1). What Cage adds is his 'joke' at the hubris of humanity 'conducting' nature. Artist Joseph Beuys created one of his most famous pieces, *I Like America and America Likes Me* (https://www.youtube.com/watch?v=r9NWCOF0c5M and https://magazine. artland.com/stories-of-iconic-artworks-joseph-beuys-i-like-america-and-amer ica-likes-me/), in which he wrapped himself in felt and stayed alone in a gallery room in New York with a wild coyote. That description of the work belies its complexity, and its symbolic value in describing through the interaction, alone with a coyote, how Beuys understood the United States of that time (1974) and how it might recover itself through understanding the 'natural' and the 'mythic' values represented by the coyote. The coyote itself takes an active part in the piece, as a coyote might: at various times it bit at Beuys's gloves and his felt covering, at times it was quiet and calm. There is something of Cage's humour in Beuys's piece, an absurdity in the relationship between the intentionality of the artist and his co-option of the non-human animal with – shall we say – a less aesthetic agenda.

A less humorous – or differently humorous – equivalent of such hubris occurred decades earlier. One of the most famous early BBC radio outside broadcasts was in 1924, just two years after the BBC had started broadcasting.

A famous cellist of the time, Beatrice Harrison, used to practice in her garden, and was often joined by a nightingale. The BBC recorded one such duet, and it became a broadcasting sensation. Repeated every year for decades, the solitary cellist and the solitary nightingale brought art and nature into a beautiful harmony (https://www.google.com/search?client=fire fox-b-d&q=cello+and+nightingale#fpstate=ive&vld=cid:a83938df,vid:Qs6V 66gsrIQ). Recently, however, it emerged that the recording crew had probably scared off the nightingale, and a (human) bird-impersonator was used as a stand-in (Alberge 2022).

Concluding Nature

Solitude in or of or with nature is liable to such hubris. It is easy to criticise Thoreau for his 'safe' solitude, or Muir and Gould for their white male privileged perspectives on natural solitude. Yet people continue to seek and find solitude in nature, and find themselves – and their own sensuous, embodied, nature in nature. As Marvell said of *The Garden*, 'Society is all but rude, / To this delicious solitude' (https://www.poetryfoundation.org/poems/44682/the-garden-56d223 dec2ced). Such delicious solitudes became so popular, however, precisely because they seemed increasingly hard to find. The capitalisation of Nature was itself a reaction to industrialisation and urbanisation. The solitudes that became most characteristic of the cities, in contrast to nature, were often described as forms of *alienation*, and that is the theme of the next chapter.

6

Alienation and Its Emotions

I work every day and lose myself in the tasks that others set me,
But it's only the money, not the work, that gets me up.

Summary

Alienation developed artistically and philosophically during the first half of the nineteenth century, from more religious meanings (in Wordsworth's pantheism, Hölderlin's Greek re-working of Christianity, Friedrich's inner visions and Hegel's phenomenology, and explored in the twenty-first century by Sacks) through ideas on human nature (in Feuerbach and in Mary Shelley) to the social and economic alienation described by Marx as central to capitalism – and artistically in Thoreau, Emily Brontë and George Eliot. Later in the nineteenth century, sexuality became more central to descriptions of alienation, accompanied by newer forms of personal, self-blaming, loneliness. One form of literature that had loneliness at its heart is the short story, and these stories are explored here.

Some key artists: Friedrich Hölderlin (1770–1843), William Wordsworth (1770–1850), Caspar David Friedrich (1774–1840), Mary Shelley (1797–1851), Henry David Thoreau (1817–1862), Emily Brontë (1818–1848), George Eliot (1819–1880), Benjamin Disraeli (1804–1881), Oscar Wilde (1854–1900), Radclyffe Hall (1880–1943), Frank O'Connor (1903–1966), Thomas Mann (1875–1955), Richard Yates (1926–1992), Raymond Carver (1938–1988)

Introduction: Changing Definitions

'Alien' and 'alienation' are long-established words, words whose meanings and use changed hugely in the nineteenth century. These changes ran parallel to changes in the use of emotion words, notably 'loneliness'. Although this book is not a history of language or of emotions, and although changes in the use of emotion words are not the same as changes in substantive emotions, the links between alienation and loneliness are interesting and very much worth a chapter. Some of the significant artists of the nineteenth century have solitude themes that seem to illustrate and help us understand and develop our ideas of alienation. These include Hölderlin, Wordsworth, Friedrich, Mary Shelley, Thoreau, Emily Brontë and George Eliot. All have roles in the themes of other chapters of this book, but the coincidence of their work and that of the (professional) philosophers of alienation, and in some cases their personal links with those philosophers, makes them particularly interesting as alienation-themed artists.

First, some definitions and a bit of philosophy. To be alien means to be 'other', so 'alienation' is roughly equivalent to 'otherness'. This is a simple etymology that underplays the different uses of the word. To be alienated in the eighteenth century generally meant to be 'out of one's mind' or more commonly to be separated from God. Within philosophy at the end of that century, alienation was central to the argument Hegel put forward in his *Phenomenology of Spirit* (Hegel 1977) and the later *Philosophy of Religion* (Hegel 1988). Hegel's various accounts of alienation combined religious and social senses of the word. In his *Phenomenology*, alienation (also translated as 'estrangement') is one of the repeated 'moments' of the dialectic of separation and togetherness. Hegel's later *Philosophy of Religion* describes in more detail estrangement from God (Hegel 1988, pp. 447–9), which is characterised by anguish and evil, and estrangement from the world (Hegel 1988, p. 449–51), characterised by unhappiness. Hegel's account of alienation seems in part a response to the 'curse' of alienation that had become a *loneliness* from which his friend Hölderlin seemed to suffer ('tell me, is it a blessing or a curse, this loneliness which is part of my nature and which … I am … irresistibly driven back into?', Hölderlin 2009, p. 197, quoted in Chapter 3). To be alienated, for Hegel, was to be out of the spirit of the age, with the expectation that the alienation may be resolved in being part of a larger 'spirit', represented in the ultimate (Prussian) state. Hegel's student Feuerbach developed the theory much further, with the idea that alienation was from a person's human nature, their essence. Modern society in Europe in the first half of the nineteenth century was described by Feuerbach as alienating, and his was not so much a religious (or anti-religious) argument as a social and political one. He criticised his old teacher and turned alienation into an explanation of, a critique of and a way of going beyond Christianity, and a critique of the state. People alienate themselves from their own species being, from their 'essential nature' (Feuerbach 1855, p. 19) and from 'Nature' (Feuerbach 1855, p. 183).

A third stage in alienation's development was the one that has become the best known of all. In the middle of the nineteenth century, Marx wrote – against both Hegel and Feuerbach – that alienation was not a spiritual matter at all but an economic and social one, and not a separation from human nature but from each other and from the products of one's work. Early in his writings, Marx had been closer to Feuerbach's views, describing how 'man [*sic*] is a species-being ... because he treats himself as a universal and therefore a free being' (Marx 2009, p. 31). At this stage, alienation is for Marx, as for Feuerbach, the separation of people from their species being, from their nature. Alienation 'estranges from man his own body, as well as external nature and his spiritual aspect, his *human* aspect ... [which in turn leads to] the *estrangement of man* from *man*' (Marx 2009, p. 32). The universality of human nature, in Feuerbach's philosophy, was later rejected by Marx, as people and alienation are historically embedded: 'the human essence is no abstraction inherent in each single individual ... [but i]n its reality it is the ensemble of the social relations' (Marx, in Marx and Engels 1970, p. 122). Alienation is retained, however, in the later more historically contingent accounts of Marx – with modern capitalist industrial societies alienating labour (including taking the products of labour away from those labouring), and in doing that alienating people from each other, from the products of their labour *and from themselves.*

Alienation Arts and Emotions

The three alienation traditions have parallels in the arts:

- Hegel's sense of alienation as a spiritual–religious condition was paralleled in the arts of contemporaries like Hölderlin, Wordsworth and Friedrich. Hölderlin and Friedrich might be described as more religiously inspired, and alienated. Wordsworth, sometimes described as a pantheist (a believer in God embedded in nature rather than separate from it), was perhaps the more spiritual, seeing solitude more positively and yet also finding himself struggling at times to connect with any sense of the spiritual.
- Feuerbach's artistic contemporaries included Mary Shelley, who had a greater focus on human nature and a sense of the failure of a creator God, and the consequent alienation of the Creature.
- Later, Marx's contemporaries included Thoreau, Emily Brontë and George Eliot, all of whom had a more social and economic sense of alienation.

Thoreau, born within a few months of Marx, explained this most fully. His account of healthy solitude by Walden Pond (Thoreau 2006) provides one of the most influential attacks on the alienation experienced in competitive crowds, a century before 'the lonely crowd' (Reisman 2000) was coined.

Clearly these artists of solitude portrayed it in many different, positive and negative, ways. Yet there is in these authors already a hint of a newer kind of alienation, expressed emotionally especially through the newly forming emotion called loneliness. But how can an emotion be 'formed' in such a way?

There are many theories of emotions, but for this work I will use a relatively conventional one as described by Spinoza in the seventeenth century. He said that every emotion is made up of two parts. One is a feeling, and he recognises only pleasure and pain as feelings, 'a force for existence ... greater or less than before' (Spinoza 1955, p. 181). The other is a cognitive element that is an interpretation accompanying the feeling, that is, 'the mind is determined to think of one thing rather than another' (Spinoza 1955, p. 185). Shame 'is pain accompanied by the idea of some action of our own, which we believe to be blamed by others' (Spinoza 1955, p. 181), envy is pain accompanied by the thought of another person's success, admiration is pleasure accompanied by the thought of another person's or object's good qualities and so on. Spinoza's theory has the advantage of simplicity, and of clearly distinguishing the affective (feeling) and cognitive (interpretative) elements. People often talk about an emotion as a 'feeling', but Spinoza's theory says it is more than this – our basic *feelings* are remarkably limited, consisting of just pleasure and pain. What his theory – in common with many other similar theories – allows for is the idea of a new emotion or the disappearance of an old emotion. There are no new feelings, but there can be new *emotions*, as new interpretations emerge. This is not about new *words* for emotions. These of course can appear and disappear over time. It is about new *emotions*. Hence, the possibility of there being a history of emotions, a history of their appearance, growth or disappearance over time, and a difference in the emotions experienced at different times and in different cultures (Plamper 2015; Bound Alberti 2019, and https://projects.history.qmul.ac.uk/emotions/).

An interesting example of this is given in a recent interpretation of a very old narrative, one that is central to one of the earliest senses of alienation. Jonathan Sacks (2021, pp. 3–7) asks a question of the Adam and Eve narrative in the Bible. What is usually understood of the account is that, by eating the 'apple' (the fruit of the tree of knowledge), Adam and Eve became aware of morality and of their responsibility for disobeying God's instruction to avoid only that fruit. However,

Sacks asks a question, one that seems an obvious problem with the narrative. (Set to one side questions like 'did this really happen?') If Adam and Eve only knew they did wrong after they ate the fruit, how could they understand that they *shouldn't* eat it, *before* they did? Surely they had to be morally aware first, before eating the fruit that makes them morally aware? Sacks has a surprising 'solution' to this problem. (There are other attempted solutions, including that the account is a story of *creativity*, Berryman 1991, p. 111, or about *boredom*, Kierkegaard 2000, p. 51, or about *learning*, Salmon 1988, pp. 18–20.) Sacks describes the difference between guilt cultures and shame cultures. Shame, he says 'has to do with how you appear (or imagine you appear) in other people's eyes', whereas guilt 'by contrast is much more internal' (Sacks 2021, p. 4).

> With this in mind, we can now understand the story of the first sin. It is all about appearances, shame, vision, and the eye. ... The key emotion in the story is shame. ... But the Torah is the supreme example of a culture of guilt, not shame, and you cannot escape guilt by hiding. Guilt has nothing to do with appearances and everything to do with conscience. ... The sin of the first humans in the Garden of Eden was that they followed their eyes, not their ears. ... The result was that they did indeed acquire a knowledge of good and evil, but it was the wrong kind. They acquired an ethic of shame, not guilt; of appearances not conscience. (Sacks 2021, p. 5)

In Spinoza's model, we might say, following Sacks, that guilt is pain accompanied by an awareness of one's *own* wrongdoing, whereas shame is more about an awareness of what *other* people think. In the Garden of Eden, *guilt* was already there, and the 'Fall' involved the invention of *shame*.

> Will our emotional horizon be bounded by honour and shame, two profoundly social feelings? Is our key value appearance? How we seem to others? Or is it something else altogether, a willingness to heed the word and will of God? Adam and Eve in Eden faced the archetypal human choice between what their eyes saw (the tree and its fruit) and what their ears heard (God's command). Because they chose the first, they felt shame, not guilt. That is one form of 'knowledge of good and evil,' but from a Jewish perspective, it is the wrong form.
>
> Judaism is a religion of listening, not seeing. (Sacks 2021, p. 6)

For Adam and Eve, nakedness became awkward: nakedness is not something that is one's own fault, it is about what other people think.

Sacks doesn't give this reading to explain the history of emotions in general, but it works for this, too. In effect, he is describing the 'invention of shame'.

And this is an emotion associated with alienation. Alienation is in this instance a separation from God. Adam wishes to hide from God, in his shame, but cannot hide from his voice and the guilt that could already be experienced, even before eating the fruit. Shame is related to 'public face', guilt to 'internal' conscience. Both can be described as a kind of alienation, for Adam and Eve. They are emotions related to this 'first' alienation – from God and from Eden. Later forms of alienation were accompanied by other emotions. Early in the nineteenth century, when more religious uses of 'alienation' were common along with those related to 'madness', some artists expressing this started using the term 'loneliness'. Hölderlin used the term (in translation, at least) of himself, Clare used it of empty places in 'nature'. Poets seemed to look to nature as a lost Garden of Eden, hence lonely because they (or we) no longer have a *place* there, in which to live. Nature was for wandering, alone, as a cloud, whilst real country living was hard work. (This also is in the Adam and Eve narrative: they were condemned to hard farming work, in contrast to simply gathering food.)

Loneliness Emerges, in Guilt and Shame

Aloneness in nature was bound to fail, in a society that had gone so far beyond simply gathering food, and in which social systems were so controlling. Clare was kept in an asylum, Hölderlin in a protected environment (protected by a caring family). Shelley's *Frankenstein* gave a more Feuerbachian account of a world in which people (represented by the Creature) were alienated from their own nature and from their creator: a more fundamental and unavoidable alienation. Later in the nineteenth century, Marx's view of alienation no longer had a religious element, nor an unavoidable human nature element: it was a social, economic, alienation. (Marx's economic history still, of course, has many echoes of the Adam and Even narrative, in the history of the change from 'primitive communism' to the class-exploitation and eventual alienation involved in settled agricultural communities.) Social and economic alienation was just as troubling as the earlier kinds, but because it was contingent on social and economic circumstances, it could therefore be overcome. The emotion that accompanied such a temporary, social, alienation was also temporary. Marx said that although alienation *could* be overcome, it would *not* be overcome until people became *conscious* of their situation. Until then, people suffered from what was later called 'false consciousness' (e.g. Marcuse 1991, pp. 148–9). The alienation-emotion suited to this situation was a newer kind of loneliness. A painful feeling, accompanied by a *separation* from other people, a *rejection* by other people (potentially a form of *shame*, in Sacks's description of that emotion) and a sense that it is one's *own* fault (potentially a form of *guilt*, in Sacks's description). It could be 'recovered' from, not simply by changing the social situation (which might mitigate shame) but also by changing one's own consciousness (which might mitigate guilt). 'Shame and its cover-up' is described by Shabad as 'the self-enclosed prison of isolation' (Shabad, in Dimitrijević and Buchholz 2022, p. 307), which contributes to 'the transformation of aloneness into loneliness' (Shabad, in Dimitrijević and Buchholz 2022, p. 312).

New forms of loneliness, socially embedded and accompanied by a sense of self-blame or guilt, were the accompaniments to the somewhat godless yet self-blaming social and economic alienation of the mid- to late nineteenth century. In the hands of the Brontë novelists, and even more the novels of George Eliot (especially *Middlemarch*, Eliot 1965) and the poems of Emily Dickinson, this was gradually established as an emotion central to European (perhaps North European) and North American culture. But for those thinking a Marxist bit of theorising is the last word, there is an additional strand of loneliness that emerged in the late nineteenth and early twentieth century.

Sexuality was written about with an intensity missing from the novels of Dickens or many earlier writers. Douglas brought gay sexuality – and the alienation and loneliness associated with it (for him) – with the phrase that became a cliché: 'the love that dare not speak its name' (Douglas 2013, p. 25). In that poem, two men walk towards the narrator, and one kisses him.

> 'Sweet youth,
> Tell me why, sad and sighing, thou dost rove
> These pleasant realms? I pray thee speak me sooth
> What is thy name?' He said, 'My name is Love.'
> Then straight the first did turn himself to me
> And cried, 'He lieth, for his name is Shame,
> But I am Love, and I was wont to be
> Alone in this fair garden, till he came
> Unasked by night; I am true Love, I fill
> The hearts of boy and girl with mutual flame.'
> Then sighing, said the other, 'Have thy will,
> I am the love that dare not speak its name.'

Douglas's lover, Oscar Wilde, wrote of *Silentium Amoris* (Wilde 1966, p. 786) in his own way, and, notwithstanding his greater qualities as a poet, said far more bluntly that 'for excess of Love my Love is dumb' (Wilde 1966, p. 786). In his *Ballad of Reading Gaol* he wrote how 'each man kills the thing he loves' (Wilde 1966, p. 843), yet 'each man does not die', as he 'does not die a death of shame' (Wilde 1966, p. 843), as Wilde presumably felt he was doing, in prison. He was alone in a crowded prison, amongst 'all the souls in pain' (Wilde 1966, p. 845). Being in prison was described as full of shame and of guilt, which were the qualities that created the isolation despite so many people being crowded together as '*he does not win who plays with Sin / In the secret House of Shame*' (Wilde 1966, p. 860, italics in original). One of his conclusions is that 'thus we rust Life's iron chain / Degraded and alone' (Wilde 1966, p. 859). Combining aloneness with guilt and shame, Wilde is shaping the emerging form of loneliness, without naming it loneliness.

It was Radclyffe Hall who gave 'loneliness' its most public form as an emotion of guilt and shame driven by social attitudes to sexuality of the late Victorian age and early twentieth century. Her best-known work was *The Well of Loneliness* (Hall 1982), first published in 1928. There were other, more celebratory, accounts of LGBTQI+ sexuality of the time, such as the wildly outrageous art of Aubrey Beardsley, but the focus here is on solitude and loneliness. In Hall's account, in particular, it was the guilt and shame accompanying the heroine's, Stephen's, sexuality that drives the novel towards loneliness. Introducing the novel, Hennegan explains how it is 'jokingly, and not so jokingly, ... known as "the Bible of lesbianism"' (in Hall 1982, p. viii), and Hall's description of loneliness is described in terms of an 'unwanted being' (Hall 1982, p. 205), a form of self-rejection. Stephen's father dead, her mother discovers the 'scandal' of her daughter, and the daughter (Stephen) realises they cannot live together.

> As though drawn there by some strong natal instinct, Stephen went straight to her father's study; and she sat in the old arm-chair that had survived him; then she buried her face in her hands.
>
> All the loneliness that had gone before was as nothing to this new loneliness of spirit. An immense desolation swept down upon her, an immense need to cry out and claim understanding for herself, an immense need to find an answer to the riddle of her unwanted being. All around her were grey and crumbling ruins, and under those ruins her love lay bleeding; shamefully wounded by Angela Crossby, shamefully soiled and defiled by her mother – a piteous, suffering, defenceless thing, it lay bleeding under the ruins.
>
> She felt blind when she tried to look into the future, stupefied when she tried to look back on the past. (Hall 1982, pp. 205–6)

In the final words of the novel, Hall addresses the God from whom she feels alienated – in the earlier use of the term 'alienation' – in her loneliness.

'God,' she gasped, 'we believe; we have told You we believe ... We have not denied You, then rise up and defend us. Acknowledge us, oh God, before the whole world. Give us also the right to our existence!' (Hall 1982, p. 447, original ellipses)

This novel is the completest and the best-known description of the form of loneliness that was related to sexuality, and was an emotion involving not just isolation, not just rejection by others, but also *self*-rejection.

What I am suggesting here, in Spinoza's model of emotions, is that a threefold form of loneliness had emerged, exemplified by Hall's novel. It was a pain, to start with. There are less painful and even quite neutral or positive uses of lonely. The exiled Coriolanus in Shakespeare's play was 'Like to a lonely Dragon, that his Fenne Makes fear'd, and talk'd of more then seene'. This implied the angry exiled anti-hero was dragon-like, a fighter, and alone (as dragons were, in the mythical accounts of the creatures), but not – in this phrase – necessarily in pain. Or Wordsworth's cloud-like loneliness, which is simply a form of being (painlessly) alone. But more painful loneliness was already implied in later nineteenth-century writers. So lonely became a pain, accompanied by the idea of separation of some kind from other people, the idea of *rejection* by other people (Sacks's social rejection associated with *shame*) and the idea that the person blames themselves for the isolation and rejection (the individual conscience or *guilt* of Sacks). This threefold emotion of loneliness was a 'new' emotion, even though the four elements (pain, separation, rejection and self-blame) were not new. It is their specific combination, strikingly so in Hall's novel, that was distinctive.

New Lonelinesses

Using the word 'lonely' or 'loneliness' – in poetry and novels – increasingly referred to this form of the emotion, and was one of the ways in which the arts helped 'create' the emotion. In Dickinson's poetry, loneliness involved pain accompanied by separation and rejection, but it is harder to find much self-blame there. Between her poetry and Hall's novel, a new alienation-emotion was established. This is not to say that the three-fold loneliness emotion was the only form of loneliness from then onwards. There is not a rule-book of emotion to which everyone must conform. In fact, by the late twentieth and early twenty-first century, the first form of loneliness as 'separation', which necessarily involved pain, became more popular in culture, with research tools such as the UCLA

Loneliness Scale (the most commonly used scale) having in its inventory a set of descriptions of separation, but none of pain or rejection or self-blame. 'How often do you feel that you are "in tune" with the people around you?', 'How often do you feel that you have a lot in common with the people around you?', 'How often do you feel left out?', or 'How often do you feel that there are people you can talk to?' (quoted from the UCLA Loneliness Scale, Cacioppo and Patrick 2008, p. 6) are all interesting questions, but they are indirect and do not address loneliness head-on. Yang's explanation of this delicacy is interesting. 'Loneliness is measured indirectly', he says, 'with the words that are thought to represent the feeling of loneliness, such as "left out", "no one to talk to", "no companion", etc.' and 'it is advantageous to do so because respondents may not want to directly refer to their lonely experiences in front of a stranger' (Yang 2019, p. 15). It would be possible, though, to score highly on the scale, yet never 'feel lonely'. Rejection, self-blame, guilt and shame are not there, either. And 'how often?' (i.e. 'never', 'rarely', 'sometimes', 'often') is an odd way to measure loneliness. I may only occasionally experience loneliness, but this may be an intense experience that shapes my life, so even if the UCLA scale *did* measure loneliness, I would end up scoring 'low' for loneliness. 'More often' and 'more' are not equivalent.

My own research with children, young people and adults was the source of the threefold description of aspects of loneliness (Stern 2014a), but that at least asked directly about loneliness – and found huge variation in how it was experienced. For respondents who said they had experienced loneliness (which was almost everyone), I asked how they knew it was loneliness and not another emotion. 'I would feel the guilt of loneliness' (Stern 2014a, p. 24), said a seven-year-old boy. An adult responded, 'I can tell when I am lonely when I begin to feel shame that I cannot share this feeling with anyone' (Stern 2014a, p. 182). These and other responses suggested a complex and varied emotion that went well beyond the isolation or not feeling in tune with people that the UCLA scale picks up. Well beyond in intensity as well as in terms of feeling active rejection rather than – or as well as – not fitting in. Alienation from the nineteenth century onwards was far more visceral that simple separation, whether that alienation is from God, from one's senses, from one's own nature or the result of capitalist economic exploitation. The visceral description of another seven-year-old seems closer to alienation than the thinner descriptions common in loneliness research. 'I felt like I didn't exist and I kept messing things up and I felt lost deep, deep deep down inside me and that hurted my feelings alot' (Annie, in Stern 2014a, p. 23).

Loneliness is not the only emotion associated with the idea of alienation as it developed over time, but it is a crucial one. Both alienation and loneliness are 'internal', concerned with conscience and consciousness (perhaps false consciousness), and both are 'external', concerned with the social and with reactions to and of other people. Gender and sexuality were not central to Marx's description of alienation. However, the character of gender and sexuality has much in common with some of the later Marxist theorising (such as Marcuse 1991) and some of the class theory of Marx himself. Unequal power relations and exploitation, a combination of social structuring and personal emotions, and, importantly, the possibility of change over time.

Some of the most powerful accounts of the emotions of alienation in literature come in short stories. One striking example is Melville's *Bartleby the Scrivener* (Melville 2016a). Bartleby, a lowly copyist, is oddly alienated through what appears rather like a one-person class war. 'I would rather not do that', he says, and this gradually leads to a sad end. A lonely life not only as a result of the work but also as a result of the objection to the work. The loneliness of the rebel, the campaigner, is an alienation that might be described as fully conscious, unlike the alienation of those who 'accept' their alienated position. Sacks describes Jews through the ages as socially 'other', and therefore always liable to shame but less likely to *suffer* it because it is a 'principled' otherness, because 'because Jews do not conform to what everyone else does' (Sacks 2021, p. 6). Yet Jews, he says, *are* liable to the more internal 'guilt'. Eliot's Jewish protagonist, Silas Marner (Eliot 1999), presents both aspects of the situation and is a model of loneliness. Marner was a weaver and as Eliot describes him he was alienated through his job as much as his religion, as 'it came to pass that those scattered linen-weavers – emigrants from the town into the country – were to the last regarded as aliens by their rustic neighbours, and usually contracted the eccentric habits which belong to a state of loneliness' (Eliot 1999, p. 4). The Jewish novelist, and later prime minister, Disraeli also juggles aspects of shame (lightly felt, unsurprisingly, for the political circles described) and guilt (more severely felt), leading to lonely if often socially and politically successful lives. A good example is the somewhat autobiographical *Vivian Grey* (Disraeli 1906) about a young man attempting to make a political career in a socially rigid England, a novel said to have influenced Wilde in writing *The Picture of Dorian Grey* (Wilde 1966). But short stories are filled with lonely characters.

Short Stories as Lonely

Frank O'Connor, himself a major contributor to the short story genre in the tradition of Joyce, describes all short stories as stories of loneliness. Short stories and novels, together, represent for him a move from 'public art' to art 'intended to satisfy the standards of the individual, solitary, critical reader' (O'Connor 1968, p. ix). The peculiarity of the short story, in particular, is that it 'never had a hero' and instead has 'a submerged population group' (O'Connor 1968, p. xii) so that 'there is this sense of outlawed figures wandering about the fringes of society' and 'as a result there is in the short story at its most characteristic something we do not often find in the novel – an intense awareness of human loneliness' (O'Connor 1968, p. xiv). Whereas the novel 'can still adhere to the classical concept of civilized society, of man [*sic*] as an animal who lives in a community, … the short story remains by its very nature remote from the community – romantic, individualistic, and intransigent' (O'Connor 1968, p. xiv). Novels can portray whole societies, even if represented by a small number of people, whilst short stories are only able to be about one person and have too little space to tie them to a society. An example he gives is of Chekhov's *The Dependents*, in which 'an old man who can no longer support his old horse and dog brings them to the knacker's yard, and when he sees their corpses goes meekly up to the stand and presents his own forehead for the blow' (O'Connor 1968, p. 105). 'Never in the history of literature', O'Connor continues, 'has human loneliness been described with such passion' (O'Connor 1968, p. 105).

When a short story shows a relationship of a person to society, it can only ever be an alienated and therefore lonely relationship, as with *Bartleby the Scrivener* (Melville 2016a), or the stories in Joyce's *Dubliners* collection (Joyce 1961). Sad or piquant, funny or dour, each complete in itself, and in its very completeness *therefore* lonely, separate, rejected and taking on some mixture of guilt and shame. O'Connor goes on to say that short stories are so lonely that their writers all try, if they can, to move on to less lonely genres, Chekhov to plays, Melville to novels.

> The saddest thing about the short story is the eagerness with which those who write it best try to escape from it. It is a lonely art, and they too are lonely. They seem forever to be looking for company, trying to get away from the submerged population that they have brought to life for us. Joyce simply stopped writing short stories. D. H. Lawrence rode off in one direction; A. E. Coppard, that other master of the English short story, in another, but they were all trying to escape. (O'Connor 1968, p. 325)

In a novel, a writer can attempt a 'bigger' completeness, without necessarily alienating its protagonists. Bakhtin's *heteroglossia* describes the many voices in a single novel (by a solitary novelists) and it is a social, dialogic, event (Bakhtin

1981, p. 263). The famous painting by Buss, *Dickens' Dream* (https://www. charlesdickenspage.com/buss.html), shows Dickens sitting in a chair near his writing desk, eyes closed and presumably sleeping, with characters from his novels appearing all around him in dream-like vignettes, including a forlorn girl sitting on his knee. This is the novelist's sociability, even when alone in their own study, even asleep. Meanwhile, a short story writer might be portrayed as unaccompanied and lonely.

Thomas Mann's *Death in Venice* (Mann 1991), a 'novella' and therefore not quite achieving novel-status (its own kind of alienation), is the account of a distinguished writer visiting Venice and 'awakened' by his attraction to a Polish boy, and eventually letting himself die alone. A tragic gay romance, and a story of loneliness of three kinds: the lonely author alienated from his emotions, the 'awakened' man failing in his love and suffering the shame of it (i.e. alienated from the society in which he lives), and the dying man, both guilty and accepting of his forthcoming alienation from life. The writer as lonely and alienated was already there in Mann's earlier novella *Tonio Kröger* (Mann 1991). (I refer to the *story* about a writer as lonely, not about the debates on how autobiographical *Death in Venice* and *Tonio Kröger* may be.) *Tonio Kröger* describes the protagonist alienated from both sides of his family, represented in his two names, and becoming a distinguished author only by finally 'exiling' himself from society, or even from reality. These two (long) short stories of Mann articulate a whole range of alienation emotions. But a collection named precisely for its loneliness was completed later, in the 1950s, by Richard Yates. Yates's *Eleven Kinds of Loneliness* (Yates 2008) is perhaps less encyclopaedic than the title might suggest, but it certainly does provide complex portraits of the loneliness experienced at different life-stages.

One of the best-known of Yates's stories is *Doctor Jack-o'-Lantern* (Yates 2008, pp. 1–20). It is a beautiful and desperately sad tale of Vincent Sabella, a poor, tough, pupil and his first few days at school. The teacher, Miss Price, makes the 'mistake' of befriending him, and Vincent gets his revenge, to everyone's disadvantage. At recess (playtime) he is left alone or rejected by the other pupils 'so he joined nobody'.

> He stayed on the apron of the playground, close to school, and for the first part of the recess he pretended to be very busy with the laces of his sneakers. He would squat to undo and retie them, straighten up and take a few experimental steps in a springy, athletic way, and then get down and go to work on them again. After five minutes of this he gave it up, picked up a handful of pebbles and began

shying them at an invisible target several yards away. That was good for another five minutes, but then there were still five minutes left, and he could think of nothing to do but stand there, first with his hands in his pockets, then with his hands on his hips, and then with his arms folded in a manly way across his chest. (Yates 2008, p. 7)

His teacher watches this and later says to him: 'The main thing to remember is that making friends is the most natural thing in the world, and it's only a question of time until you have all the friends you want', finishing with the dangerous statement 'and in the meantime, Vincent, I hope you'll consider *me* your friend' (Yates 2008, p. 9). He later writes some graffiti, and is found out by the teacher. 'Perhaps, after all, she should never have undertaken the responsibility of Vincent Sabella's loneliness' (p. 9). After being told off, he leaves.

> He got his windbreaker out of the cloakroom and left, avoiding the tired uncertainty of her eyes. The corridors were deserted, and dead silent except for the hollow, rhythmic knocking of a janitor's push-broom against some distant wall. His own rubber-soled tread only added to the silence; so did the lonely little noise made by the zipping-up of his windbreaker, and so did the faint mechanical sigh of the heavy front door. (Yates 2008, p. 16)

In this story, Yates describes with beautiful accuracy what it is like standing alone in a playground, what it is like to be a child alienated from other children and failing to benefit from the closeness of a kind teacher. Vincent gets his revenge on Miss Price, and although he may still be lonely, he perhaps feels he has some more self-determination.

There is another school-based story in Yates's collection – it appears to be the same school – that focuses on the loneliness of a teacher, close to Christmas: *Fun with a Stranger* (Yates 2008, pp. 106–17). Why does one teacher seem able to have an exciting pre-Christmas party, when another can't? This is a story of work-based alienation, showing some of the social competitiveness of workplaces, but hardly of the form described by Marx. It is a much more intimate kind of alienation. Yates also gives us a remarkable tale of clothing-related loneliness, in *Out with the Old* (Yates 2008, pp. 159–78). Sitting around in a ward for patients with tuberculosis, the men are living rather well together, even if they are dying. The loneliness of facing death is there but more as a background hum. The most striking moment is when the men are getting changed to go home for the holidays. As they put on their clothes, their class and racial identities become more obvious – each to the other men, and each to himself. As if by magic, the men fall into snobberies and racism, other-directed or self-directed. All become alienated from others and from themselves. The clothing of the sanatorium equalises: everyday 'healthy' clothing separates.

> Many of the men were a revelation in one way or another when they appeared in their street clothes. McIntyre had grown surprisingly humble, incapable of sarcasm or pranks, when he put on his scarcely worn accounting clerk's costume of blue serge, and Jones had grown surprisingly tough in his old Navy foul-weather jacket. Young Krebs, whom everybody called junior, had assumed a portly maturity with his double-breasted business suit, and Travers, who most people had forgotten was a Yale man, looked oddly effete in his J. Press flannels and his button-down collar. Several of the [African Americans] had suddenly become [African Americans] again, instead of ordinary men, when they appeared in their sharply pegged trousers, draped coats and huge Windsor knots, and they even seemed embarrassed to be talking to the white men on the old familiar terms. (Yates 2008, pp. 163–4)

The loneliness of clothing, in Yates's story, can be compared to Maupassant's *Boule de Suif* (Maupassant 1996, pp. 2–69), in which the prostitute who is the 'heroine' of the story is only recognised (and then despised) as a prostitute after she has completed her helpful acts: her clothes eventually give her away. Yates doesn't explicitly address some of the major loneliness themes, such as those related to sexuality or mental health challenges, yet the very ordinariness of his situations adds to their poignancy. There are no heroes or villains. A lonely wife-to-be, an army officer who is good at his job and therefore makes others jealous, a man who gets sacked from his job, a journalist who has big ideas and walks out of a job, someone who incites a riot and gains 'absolute fulfilment and relief' (Yates 2008, p. 134), a 'loser' who, conversing with his apparently more sociable friend, finds that he too is 'haunted and vulnerable and terribly dependent, trying to smile, a look that said Please don't leave me alone' (Yates 2008 p. 157), a taxi driver telling stories. But that too is of the nature of the short story: it takes a society to make the heroic or tragic; a short story can achieve a small, sometimes pathetic, emotion like loneliness, the loneliness that comes out of small, simple, forms of alienation in the workplace and home.

Perhaps O'Connor was right, and all short stories are lonely? Mary Lavin wrote a story with the title *Happiness*, yet manages to describe a priest who 'took to dropping in to see us, with the idea of filling the crater of loneliness left at our centre' yet who 'did not know that there was a cavity in his own life' (Lavin 2011, p. 5). The title carries its irony lightly. The specialist in happiness dies, not quite happy, with a sigh. Even the dog in Chekhov's audacious short story of a canine circus performer is a lonely figure. *Kashtanka* (Chekhov 1974, pp. 36–57) is a dog taken from her owners by a circus trainer. One day the original owner and his child see Kashtanka in the circus and call out her name, so she returns to them. It is almost as if she'd never been away. 'She recollected the small room with the dirty wallpaper, the goose, Fyódor Timofyéich, tasty dinners, the lessons, the circus, but all this now appeared to her as a long, confused and depressing dream' (Chekhov 1974, p. 57).

Why, then, do we *read* all these lonely short stories? Are lonely stories a cure for loneliness? Or is loneliness shared thereby mitigated? There is a softness to a short story, a pain that is bearable, leaving the reader rarely more than a *little* sad. *Another* loneliness, perhaps, as Dickinson had it, that makes us 'richer', resulting from 'thought' (Dickinson 1970, p. 502). And just as Dickinson ends her lines with a dash (–) to indicate an uncertainty (as with *The Loneliness One dare not sound* –, Dickinson 1970, p. 379), so do many short stories end with such an uncertainty or ambiguity. Raymond Carver's magnificent *One More Thing* is a perfect example, ending a tale of L.D. being thrown out of the apartment in which he has been living with his girlfriend and her daughter:

> L.D. put the shaving bag under his arm and picked up the suitcase.
>
> He said, 'I just want to say one more thing.'
>
> But then he could not think what it could possibly be. (Carver 1991, p. 122)

The loneliness that seems to emerge out of alienation is well-represented in these accounts. But there is more to be said of the solitudes that are related to different forms of conflict and discord, not always mediated by alienation, and these are the subject of the next chapter.

7

Solitudes of Conflict and Discord

So many clashes, so many fights all round and I hear them all.
Inside I don't know whether to take a side or opt out.

Summary

Novels describe large-scale social developments, even if these are described through apparently small-scale domestic settings. They therefore articulate how different forms of conflict (war, civil war, racism and other forms of exploitation and oppression) are experienced, and how they can isolate individuals. Moving from the novels of Dickens and Hugo to those of George Eliot and Hardy, and exploring American novels by Melville or Sinclair, there is a consideration of the more 'lonesome' portrayals in Twain's novels set before but written after the Civil War. Turgenev represents generational conflicts, as part of larger-scale social conflicts, and the chapter goes on to those novels and plays (of Kafka or Brecht) that seem to attempt to empty life of emotion. However, concord and discord are much more openly portrayed in music, as central to the music itself, as well as in its attempts to break away from the previous generation's tastes, or – as with Nancarrow or the blues of Robert Johnson – represent the musician's own response to social conflict.

Some key artists: Charles Dickens (1812–1870), Victor Hugo (1802–1885), George Eliot (1819–1880), Thomas Hardy (1840–1928), Herman Melville (1819–1891), Upton Sinclair (1878–1968), Mark Twain (1835–1910), Ivan Turgenev (1818–1883), Franz Kafka (1883–1924), Bertolt Brecht (1898–1956), Camile Saint-Saëns (1835–1921), Tony Iommi (1948–), Conlon Nancarrow (1912–1997), Robert Johnson (1911–1938)

Introduction: Novel Solitudes

Short stories are peculiarly suited to the expression of loneliness in its threefold alienated form. But there are other solitudes that are not so clearly mediated through alienation and that are not all experienced as loneliness. These other solitudes were being expressed, especially in the form of novels, and I characterise these as emerging out of conflict and discord. Social conflict is implied by alienation in its various forms, but alienation remains a particular individual response to a situation. It is therefore worth considering how else broad social conflict may be described and experienced solitudinously. In the mid-nineteenth century, novels often had isolated figures, not all of whom were alienated in the religious, mental health or 'human nature' senses described in Chapter 6. In Dickens's novels, for example, there are many separated characters, too many to need mentioning, and the isolation of orphans, widowed, imprisoned or miserly is wonderfully described. They are all described in contexts of societies divided and internally or externally conflicting – generating different solitudes. Rarely using 'loneliness' to describe the emotions of his characters, there is more on sin and redemption than there is on internal emotions combining shame and guilt with the sense of rejection and isolation. And there is often a meeting, later in the novel, that resolves the isolation, at least for the 'deserving' characters. (Death is the other 'resolution' Dickens offered the isolated.) But it rarely seems anything like the alienation described by Hegel, Feuerbach or Marx, or like modern forms of loneliness.

To an extent, the novels of Dickens tackled social class issues, but unaccompanied by collective attempts at social change. Victor Hugo, similarly, has subtle accounts of the morality of social isolation, whether through crime (most obviously in *Les Miserables*, Hugo 1976) or disability (with *Notre-Dame de Paris*, Hugo 2004, combining crime and disability). The religious framing of alienation is important to Hugo's novels, and sin and redemption – as with Dickens – are more central than any sense of loneliness. There is much on social, political and industrial change and conflict, but the emotional response is not so much a lonely one as a range from anger to despair. Describing Dickens and Hugo is valuable to illuminate the contrasting approach to novels *later* in the nineteenth century, and these are fine accounts of social conflict of a different kind to the earlier 'alienating' emotional presentations given in the previous chapter. In Eliot's novels, for example, there is more concern with tying large-scale social and class movements to individual, personal, emotions. *Middlemarch* (Eliot 1965) describes how both Dorothea Brooke and the man who becomes her husband, Edward Casaubon, fall into loneliness through their social as much as personal circumstances. Their failure to reach each other is a lonely form of solitude, but they are also affected by social forces that encourage their – as it is called – stupidity:

> If we had a keen vision and feeling of all ordinary human life, it would be like hearing the grass grow and the squirrel's heart beat, and we should die of that roar which lies on the other side of silence. As it is, the quickest of us walk about well wadded with stupidity. (Eliot 1965, p. 162)

Later in the nineteenth century, Hardy's novels described the individuals caught up in the massive social conflicts resulting from industrialisation and urbanisation. His first novel of Wessex, *Under the Greenwood Tree or the Mellstock Quire: A Rural Painting of the Dutch School* (Hardy 1989), is more piquant, starting from the unemployment of the church band as a result of the introduction of a church organ which could be played by a single musician. As Hardy's novel series progressed, other big social issues were central, with the loneliness experienced by women (Tess of the d'Urbervilles, in Hardy 1912b, Bathsheba Everdene, in Hardy 1912a) and by those transgressing with respect to social class (Jude the Obscure, in Hardy 1993). Early in the twentieth century, Arnold Bennett's novels explore the newly emerging social classes as they are changing, with intergenerational tensions and alienations associated with loneliness and despair.

Melville was only a few years younger than Dickens, but he seemed to be of a different generation when it comes to the 'desolation of solitude'. There are religious themes, as in earlier novels, but the combination of guilt and shame and self-blame is much stronger, with sexuality – especially in *Moby-Dick* (the crew of the Pequod are described as 'isolates', Melville 2016b, p. 202) and *Billy Budd* (Melville 2016a) – as one source of what seems like loneliness in its modern form. Melville's *Bartleby*, mentioned in Chapter 6, is another unredeemed and therefore more likely lonely figure. Zola's *Germinal* (Zola 1993), along with many of his works, has the social conflicts that lead to lonely solitudes. Yet they do not seem to describe loneliness in the way that his near-contemporary Maupassant does. In the United States, Sinclair Lewis has novels filled with isolated rebels, but the loneliness is the consequence of rebelling, not directly of the alienation against which the workers are rebelling. Upton Sinclair's *The Jungle* (Sinclair 1988) is even fuller of realistic accounts of capitalist exploitation in the meat industry, with despair and anger as the dominant emotions. Perhaps the journalist Doremus Jessup in Sinclair Lewis's *It Can't Happen Here* (Lewis

1963) is the closest to a lonely figure in these French and American novels. He feels sufficiently independent of the political events to survive as an independent figure, but gradually gets drawn in and, suffering, blames himself. Heroism and tragedy move the novel into more conventional political allegory, centred on an incipient civil war.

It is in the novels with less obviously 'big' social conflict that loneliness more often appears. Mark Twain's *The Adventures of Tom Sawyer* and *Huckleberry Finn* (Twain 2001) are lighter and often humous novels, but they vividly describe both loneliness and its cousin 'lonesomeness'. These emotions do not seem to result from the urban alienation of more 'industrial' novels but from poverty, youth and various class and racial divisions and conflicts. Being lonely to the point of wanting to die, but not harming himself, Huckleberry Finn is sometimes lonely but also experiences the distinctively American emotion of lonesomeness. This is described by the critic Lewis (2009) as a mixture of negative and positive characteristics, including a longing – associated with the American West, and found in the 'country and western' songs of Hank Williams as well as the poetry of Dickinson. Lewis focuses on Twain's description of Huck Finn: 'and then for about an hour there wouldn't be nothing to hear nor nothing to see – just solid lonesomeness' (Lewis 2009, p. 54).

> Huck's lonesomeness here, as morning comes, touches the spiritual dimension of the self in a feeling of rapt attunement to no particular thing and to no particular transcendent being or order of things, but simply to the fullness and splendor of the creation before his eyes. (Lewis 2009, p. 55)

Lewis's description has echoes of the enstatic 'oneness' of Buddhist traditions as much as the immediate influence of the American transcendentalism of Thoreau or Emerson, as he notes 'the feeling or perception – it is both, of course – … of unobstructed integration into that plenitude of being' (Lewis 2009, p. 55).

> This is the open-endedness of the American lonesome, taking the particular form of the individual's own responding subjectivity at a 'peak' moment. It is composed here of becalmed watching and the kind of reflective 'listening' we meet in Emily Dickinson. (Lewis 2009, p. 55)

The lonesomeness here 'occurs not in solitude but in the company of Jim', and therefore has 'a social component' contributing to 'the amazing grace of the partnership' such that 'spontaneously Huck employs the pronoun "we"' (Lewis 2009, p. 55). Notwithstanding Lewis's claim of a spiritual character of lonesomeness in such literature, it is possible to see a more socially and politically engaged character to the novel, in the realism of its description of how the protagonists interact with each other and with the conventional society they keep bumping into on their adventures. This is why I suggest it is a novel of solitudinous response to a conflicted wider society, more than enstatic lonesomeness, represented not least by the two protagonists, living before but written after the American Civil War. The same might be said of Dickinson's poetry, certainly in its *suffering* loneliness, a loneliness that is far less piquant and longing than the lonesomeness of Twain's novels, a kind of solitude with a sad edge to it rather than full-on, painful, loneliness.

A mixture of the longing of lonesomeness and the loneliness derived from social conflict can also be found in the novels of Turgenev. He wrote of the divisions of Russian society, including its experience within families, as in *Fathers and Sons* (Turgenev 1991). The different views of social change, conservative traditionalists in the background, and 'liberal' fathers and 'nihilist' sons, and divided in different ways, with love and death also dividing people. He gets closer to loneliness, both as a result of the fracturing of relationships and of choices to follow nihilist 'rejecting' principles. (Horowski 2020 writes of the need to be prepared to be lonely, if one is to follow one's principles, and Dyal 2022 writes of Sophocles's eponymous *Antigone* as choosing alienation, for a similar reason.) Although Russia's society in the nineteenth century was far from that of industrial Germany and the UK described by Marx, it is worth remembering that Russia hosted the first successful Marxism-inspired revolution. Turgenev's education, too, included a healthy appreciation of German society and philosophy. His short stories or novellas had more alienation and loneliness, notably in *The Diary of a Superfluous Man* (Turgenev 2013), where the protagonist begins a diary of his rather lonely (and superfluous) life just a few days before he is expecting to die.

Solitude Beyond Emotion?

Half a century after Turgenev, Conrad wrote *Nostromo* (Conrad 1917), describing a prescient postcolonial future for Caribbean countries just as Turgenev described a prescient post-feudal Russia. The eponymous Nostromo is isolated and conflicted by a system that makes everyone a lesser person, isolated from each other and from their own natures, as a result of colonialism. Many of Conrad's protagonists are isolated and solitudinous, whether this results in the frustrated loneliness of Nostromo or in the megalomaniac madness of Kurz in *The Heart of Darkness* (Conrad 2002). Conrad prefigures the protagonists of

Camus or Sartre, and is described by Romano as having 'sounded the loneliest notes of any novelist in his time' (Romano 1979, p. 1), channelling the 'strange, potentially disabling environment of illness and exile, loss and oppression in which Conrad gets his start', in the oppressed and divided Poland of his youth (Romano 1979, p. 1).

Whereas Kafka's protagonists are undoubtedly isolated, they are less often described as blaming themselves or in any way responsible for their isolation. That is what distinguishes them from the people in the novels of Conrad or Turgenev, or almost any figure in short stories – at least in O'Connor's model – who more often seem divided against themselves, reflecting wider social divisions. Kafka's characters simply don't know – any more than his readers know – what exactly the situation is. In Kafka, the wider conflicts 'freeze' the emotions of the protagonist, so the dominant emotion is no emotion at all. Perhaps it is a form of de-emotionedness, a kind of depression? This might help explain Kafka's wish for art to be like an ice axe cracking through one's skull, like suicide, even:

> If the book we are reading does not wake us, as with a fist hammering on our skull, why then do we read it? So that it shall make us happy? Good God, we would also be happy if we had no books, and such books as make us happy we could, if need be, write ourselves. But what we must have are those books which come upon us like ill-fortune, and distress us deeply, like the death of one we love better than ourselves, like suicide. A book must be an ice-axe to break the sea frozen inside us. (Kafka, in a letter written when aged twenty in 1904, quoted in Steiner 1967, p. 67)

Kafka – as himself, in his correspondence, and in his novels – is a genius of solitude. On emotion, he seemed to suppress any expression of it, although in its very suppression, it seems to express social conflicts all the more powerfully.

In theatre and cinema in the twentieth century, solitude resulting from social conflict moved centre stage. There were campaigning, strident, anti-establishment plays of Shaw and of Brecht. Brecht's 'alienation effects' were not quite the alienation of Marx, but a distancing from the artifice of theatre, a lifting of the mask. Brecht himself drew on the German expressionism of earlier art, theatre and cinema. Anti-realism, unreal or surreal, combined with nightmarish social visions to show the isolation of characters in part by acting as though the audience is the enemy. It is a commonplace of clinical psychology that the way a person makes *you* feel is the best guide to how *they* feel.

Once the teachers' group came to realise that their feeling response could provide an important clue to the understanding of others, they were able to take much more note of which students made them irritated, who made them angry, depressed, unable to think. (Salzberger-Wittenberg et al. 1983, p. 62)

The theatrical alienation effects therefore represent social and political conflict – and the need for reform – by making the audience *feel* conflicted themselves, rather than simply recognising the characters' situations. Before returning to Brecht, let's try some German expressionist cinema. Wegener's *The Golem* (1920) is one of the best-known of all silent films. It tells the tale of a golem, popularised in late-nineteenth-century literature (Rosenberg, in Neugroschel 2006) that drew on older Jewish folk tales. The word 'golem' can be translated as an 'animated clod without soul' (as in Buber 2002a, p. 248), and it is used in the Bible of the 'clay' out of which Adam was said to be created. In the nineteenth century, and in *The Golem*, it is a clay creature brought to life by a rabbi to protect the Jewish community from persecution. Initially helpful, the creature later becomes destructive and has to be destroyed.

The lumbering creature was not just a model of a creature cut off from those around him but also of the hubris of humanity creating things that get out of control. A metaphor, therefore, of technology-gone-wrong, and of the destructive effects of modern institutions. Drawing on the golem stories, Čapek wrote of a group of such creatures, referred to as Rossum's Universal Robots, introducing the world to the *robot*. Creature and creator, hubris and conflict, the relationship between the golem accounts and Shelley's *Frankenstein* (1999) is clear. Even clearer, the relationship between *The Golem* and Whale's 1931 film, *Frankenstein*. The monster in Whale's film bears little resemblance to Shelley's creature, slow and inarticulate rather than fast and articulate. But Whale's creature, and the whole style of his film, is a homage to Wegener's silent film of a decade earlier. The Golem, like Whale's monster, makes the audience both frightened and sympathetic, saddened by the inevitable sad ending of the story, without wishing for more monsters/golems.

Although Brecht's theatrical style is known (in English) for its 'alienation effects', these are really just the distancing from the 'reality' pretended by conventional theatre. It is a way of saying 'we are involved in a stage performance: think about the ideas we are presenting, do not lose yourself in the (pretended) lives being presented'. The audience become like strangers in a strange land, trying to puzzle out what is meant by what is happening. The sociologist Schutz describes being a stranger in such a way (Schutz 1976,

p. 91), based on the experiences of European exiles in the United States, and Brecht himself was one of the writers known in the German National Socialist period as the *Exilliteratur*. This is therefore related to various solitude themes, of exile, alienation and conflict. It is also related to cynicism, the emotional disconnectedness of Shakespeare's cynic Jaques in *As You Like It*, for whom all the world's a stage, and all the men and women merely players (i.e. 'look at us: we are just actors'). But the social conflict in Brecht's plays is closer to that described by Marx. Marx and Brecht both wrote polemically about the proletariat and, even more, the *lumpenproletariat* (the 'underclass' of the unemployed, criminals, sex workers and so on) who were variously tricked, exploited and often complicit in their very exploitation. *The Good Person of Szechwan* (Brecht 1962) is an account of 'goodness' subject to, and largely defined by, the economic system, leaving the audience to try to find a solution to the goodness that is patently not good. We are all 'merely players'. *Mother Courage* (Brecht 1962), set in wartime (of the seventeenth century, but written and performed in 1939 as war was growing in Europe) tells of the Mother who continues trading through years of war and conflict that tied war into yet another terrible economic system.

Working hard to avoid 'romantic' ideas of theatre as emotional escapism, the harsh intellectualism of Brecht of course ended up having an emotional impact, even if that was not intended and perhaps unwelcome. Disgust and anger and fear, as also evoked by much of the German Expressionist style, are emotions like any other. Everyone is separated from everyone else, relationships are only ever transactional and intimacy can never be sincere. Are Brecht's characters lonely? Brecht wouldn't want to tell us. It is a comprehensively divided world. Brecht's characters, like those of Kafka, are unable to understand their situation and do not – quite – blame anyone. If they survive, they will. Brecht's plays, like Kafka's novels, are there to break through, like ice picks. *Afterwards*, we may achieve the emotional state of self- and social awareness, sufficient to feel lonely or perhaps in comfortable solitude – although the latter seems unlikely.

Before and After: Concord and Discord

'Afterwards' is an important quality of various forms of solitude and loneliness. Wordsworth only realises long after he spies the daffodils that they can be recalled in the 'bliss of solitude'. Wilde and Hall long for 'after', after prison or even after (beyond?) sexuality. Yates's short stories – in a sense, *all* short stories – are of times of loneliness stuck in the present and without a view of a future.

Psychologists have noted how loneliness is rarely remembered. It is a 'present' emotion more than a remembered one. In the middle of loneliness it may feel permanent, but it typically ends in the blink of an eye and is forgotten like a dream may be lost on awakening. So loneliness itself has little existence outside the present tense. (This makes it hard to research, of course.) But solitude is enjoyed and suffered in the past, present and future tenses. People remember past solitudes, fondly or not, and look forward to future solitudes (or not). But 'many of us severely underestimate our own past experience with loneliness and as a result underestimate the role it has played in the lives of others' (Weiss 1973, p. 10).

> Sullivan believed that loneliness was an experience so different from the ordinary that its intensity could later not be entirely credited. He said it was 'an experience which has been so terrible that it practically baffles clear recall.' Fromm-Reichmann believed that there was active rejection of the memory of loneliness, and not simply passive inability to recall. She believed that many of those who had once been lonely were aware that memory of that state would be threatening to their current well-being. She said, 'It is so frightening and uncanny in character that they … try to dissociate the memory of what it was like and even the fear of it.' (Weiss 1973, pp. 10–11)

Weiss goes on to say that when he has asked people to recall a time when they were lonely, they have sometimes said to him 'Yes, I suppose I was lonely', and continued 'but I wasn't *myself* then' (Weiss 1973, p. 11). He goes on to say that this may explain why people who are not at that time lonely have little empathy for those who are. People find loneliness difficult to recall, unlike solitude. In my own research, when I have asked people about positive experiences of solitude, rather than loneliness, another dimension emerged. Children and adults alike often enjoy solitude *after* an event, after the end of the school day, the day after a birthday, after completing homework, the day after Christmas Day (Stern 2014a, p. 172). Paintings such as *Après Le Bain* by Jean Jacques Henner or, with the same title, by William Bouguereau may have the voyeurism of the male artist observing a female nude, but both also portray a peaceful solitude of the figure portrayed, after bathing.

There are strong past- and future-tense solitudes, and some reflect exile – the solitudinous remembrance of previous homes – but they are hardly 'alienation'. The alienation of the early- to mid-nineteenth century overlapped in the arts with solitude themes derived from social conflicts that were not only experienced as alienation or emotionally as loneliness. But I have not yet explored how conflict is presented musically. During this same period (from the mid-nineteenth century onwards) there was a growth in the idea of the solo musical 'star', developed by musicians such as Liszt and Paganini, described in Chapter 4. Within each musical tradition around the world, there are forms of 'concord' and 'discord'. Concord represents sounds that are said to go well together, discord to sounds that clash. Both concord and discord will be used in a single musical piece, typically with discord being resolved into concord. Within classical and popular music in Europe, there is a long tradition of harmony, including rules about concord and discord, that was well-established by the seventeenth century and continues to this day. However, even this dominant system – by the nineteenth century, influencing music in many other parts of the world – had a number of exceptions. I have family in Scotland and have spent a lot of time there, but I live in England. Here, Scottish bagpipe music is often derided as 'out of tune' and therefore wholly discordant. This is not an anti-Scottish sentiment, but a 'recognition' that some of the notes played by a Scottish bagpipe do not fit on the twelve notes of conventional harmony (i.e. the twelve different notes of each octave on a piano keyboard). Disagreement over what counts as concord and discord happens across cultures, even those as close in other ways as England and Scotland. Intercultural conflict is presented musically in the persistence of music of one culture that 'offends' the ear of another culture. That also happens across generations.

Generational division is a significant theme in literature. Turgenev's *Fathers and Sons* (1991), earlier in this chapter, and Arnold Bennett's *Clayhanger* trilogy (Bennett 1954, 1975a, 1975b) show in different ways how the younger generation with its new or rebellious ways clashes with the older people who usually represent the old-fashioned or conservative values. This can be described as intergenerational conflict: separation, mutual rejection, with feelings of guilt and/or shame on each side of the relationship. For many, the generational clash can best be represented musically, as each younger generation can 'shock' the older generation with their new music, and each older generation complains of the discordant noise of the younger generation's music. In my own early teens, I was a fan of the heavy metal group *Black Sabbath*, a loud, noisy, disruptive snub to my parents' generation's music. I didn't know at the time that the composer of the group's eponymous 'theme song' of 1970 (Black Sabbath 2009 and https://www.youtube.com/watch?v=0lVdMbUx1_k) was itself a playful reference to a similar musical generational rebellion almost a century earlier. In conventional European harmony, the most discordant interval has been considered the tritone. This is three full tones, for example, from C to F#. Guides to composition made the tritone a taboo. Indeed, such was its discordant sound, it became known as *diabolus in musica*, the devil's interval. Black Sabbath's piece was based on one of the early classical composers to break the taboo, Saint-Saëns, in his *Dans Macabre* (*Dance of Death*) of 1874 (Saint-Saëns 1994 and https://www.youtube.com/watch?v=71fZhMXlGT4). That piece starts with the midnight chimes, after which the violin starts a diabolical dance, using the tritone to announce its devilish character. It is a dance of the dead, only ended by a cockerel crowing and the rising sun. A good way to show the older more conservative composers how to be modern, and how to snub your nose at religious orthodoxy, too. The composition was badly received when first performed, but has become a concert staple since then, widely used in films and television too. Black Sabbath's song starts with the same midnight chimes, followed by a discordant guitar solo by the composer, Tony Iommi, using the tritone once again to demonstrate diabolical intentions of a devilish sabbath.

Between Saint-Saëns and Iommi, the tritone had lost some of its taboo character. Liszt, an older friend of Saint-Saëns, had used the interval in his *Dante sonata* (*Après une Lecture du Dante: Fantasia quasi Sonata*, of 1849, Liszt 2001 and https://www.youtube.com/watch?v=KB59i99Wxc4) to indicate the descent into hell. But by the mid-twentieth century, following the harmonic shocks of twelve-tone and other 'discordant' musical styles, the tritone was being used in different ways. Bernstein used the tritone interval for the first two syllables of the name in the song *Maria* in his 1957 musical *West Side Story* (Bernstein 1998 and https://www.youtube.com/watch?v=DyofWTw0bqY), without devilish implications – albeit to the annoyance of singers, for whom it was an unfamiliar and therefore difficult interval to sing. Even more innocently, it was later used by Danny Elfman for the first two notes of *The Simpsons* theme tune of 1989 (The Simpsons 1998 and https://www.youtube.com/watch?v=Fttst9dG6Ko). So Black Sabbath's use of the tritone was something of a last gasp of discordant shock, before the Simpsons softened it for good. Still, Black Sabbath records were banned by a number of radio stations, for their religious heterodoxy (already implied by their name) and their apparent tendency to corrupt youth. It certainly worked for me.

Being able to separate yourself from older people is not, of course, always based on radical social conflict. But it is part of the wider network of conflicts, also including religious conflict (playfully exploited by Liszt, Saint-Saëns and Black Sabbath), mental health-related troubles (as in the poetry of John Clare, perhaps, or Hölderlin), generational division (Turgenev, Bennett), oppression related to sexuality (Hall, Douglas, Wilde) or colonial exploitation (Conrad,

Camus). The experiences related to these different forms of conflict are similarly varied. Guilt and/or shame is often in the mix, as in the alienation examples of Chapter 6, along with anger, despair and, especially in the arts of the late nineteenth century through to the mid-twentieth century, loneliness and the 'lost' sense of *anomie*. Some of the arts of conflict, however, seem to be anti-emotional. I might include Brecht's characters in this group, or those of Kafka. These authors *demonstrate*, as much as *describe*, conflict, so it is the audience's emotions that might be more significant than those of the characters within the writing. And, especially in the case of Brecht, it is an intellectual reaction that is intended, more than an emotional one.

Given the breadth of conflict generated, there are almost too many examples of art, literature and music expressing it, more or less emotionally. Is da Vinci's *Jerome in the Wilderness* a perfect picture of loneliness, or is the full 'three-dimensional' loneliness better painted by Hopper's pictures of diners or of separated couples? Or the loneliness-inspired Lowry's paintings such as *Three Men and a Cat*, described in Chapter 3? Larkin has a bigger role in the next chapter on Modernism and Postmodernism. But I will finish this chapter with two contrasting examples of the music of discord that speak of social conflict. One is the composer Conlon Nancarrow, the other is the American blues tradition. Each provides interesting links to other forms of solitude, in particular the exiles that feature in Chapter 2, but both also evoke and represent specific forms of conflict.

Nancarrow's Communist Party membership led him to exile himself from his US home to Mexico in 1940, and he lived there for the rest of his life. In Mexico, he specialised in composition for the player-piano. This was, and is, a remarkable instrument for the pre-electronic age. A player-piano plays from a piano-roll, a roll of stiff paper with holes in it that, as it turns, triggers the notes of the piano. Some famous pianists of the early twentieth century had piano rolls made of their performances. Classical pianists like Eugen D'Albert (1992) and jazz pianists like Gershwin (2004) had their performances directly captured onto piano rolls, and 'playing' the rolls thereafter reproduced the original playing with uncanny accuracy. The reproduction of the sound is 'as live' and therefore of a much higher quality than any contemporary musical reproduction on records or radio, or even the most modern sound systems. This is possible because the piano, although a complex machine, only allows the player to affect the timing and the speed with which the hammer is 'thrown' at the strings: there is no direct contact between player and strings. Nancarrow (1999) subverted this mechanical innovation. He composed directly for the player-piano and avoided altogether trying to reproduce conventional pianism. His compositions are patterns of overlapping themes, themes that seem geometrically composed, making regular patterns on the piano rolls. They double and halve speeds and invert patterns, just as Bach did in his fugal writing. But unlike Bach, Nancarrow made no attempt to create any harmonic sympathies to go along with the mathematical complications. The pieces sound like being drowned in a waterfall of notes. So rapid and multilayered are the pieces, most would be impossible to play by a human pianist. If the piano was Weber's 'bourgeois domestic instrument' (Weber 1978, p. 382), an individualist and domesticated machine that could put whole orchestras and other communal groups of musicians out of work, Nancarrow put the pianist, too, out of work. His is the final stage of industrialisation, making human workers entirely redundant. An exiled communist demonstrates the frightening power of industrialisation, therefore, in its listening experience, and in replacing the need for a human performer, Nancarrow does more to demonstrate the industrialisation of music than anyone until the electronic and computer-aided composers of later in the century. The emotions evoked by his music include anxiety and puzzlement, along with a lot of humour at the absurdity of the pieces. His is a somewhat under-appreciated high point of Modernism, and therefore a perfect introduction to the following chapter of this book.

Conclusion: Lamenting the Blues

However, the second and final of these 'musics of conflict' is the blues, especially those of the United States in the early- to mid-twentieth century. Musically, there are roots in West African music, forced into the Americas by the slave trade, along with some influence from European folk music, brought to the Americas by colonisers and refugees. The blues is the most important of the musical genres of African American people in the United States in its emotional expression of loss, despair and hopelessness in the face of slavery and the exploitation and poverty that followed after the ending of slavery. The losses are typically described in the song lyrics very individually and personally: the singer wakes up and their partner has gone, is homeless with a matchbox for their clothes and so on (e.g. Johnson 2008). But the personal themes are echoes of larger social issues, as these personal sadnesses are not seen as resolvable or redeemable, except in death. The English folk singer Norma Waterson, who also worked and lived in Montserrat in the Caribbean for several years, said that some English folk songs about dying and death were transferred to the Americas. In the translation, they became more upbeat and positive. Waterson said that this was because death was a loss to a person with a reasonably secure life, but a relief to a person with a life of slavery and exploitation. So blues songs were most positive in describing death as relief. The emotions of blues include a large dose of loneliness and lonesomeness, making it an excellent example of solitudinous suffering in the face of racist conflict.

'Don't the world seem lonely', says the scholar McGeachy, comparing the blues with the Old English lament of a millennium earlier:

> Strange yet familiar, the lonely voices of the Old English lament and the African American blues call beyond the walls of the text, captivating audiences, engaging listeners in a dialogue of longing. Although the lyrics of each poetry speak the language of a poetic tradition that evolved within a distinct history and culture, the voices are remarkably similar in their emotive expression of personal and social struggle. (McGeachy 2006, p. 1)

Blues lyrics return to loneliness more than any other terms, after 'blues' itself, and 'worried': 'Baby I'm feeling so lonely: and I'm feeling so blue … I'm so sad and lonely: love has been refused' (McGeachy 2006, p. 64). One of the distinctions between the blues and Old English lament, as also between the blues and other African American song lyrics, is that there is less memory of a better past and less hope for a better future. It is therefore a stronger representation of the terrible legacy of slavery and established racism. 'The blues speaker has little memory of better time' (McGeachy 2006, p. 69), and 'where Spirituals move the group heavenward (and northward), blues songs move the displaced individual hellward' (McGeachy 2006, p. 87). Blues lyrics are cut off from a future and a past in a way that is characteristic of both loneliness and, even more, depression. When translated to English musical contexts, the blues can be 'renamed' as loneliness. The often-suicidal John Lennon wrote a Liverpool version of the blues, called *Yer Blues* (The Beatles 2009 with a 1968 version with Eric Clapton on guitar at https://www.youtube.com/watch?v=JeFwaWFTGYU). Only the title mentions the blues. For the rest of the song, Lennon simply says that he is *lonely*, and wants to die.

For all the examples in Chapter 6 of alienation and in this chapter on social conflict, the extreme emotions of solitude really came into their own in Modernism.

8

Individualism and Death from Modernism to Postmodernism

Some people hate me. I used to think they were fools with no taste at all.
Now I think they may be right, and hate that I'm agreeing.

Summary

The high point, or should that be low point, of individualism seemed to be found in Modernist arts, which became increasingly concerned not only with the modern mechanised world hoping for a utopian future but also with the presence of mass industrial-scale slaughter of the world wars and the Shoah. Modernist literature as represented by T. S. Eliot, and philosophically by the early Wittgenstein, was more solipsistic and developed into the existentialist individualism of Camus and Sartre, in turn merging into the Postmodernism of Beckett. Later Postmoderns such as Pärt or Kusama have different ways of dealing with solitude. They sit alongside those who were more or less intentionally outside Modernist and Postmodernist 'camps', writers such as Arnold Bennett or Larkin, or those like Buber (as novelist as well as philosopher) who critiqued both camps and attempted a route beyond them.

Some key artists: T. S. Eliot (1888–1965), Albert Camus (1913–1960), Samuel Beckett (1906–1989), Virginia Woolf (1882–1941), Yayoi Kusama (1929–), Arvo Pärt (1935–), Arnold Bennett (1867–1931), Philip Larkin (1922–1985)

Introduction

Why choose Modernism and Postmodern as the focus of this chapter? It is proposed that these artistic movements present a culmination and ultimately a disintegration of the alienated individualist loneliness that grew out of European and North American industrialisation and colonisation, and developed into a new emphasis on death, in the light of the industrial-scale mass slaughter of the twentieth century. Presenting 'the modern' and its artistic form in Modernism as the loss of the personal, a confident individualist utopianism and death, the argument moves on to the emergence of Postmodernism and its critics. Sitting to the side of Modernism and Postmodernism were less 'on-trend' artists, from Arnold Bennett and Vaughan Williams to Philip Larkin, who by their very 'outsider' status further illustrated the significance of Modernist solitudes, and who also point the way to how solitude might be 'recovered' from its lonely, individualist, death-fuelled Modernist and Postmodernist forms. The job of recovery is started, but remains incomplete.

The Modern

This chapter was first drafted in 2022, the centenary of 'ground zero' for Modernism. The year 1922 saw the publication of Joyce's *Ulysses* (2000) and Eliot's *The Waste Land* (2015, pp. 53–71, https://youtu.be/Hcj4G45F9pw), Woolf's *Jacob's Room* (2022a) and Scott Fitzgerald's *Tales of the Jazz Age* (2013). Wittgenstein's *Tractatus Logico-Philosophicus* came out in the same year (Wittgenstein 1961), along with paintings by Klee, Miró, Léger and Picabia, and Picasso's *Four Bathers*. Cocteau's *Antigone* was performed with sets by Picasso and music by Honegger, and Walton's *Façade* was performed with Sitwell's poems (see McCarthy, in London Review of Books 2022, p. 1). The Great War was over, and although it was said at the time that this was the war to end wars, an industrialised and, thanks to European colonialism, globalised conflict, this may have been a 'decadent' time for some, but it was hardly settled. The year 1922 saw hyperinflation in Germany, and the election of the fascist Mussolini in Italy, bad omens both – with growing inflation and a neo-fascist government in Italy evident during Modernism's centenary. Was Modernism a high point or a sign of terrors to come? No doubt it was both. And solitude was at its heart. If it had a heart.

What made Modernism distinctive? It marked itself out from what was 'old', but every age does that. It was a generational shift, but again that is true of every generation. Historically, after more-or-less a century of rapid industrialisation, urbanisation and globalisation, the Great War was a kind of culmination, bringing much of the world together, albeit in bloodshed. Artists were making sense of this brave new world, or just as often, showing it to be nonsense. Eliot wrote of

Cousin Nancy that 'her aunts were not quite sure what they felt about it, / But they knew that is was modern' (Eliot 2015, p. 24). The older generation knew the younger generation was modern. This gives an important clue to Modernism: it was self-conscious of its modernity and was self-consciously reacting against the last vestiges of the old. Every war gives people a sense of new times, even if, with hindsight, it doesn't always look so new. The Great War gave an even greater sense of new times, and so the modern was capitalised into Modernism. Yeats, dating the Modern to the end of Victorianism, describes how, 'in 1900 everybody got down off his stilts; henceforth nobody drank absinthe with his black coffee; nobody went mad; nobody committed suicide; nobody joined the Catholic church; or if they did I have forgotten … [as] Victorianism had been defeated' (Yeats 1936, p. xi).

The Loss of the Personal in Utopia and Death

In Chapter 6, I argued that alienation developed in various ways and was, through the arts, developed in various *emotional* ways, notably the emotion known as *loneliness* that was articulated in new forms. The social conflicts described in Chapter 7 provide further examples of how people were separated and divided, in the arts as in life. Modernism was in many ways the final outcome or culmination of alienation, loneliness and conflict. This started with a loss of the personal in innovative art forms. The paintings of Mondrian, for example, were often of blocks of colour in a grid. The personal as representational was suppressed. These were utopian innovations, utopian in seeing themselves as 'final solutions' to artistic expression. It was Wittgenstein's disturbing boast that his *Tractatus* was philosophy's 'final solution' (Wittgenstein 1961, p. 4). But alongside such depersonalised utopianism and innovation was an individualism that, in its artistic forms, rarely hid how problematic the (usually lonely) individual was. The characters in Picasso's *Tragedia* stand on a beach by the sea. It is an example of his 'blue period', following the suicide of his friend Carles Casagemas (after Casagemas attempted to murder a mutual friend). In *Tragedia*, two adults, male and female, almost face each other, but both look down at the ground and both cross their arms. A boy stands to the side, looking across and down, with his hands held out, one palm-upward, one palm-forward. Their unconnectedness seems worse because they look so much like a family group. When children in my research were asked to add thought bubbles to this picture, their responses were fascinating. Cary (aged eight) thought the woman felt 'sad, lost and cold', whilst Carol (aged eight) thought 'She is sad she is thinking of the past'. The man is described similarly, with Rian (aged eight) suggesting 'Why are we out here, it's so lonley?', and Annie (aged seven) suggesting 'I am cold and I don't want to die', with Alfie (aged eight) indicating him as thinking simply 'I want to live'. There are some more 'active' suggestions for the boy. Jeremy (aged seven) says 'he is ~~looking~~ Trying To xPlane something', and Kadir (aged eight) says 'It looks like he wants to tell the man something'. Amina and Ophelia (both aged seven) give him the words 'please help me papa carry me I am cold', and 'I don't have a mother could she be our's?' The older Terri (aged 16) provides a similar range of ideas, describing the woman as 'cold and empty craving company', the man as having 'let his self go' and 'looks insecure', whilst the child 'wants to be loved' (all reported in Stern 2014a, p. 157).

The 'blue period' pictures of Picasso, like the art of Munch (notably *The Scream*, in its various forms), have become so familiar it is difficult to see their original shock value, presenting alienated tragic modern figures without any of the Romantic softening of tragedy. As Paul describes it, for example, 'Munch's strength is to inhabit the lonely soul of an "other"' (Paul 2022, p. 10). So there is a tension between Modernist utopianism – seen in the perfect-seeming structures of *Ulysses*, Wittgenstein's *Tractatus*, the Modernist architecture of Le Corbusier or Bauhaus design – and Modernist end-times alienation of Picasso's 'blue period', Munch's *The Scream* or Eliot's *The Waste Land*. Yet the tension is present in each of these works. For all its stylistic perfections, *Ulysses* is also filled with unheroic and variously 'impure' actions and thoughts. Joyce plays with readers' intellects and their taboos. Wittgenstein's 'final solution' to all of philosophy is also a demonstration (or attempted proof) that philosophy has nothing to say about beauty, morality or religion: on those, we must remain silent. Le Corbusier was so utopian, in contrast, that the real buildings he designed were sometimes less important than the perfection of his architect's drawings. There is in many Modernist works a combination of style, wealth, corruption and death. It is elegantly portrayed in Fitzgerald's writings, for example. Meanwhile, Cocteau's *Antigone* (Cocteau 2015), like that of Anouilh (1987) and Joyce's *Ulysses*, drew on ancient authority whilst being thoroughly modern. All in their own ways are expressive of loneliness and related sadnesses. *Ulysses* is a sociable enough novel but one with as much of a stream of loneliness running through it as a stream of consciousness.

(Dis)solving Modernism

Sartre wrote elegantly of this kind of tension, the individual torn by the tensions between utopianism and loneliness in Modernism, in all his novels as well as – with a somewhat more upbeat if hardly jolly character – in his philosophy. 'Is this what freedom is?' asks the protagonist in *Nausea*. 'I am free; I haven't a single reason for living left.' He is 'alone and free', yet 'this freedom is rather like death' (Sartre 2000, p. 223). The victory of the modern world of industry, of political freedom and of social advance is rather like death. Such is Modernism, at least when looked at through a solitudinous lens. Perhaps the final stage of all these final solutions was the most appalling of all the achievements of the modern world, the Final Solution attempted to what Hitler's government referred to as 'the Jewish question'. The second of the wars to end all wars was also the period of the second culmination of nineteenth-century industrial, social and economic development. And, much as art became almost impossible in the wake of the Shoah (Simpson and Stern 2018), a final twist to Modernism saw it drop all its elements of utopianism to express all the lonely despair of the modern world. There is no better representative of this late-stage, almost post-mortem, lonely Modernism than Samuel Beckett. 'But what matter whether I was born or not, have lived or not, am dead or merely dying, I shall go on doing as I have always done, not knowing what it is I do, nor who I am, nor where I am, nor if I am' (Beckett 2010a, p. 53).

Asking what exactly Beckett meant by this is missing (some of) the point. Joyce was setting puzzles for his readers and for the professors who would spend years analysing his texts. Joyce played games and created huge, arcane, systems. Beckett recognised Joyce's genius but didn't ever attempt the same 'pure' Modernist utopian task. He was still a Modernist, though, in pushing even further with the alienation, loneliness and loss of the personal. In his trilogy of novels, by the third one, the protagonist was eponymously *Unnamable* (Beckett 2010b). Sartre's comparison of freedom and death seems positively neat and tidy when set alongside Beckett's 'nor if I am'. Beckett's is the *experience* of angst, more than a *description* of it. Perhaps this relates to Beckett's own experience, especially his lifelong experience of panic attacks. 'Since the age of 20, Beckett had suffered from anxiety attacks which set his heart racing in panic' (Wimbush 2020, p. 52), and this condition, 'so ambiguously poised between body and mind' led Beckett to consult 'both physicians and psychologists' (Wimbush 2020, p. 53). Beckett draws on Burton's *Anatomy of Melancholy* (Burton 2021) to write of the 'fetid heart' in *Dream of Fair to Middling Women* (Wimbush 2020, p. 55).

The angst, panic and/or anxiety are Beckett's own, and infuse his literature. Seeking treatment from medical doctors and from psychoanalysts, he also sought mitigation in religion and philosophy. His main religious source, according to Wimbush (2020), was Quietism, his philosophical source Schopenhauer, and these are complementary approaches. Quietism was a Catholic tradition (later rejected by the church) initiated by Molinos in the seventeenth century. It is a tradition suited to, but not exclusively for, solitaries. There are spiritual exercises that attempt to avoid becoming fixed models. Molinos wrote a book saying that following books could never help you achieve the highest levels of spirituality: 'You enter the mystical science of the soul not by hearing or by the continuous reading of books, but by the liberal infusion of the divine Spirit' (Molinos 2010, p. 51), and though 'the soul itself may learn through some book that treats of these matters', one of 'the signs by which one may recognize [… a] vocation for contemplation … [is that] the soul finds reading spiritual books to be tedious because they do not speak of the interior gentleness that the soul has in its interior without knowing' (Molinos 2010, pp. 60–1). What was most important – and gave the religious movement its name – was staying quiet in the face of temptation or enlightenment alike. Rather than *fighting* temptation and *straining* for enlightenment, one should *be*, quietly, and God may be close. Or not. It is easy to see how this influenced the Beckett of 'nor if I am' (Beckett 2010a, p. 53).

Avoiding or mitigating panic through a quietist approach to life may have helped Beckett, and certainly influenced a great deal of his writing. Quietism was sidelined in Catholicism and also by many modern writers on religion and philosophy, as being more nihilist and 'hopeless' than even the most angst-ridden writers. (William James was said to be one of the few modern writers other than Beckett who recognised a value in Quietism, Wimbush 2020, p. 29.) Beckett went further than most Modernists and other artists since the seventeenth century in his search for something-other-than-panic. (It was a search without a conventional end-point, a kind of anti-search, not so much a 'solution' to Modernist tensions as a 'dissolution' of them.) He also drew on the similarly unconventional philosophy of Schopenhauer. Schopenhauer treated his own philosophy as theoretical and untied to practice. According to Berman: 'there is little connection between it and any practice' (Berman, in Schopenhauer 1995, p. xviii). Yet the 'practical' wisdom in Schopenhauer is evident across Beckett's work. 'Every breath we draw fends off death, the persistent intruder with whom we struggle in this way at every moment, and then again at longer intervals, through every meal we eat, every sleep we take, every time we warm ourselves, etc', Schopenhauer tells us, yet 'in the end, death must conquer, for we fell into his clutches through birth, and he plays only for a little while with his prey before he devours it' (Schopenhauer 1995, p. 197). This could be put directly into one of Beckett's plays or novels.

Beckett treats Schopenhauer's philosophy, like Molinos's spiritual guidance, as practical rather than as 'theories' or as intellectual exercises. (Within contemporary philosophy, Beckett could have found some comfort, perhaps, in the 'new philosophy' of the personalist Rosenzweig, who advises philosophers to avoid reading his philosophy, and accuses them of suffering from 'acute *apoplexia philosophica*', Rosenzweig 1999, p. 59.) Schopenhauer describes human mortality as the greatest gift: who would want to continue suffering for ever? 'In *Cinderella*', Berman writes, the protagonists 'live happily ever after, and the story ends', but 'why is so little space given over to their happy life ever after?' (Berman, in Schopenhauer 1995, p. xxviii).

> Schopenhauer answers that it would be incredible, even to children; for life is not about happiness or satisfaction, but about desiring, striving, longing, craving, and hence suffering. (Berman, in Schopenhauer 1995, p. xxviii)

Postmodernism

If Beckett did an excellent job of pushing Modernism to its individualist, lonely, limits, providing Modernism's obituary and *dissolving* as much as *resolving* its tensions, he also seemed, through his disconnected, absurdist, confused and 'untidy' style, to give birth to Postmodernism. In *The Unnamable* his protagonist flip-flops through moods with a ghoulish humour. 'If it opens, it will be I, it will be the silence, where I am, I don't know, I'll never know, in the silence you don't know, you must go on, I can't go on, I'll go on' (Beckett 2010b, p. 134), he says, the final words of the book. This goes beyond Modernism to the overflowing ambiguity of Postmodernism. The Postmodern attitude adds irony to scepticism, and has difficulty holding on to truth and reality, and definitely (as much as it is ever definite) gives up on utopianism. Beckett himself distances his work from the more neat and complete works of Joyce or Kafka. They may have their fair share of alienation and misery, but this is placed in an artfully constructed coherent – even if terrifying (in Kafka's case) and/or lonely (in Joyce's case) – world. Beckett breaks with coherence, even though each of his novels and plays is complete and stands alongside any writing of the twentieth century. His odd attitude to theology and philosophy helps explain the odd position he holds in literature. Very well read, he is a 'user' of theology and philosophy more than a theologian-philosopher, and he is attracted to theology and philosophy that can be 'used' rather than 'understood'.

The Postmodernism that Beckett helped birth is hardly a neat category. By its nature in rejecting 'grand narratives', metaphysics and comprehensive theories, it is more a cluster than a movement. One of the artists associated with Postmodernism seemed to have had a similar way into the approach as Beckett's. That is Yayoi Kusama (Kusama 2019, http://yayoi-kusama.jp/ and https://www.tate.org.uk/art/artists/yayoi-kusama-8094). Like Beckett, she describes her art as, in part, a way to mitigate her anxiety and fear. Experiencing hallucinations from her troubled childhood onwards, these fed into her art. A characteristic feature is polka dots, with 'infinity nets' of dots and nets, and visions of flower patterns. Hers is a solitude at least as extreme as that of Beckett, and her visions are self-obliterating in intention, an attempt to escape from suffering. Her installations, combining art and sculpture and music – combinations being features of Postmodernism – create almost-worlds, without obvious meaning. Organising 'happenings', including one at the Church of Self-Obliteration in New York, broke taboos of the time and helped establish her anti-establishment credentials. However, whereas some artists and others were happily anti-establishment, Kusama has always appeared to be genuinely estranged and isolated. Estranged from Japan for much of the middle of her life, she was estranged from the establishment, yet never wholly accepted by the anti-establishment. Self-estranged and often suicidal, Kusama has for many years of her later life protected herself in a hospital in Japan for those with mental health issues, leaving only to set up and visit her exhibitions.

Kusama's installation *Aching Chandelier* of 2011 (Kusama 2019, pp. 142–3) involves being in a room with a chandelier and mirrors, vertical and horizontal, leaving the viewer to look into the depths and heights of grief and, finally, darkness. *Walking Piece* of 1966 (Kusama 2019, pp. 78–9) has a series of photographs of Kusama walking around New York, on her own and out of place and time, in a kimono and carrying a parasol. Each piece expresses feelings and emotions, and each avoids any clear theory or narrative. These are models of Postmodern solitude. Kusama also seems to share with Beckett a sense of humour in such anxious and despairing emotions. Not just the slight, ironic, humour of less substantial artists but real laugh-out-loud humour – in Kusama's case, for example, posing on a bed of polka dot-covered phalluses; in Beckett's case, for example, recommending comic actors for his plays (as also mentioned in Chapter 3), with distinguished Beckett actors including Bert Lahr (who debuted *Waiting for Godot* on Broadway), Buster Keaton (who starred in Beckett's film, *Film*) (Lahr 2023, p. 3), Steve Martin, Robin Williams and many others.

A contrast with these Postmodern despairing artists might be a composer often categorised as Postmodern, but who expresses a much more meditative and calm solitude. Arvo Pärt (2021 and https://www.arvopart.ee/en/arvo-part/) began his career drawing on the neoclassicism of major composers of the early twentieth century such as Prokofiev or Shostakovich, before moving on to the serialism of Modernists like Schoenburg. Becoming politically unpopular and creatively blocked, he fell into a despairing silence. Pärt broke his silence through his exploration of medieval Gregorian chant and through a meditative engagement with his strongly held Christianity. What emerged was a minimalist approach that is not making an intellectual statement about music (which might be said of Nancarrow 1999, for example), but expressing emotions of contemplation, ecstasy and perhaps enstasy. It is remarkable that this dour classical composer should become as popular as he has, but he is one of the most played composers of the late twentieth and early twenty-first centuries. Pärt combines features of medieval church music with avant-garde techniques from the twentieth century, along with 'conventional' classical elements. It is this bricolage of styles that qualifies him as Postmodern, although he might well be expelled from the club for his consistent expression of the Christian grand narrative. One of his best-known religious works is *Litany* (2000), a setting of the liturgy of the ascetic, eremitic, fourth-century John Chrysostom, previously set by Tchaikovsky and Rachmaninov. However odd it is that a quiet, meditative and deeply serious classical composer, who assiduously avoids fashions in music, should end up so popular, Pärt has managed that. His expression of, and his music's evocation of, a quietude – the quietness that Beckett, one might say, never found – may be part of the reason for his popularity. The popularity of Pärt's music and its postsecular explicit religiosity and spirituality takes Pärt somewhat beyond Postmodernism, rather as Beckett's extreme version of Modernism pushed him, and art, beyond Modernism and into Postmodernism. But before moving on to post-Postmodernism, it is worth considering some of the contemporary critiques of, and alternatives to, both Modernism and Postmodernism.

Beyond Postmodernism

No approach to the arts is universal, however much textbooks like to characterise each period as exhibiting a single, singular, style. One of the central philosophers of the twentieth century, Martin Buber, managed in his philosophy to critique both Modernism and Postmodernism. Both solipsism and hyper-rationalism are evidenced in Modernism. Both were characterised by Buber as impersonal, as examples of *I-It* relationships, typical of industrialisation and of capitalism

(Buber 1958). This is a direct critique of ahistorical utopianism, as well as the individualism of art such as *Robinson Crusoe* along with the twentieth-century Modernist arts. *Robinson Crusoe* (Defoe 2001, first published in 1719), Defoe's chameleon-like novel, appeared well before the Romantic period, yet seems to express a heroic Romantic model of spiritually significant solitude, reframed by Marx as a model of the capitalist economics (Marx 1973, p. 83), and into the twentieth century, Crusoe could be seen – and is seen by Engelberg (2001) – as a *Modernist* novel. Its utopian, individualist, scientistic structure (Crusoe is an arch-experimenter, and 'lone-scientist', in developing his island life) suits this interpretation. Buber's criticism of societies based on only *I-It* relationships undermines Defoe's model of human nature.

The critique of Modernist, capitalist, *I-It* relationships is only half of Buber's philosophy, as *I-It* relationships are complemented by *I-Thou* relationships. Many people write about Buber as though he *only* valued *I-Thou* relationships, and as though all *I-Thou* relationships are entirely positive. Both ideas are incorrect. *I-Thou* relationships include people trying to kill each other, as in a duel rather than a mere play-fight (Buber 2002a, p. 241). He even talked of demonic *I-Thou* relationships (Putnam et al. 2014, p. 15). And a life of only *I-Thou* relationships is just as false as one of only *I-It* relationships. The modern world (modern, not just Modernist) tended to separate *I-It* from *I-Thou* relationships. Institutions, modern bureaucratic systems of impersonal structures, were *I-It* places; homes where people relaxed in protected emotionally charged but unconnected beyond the walls were *I-Thou* places. 'Institutions are "outside," where all sorts of aims are pursued, where a man works, negotiates, bears influence, undertakes, concurs, organises, conducts business, officiates, preaches', he said, and 'feelings are "within," where life is lived and man recovers from institutions', but 'the separated *It* of institutions is an animated clod without soul, and the separated *I* of feelings an uneasily-fluttering soul-bird' (Buber 2002a, pp. 62–3). Modern institutions, then, tend to be robotic and golem-like (with 'animated clods without souls' being the translator's version of the Hebrew 'Golem'), modern homes are occupied by uneasily-fluttering soul-birds. 'Neither of them knows man: institutions know only the specimen, feelings only the "object"; neither knows the person, or mutual life' (Buber 2002a, p. 63). If Buber can be seen as critiquing Modernism in *I-It* formations, he can equally well be seen as critiquing Postmodernism for its having fallen into a false emotionalism of feelings without historical, social and political contexts or significance. In this way, Buber critiques the solitudes of both Modernism and of Postmodernism.

Buber's own novel, *Gog and Magog* (Buber 1999), is a good expression of his 'artistic' attitude to Modernism and Postmodernism as it was emerging, illustrated through two differently isolated protagonists. A story nominally set during the Napoleonic wars when a number of religious people thought the end of the world (and therefore the biblical prophecy of a battle between Gog and Magog) was close at hand, the novel was written in 1941, at another end-of-the-world moment. The two protagonists are rabbis and both have visions. One asks not to have such visions:

> Jaacob Yitzchak was called the 'Seer' because in truth he 'saw'. It was told that, when he was born, he had been able to see from world's end to world's end. Thus had man been destined to see when on that first day of Creation, ere yet a constellation was in the firmament, God's Word caused to arise the Original Light. ... The child who 'saw', however, was so dismayed by the flood of evil which he beheld engulfing the earth, that he besought the gift to be taken from him and his vision to be restricted to a narrower span. (Buber 1999, p. 4)

The other rabbi exploits his visions and gains fame for it. In an earlier essay, *The Man of Today and the Jewish Bible*, Buber contrasts a 'freethinking' view of history as 'a promiscuous agglomeration of happenings' and 'meaningless hodgepodge', with a 'dogmatic view of history able to "derive laws" from which we could "calculate future events"' (Buber 2002b, p. 54). Both, he says, miss out 'the vital living' that is 'constantly moving from decision to decision' (Buber 2002b, p. 54). This contrast – related to his *I-It-I-Thou* contrast – helpfully explains the significance of his two visionary and isolated rabbis. History is not clearly seen, and neither is the future, but people live and make real decisions to act in the world. Buber makes an artistic case, both in the essay and in the novel, to avoid a Modernist clear view *and* a Postmodern hodgepodge. The 'monumental' Modernism and the 'antiquarian'/collector Postmodernism are both to be replaced by a 'living', critical, activist history or, rather, philosophical anthropology.

Both protagonists in *Gog and Magog* are struggling with these views of history and society, and end up subjects with a 'living' critical present. It is as though aspects of Modernism/*I-It* and aspects of Postmodernist/*I-Thou* philosophical anthropologies are themselves worked out through the novel. The protagonists, despite being intensely socially engaged, are isolated by their respective philosophies, and left lonely. This is a remarkable artistic achievement, prescient (visionary, one might dare say) in its critique of mid-twentieth-century history (the war and the ongoing systematic persecution of Jews and others, even if the

Shoah was not yet as clear as it later became), but also critiquing the loneliness of historical, social, religious and artistic expressions of the two inadequate ways of being. In contrast to many publications about Buber, this is *not* saying that *I-Thou* relationships trump *I-It* relationships and should be central to all social relationships. Rather, I am claiming, alongside Buber, that people should, if they can, live *at the same time* with both *I-It* and *I-Thou* relationships.

Solitude to the Side of Modernism and Postmodernism

There is a sense, therefore, of Buber swallowing up both Modernism and Postmodernism, not dialectically but by drawing on the valuable elements of each. But through the twentieth century there were also writers, artists and musicians who, instead, *stood to one side* of Modernism and Postmodernism. Some have been mentioned in previous chapters. Vaughan Williams, for example, was criticised by contemporary Modernist musicians as being part of the 'cow pat school' (Rayborn 2016, p. 111), particularly for his folk-song arrangements. Arnold Bennett was insulted for his provincialism. Virginia Woolf described him as 'coarse; … dimly floundering and feeling for something else; glutted with success; wounded in his feelings; avid; thicklipped; prosaic intolerably; … deluded by splendour and success; but naive; an old bore; an egotist; … a shopkeeper's view of literature; yet with the rudiments, covered over with fat and prosperity and the desire for hideous Empire furniture' (Woolf 1982, pp. 165–6). Both Vaughan Williams and Bennett were outside the Modernist club, and both were nevertheless successful. (The public do not always agree with literary fashions.) A later example of someone who stood to one side of both Modernism and Postmodernism, and who relished his provincialism, was Philip Larkin. His place in an account of Modernism and Postmodernism is justified by his *curating* of poetry of these movements, as well as his poetry's contrast with that of the more 'fashionable' poets – a kind of *apophatic* illustration of them, by showing what they are *not*. (Perhaps he deserves a chapter all to himself, as his writing is also apophatically related to exile, ecstasy and enstasy, nature and alienation.) And, well, he is one of the finest poets of solitude.

Larkin was brought up in Leicester, and spent much of his life in (equally provincial) Hull, as university librarian. His curatorial role in the library was complemented by his editing of the *Oxford Book of Twentieth Century English Verse* (Larkin 1973). A loneful curator of literature, especially of the twentieth century, he was also a novelist and a part-time music critic. Larkin was a collector of art related to the more vicious of his solitudes. Larkin makes a good culmination of this chapter. Two poems to start with. One is about being at one, or more. *Counting* (Larkin 1988, p. 108) is perhaps the best poem on oneness since Hölderlin's *Root of All Evil* (Hölderlin 1990, p. 139). Counting to one is easily done, he tells us, one chair, one bed, one coffin filled. He has difficulty, though, in counting up to two, because 'one must be denied / Before it's tried'. Oneness, or solitude, is weakened by addition. This is in stark contrast to the solitude of Thoreau, who had *three* chairs in his hut ('one for solitude, two for friendship, three for society', Thoreau 2006, p. 151, quoted in Chapter 5). In *Dockery and Son* (Larkin 1988, pp. 152–3), Larkin writes of a college friend who had a child: 'Why did he think adding meant increase? / To me it was dilution'. Being at one, for Larkin, was what he sought and was where he was trapped: one coffin filled, and too selfish, too, to love (in *Love*, Larkin 1988, p. 150). He had much in common with Hölderlin, finding himself wanting and hating solitude, and failing to achieve a successful 'twoness'.

It was not that Larkin lived the life of a Romantic poet like Hölderlin. He was sociable and humorous, he had many sexual relationships and lived his last years with one of his partners. And unlike the stereotypical poet starving alone in an attic, he had a secure and well-paid job working with many colleagues and thousands of students. So Larkin shared some suicidal feelings with some Romantic poets, but not the whole lifestyle or approach to poetry. He shared a thanatological obsession with Samuel Beckett, but not enough to be a nihilist or Postmodernist. He was modern but not experimental or utopian or a victim of alienation or exile. He enjoyed living in Hull because it was at the end of the railway line: he was not complaining of living at the end of the world, as Ovid did. Larkin rather enjoyed being away from the temptations of the capital city. His was a small and undramatic loneliness. He once almost proposed marriage, and wrote to a friend:

> Now today I cannot think what maggot was in my brain to produce such a monstrous egg. Or rather I *can* think: several maggots: – the maggot of loneliness, the maggot of romantic illusion, the maggot of sexual desire. I am not engaged, but heaven knows how I can get out of it now, decently or indecently. (Thwaite 1992, p. 165)

Larkin's solitude vision is closest to that of Dickinson, domestic and ordinary, sought and feared, hell, perhaps, but not as hellish as the alternative. 'The hell of loneliness, while still hell, is not so bad as the hell of marriage', he wrote (in

Thwaite 1992, p. 166). His was a balancing act between alienation and quiet affirmation (Spurr 2008).

Another Larkin poem speaks to his attitude to solitude, and speaks, also, to Wordsworth and Milton. *Best Society* (Larkin 1988, pp. 56–7) describes how as a child the narrator (usually considered to be Larkin) thought solitude would be easy to find, but that as an adult, it is hard to find. It is not a matter of geography – either in the poem or in Larkin's life. (Larkin spent most of his adult life living on his own, and travelled comfortably to the nearby countryside and coast.) It is a matter of social expectations and, in particular, virtues and vices. To be a virtuous person means demonstrating social qualities: all virtues are social, he tells us. As a child, you might expect adulthood to be freer than childhood, and full of choices to be made. This is a common belief of children, as they are subject to instructions from adults (what to eat, when to sleep, where to go) whilst those same adults seem to have no-one telling *them* what to do. And it is one of the most common disappointments of adulthood, to find it is not such a free time, with many adults, ironically, looking back at *childhood* as a time of greater freedom. What is unusual is Larkin's association of solitude and *vice*. Are all virtues sociable? There is some validity in such a claim. For myself, having started to research solitude and loneliness, and having been influenced by positive psychology (which focuses on character strengths or virtues), I could not find a virtue-word for someone who is good at solitude. Eventually, I found the obscure word 'enstasy' in a translation of the *Bhagavad-Gītā* (Zaehner 1969, p. 149), as described in Chapter 3.

Larkin did not find enstasy, the word or, presumably, the virtue. So when he was on his own, he felt he was vicious not virtuous. Viciously, he says, I close the door. There is a humorous theme, barely hidden under the surface of the poem. In English, the phrase 'solitary vice' refers to masturbation. Larkin wrote to his friend Kingsley Amis, and in notebooks, about his enjoyment of masturbating. A girlfriend read this in a notebook and was vaguely amused, but Larkin was furious. This aspect of his solitude was not for others to read unless he was completely in control of the telling (Bradford 2005, p. 97). He broke up with the woman, and then wrote *Best Society*. The title is taken from Milton ('solitude is sometimes best society', Milton 1980, p. 311, from *Paradise Lost*, book IX, line 249, with Adam suggesting a quick break to Eve) and is then quoted by Wordsworth, asking for:

> solitude
> More active even than 'best society' –

Society made sweet as solitude
By silent inobtrusive sympathies,
And gentle agitations of the mind
From manifold distinctions (Wordsworth 1994, p. 767)

For Milton (or Adam) and Wordsworth, perhaps solitude was indeed being in good company, with themselves, and in Milton's (Adam's) case was a wish for a mere 'short retirement' followed by a 'sweet return' (Milton 1980, p. 311). The final lines of Larkin's poem suggest to several critics that this poem is indeed in praise of solitude, like those earlier ones. But Larkin was a poet who often made a statement in the final line or two of a poem that was undermined by what was said earlier in the poem. (A good example is the much quoted 'What will survive of us is love', from *An Arundel Tomb*, Larkin 1988, p. 111, undermined by the earlier line saying this was 'almost true', i.e. *not* true, Axelrod n.d., Bradford 2005, p. 153.) So the earlier parts of *Best Society* about all virtues being sociable, and about solitude being achieved 'viciously' by closing the door, undermine the Romantic conceit of the final lines that 'there cautiously / Unfolds, emerges, what I am'. This is not Clare's 'I am' (Clare 2004, p. 361), but an already-undermined existential claim. And, incidentally, another barely disguised reference to self-abuse.

Conclusion

Larkin and Beckett can both be described as 'failed' enstatic writers (as in Chapter 3), and both here fit, if oddly, the theme of Postmodernism. They both also illustrate an old idea, expressed in the twelfth century by William of St-Thierry (and quoted in Chapter 4). Why, he asks, does a monk live in a cell, as does a criminal? In a cell, he says, you only have yourself for company, so a cell is a reward for a good person (who has a good person for company) and a punishment for a bad person (who has a bad person for company). 'A bad man can never safely live with himself, because he lives with a bad man and no one is more harmful to him that he is to himself' (in Webb 2007, p. 72), he concludes. Larkin wishes for an easy solitude, but in solitude finds he has a bad (vicious) person for company. That is why Bradford describes Larkin's as 'a kind of lewd masochism' (Bradford 2005, p. 99). Solitude, in other words, is only 'best society' for good people.

Modernism had 'solutions' and great works of art that often combined a utopianism with a rather cold individualism. Into Postmodernism, things fall apart, the centre cannot hold, and the sheer industrial terror of the Shoah and the Second World War (for Yeats, the First World War) led to artistic disintegration and irony. Larkin is part of the post-Postmodernist return to ordinary, provincial, life. As a novelist, Larkin has been compared to Arnold Bennett, that other author sitting to one side of literary fashion, addressed in Chapter 6 on alienation. Larkin and Bennett were both provincial novelists who wrote of mundane alienation and loneliness in domestic settings. The value of Larkin's position is complemented by his curatorial roles as librarian and anthologiser. *The Oxford Book of Twentieth Century English Verse* (Larkin 1973) does a surprisingly good job of covering the various trends across the century to the 1970s. I say 'surprising' as Larkin himself was surprised that the book worked for him. His skill as a librarian – building up the collection and guarding it conscientiously (he was of a generation of librarians who didn't like to see people borrowing books) – adds to his anthologising, to hint at a rather Modernist tendency. Holding literature together, and creating a complete and more-or-less coherent system, this was his task, albeit undercut by his own claim that 'I have acted not so much critically, or even historically, but as someone wanting to bring together poems that will give pleasure to their readers both separately and as a collection' (Larkin 1973, p. vi). It is in his even more solitudinous writing of novels and poetry that he really took the edge off any grand visions, in awkward reverence for the ordinary sadnesses of life. 'I shouldn't like to arrogate a "philosophy" to myself', he writes to a friend, as 'a poem is just a thought of the imagination – not really logical at all' and 'I shd like to make it quite clear to my generation & all subsequent generations that I have no ideas about poetry at all' (Larkin, in Thwaite 1992, p. 173).

The post-Postmodernist refocusing of Larkin points to a more personal – if not necessarily happy – artistic world, in which solitude can be positively therapeutic as well as pathologically troubling. Older solitudes are being revisited, as Pärt is doing, and it is the therapeutic value of, and response to, solitude and loneliness that starts to emerge, and is the subject of the following chapter.

9

Conclusion: New Solitudes for Old

If I feel lonely I may not be strong enough for the 'solution',
So mindfulness, colouring, and yoga will have to wait.

Summary

There has been a therapeutic turn in how solitude is seen, with Fromm-Reichmann a key figure in therapy and as fictionalised by Greenberg. The use of silence in therapy is as significant as its use in music, with examples of J. S. Bach's silences particularly powerful. Even children's literature is being written by therapists, and the sense of individual responsibility for, and the possibility of individual recovery from, loneliness is traced back to Shakespeare's Cordelia, and contemporaries such as Burton, Cervantes and Góngora, who all present starting points for new understandings of solitude. People are alone together, and can understand solitude in and through community, with the phrase 'alone together' used by Woolf, and later by the philosopher Macmurray and then the computing guru Turkle. Computing has helped change how solitudes are understood and experienced in recent years. The book's themes are therefore revisited in the light of newer developments, also with a consideration of the literature related to the autism spectrum.

Some key artists: Joanne Greenberg (1932-), J. S. Bach (1685-1750), Catherine Storr (1913-2001), William Shakespeare (1564-1616), Miguel de Cervantes (1547-1616), Luis de Góngora (1561-1627), Virginia Woolf (1882-1941)

Introduction: Listening and Waiting

The starting point for this chapter is an odd one, as it is not an artist but a therapeutic approach to loneliness, one that consciously goes beyond both Modernism and Postmodernism. Frieda Fromm-Reichmann was a psychoanalyst with an unusual place in her own profession and also in solitude studies. She was one of the few psychoanalysts to write about loneliness, but that is not why she is this chapter's jumping-off point. Rather, it is her rejection of grand theorising, either of the Modernist style of Freud and Jung or the Postmodernist style of Laing or Lacan. (Just because Postmodernism nominally rejects grand narratives, it is difficult to avoid saying that most Postmodern *theorists* – if not artists like Beckett – produced theories of pretty grand stature.) Freud could be said to be one of the great utopian, rationalist, Modernists (Tauber 2012, p. 43), even if it has also been said that Freud could earn a better place as a short story writer than as a scientist, with his qualities as 'a mythologizing dramatist of the inner life' (Bloom 1986, p. 1) whose 'genius lay as much in the elegance of his writing as in the content of his prose' (Hornstein 2000, p. 297) and who can be thought of as a 'late romantic writer' (Phillips 1999, p. 81). Later 'anti-psychiatrists' such as R. D. Laing (1971) and Thomas Szasz (2010) are central to Postmodernism, with Jacques Lacan having an important role in and beyond psychiatry and psychoanalysis. R. D. Laing was known as an 'anti-psychiatrist', but still practised, so his position was not against treatment itself, just the mistreatment, as he saw it, in much of the sector. He published books of poetry, including *Knots* (Laing 1999), which was also set to music and released as a record performed by Laing (with examples currently on YouTube https://www.youtube.com/watch?v=BKJV aI_Q5go). Isolated – exiled – from mainstream psychiatry, he was expelled from the profession. However, his views on the everyday relational problems – the 'knots' and 'double-binds' – that lead to distress were as known through his poetry as through his accounts of his psychiatric practice.

Fromm-Reichmann went beyond both these psychiatric traditions. She had an impressive career, especially given the greater barriers for women in medicine when she was young. She practised as a psychiatrist in Germany and then established herself in the United States – self-identifying as a 'therapist' rather than 'psychoanalyst'. Treating patients whom most analysts would say were untreatable (at least by analysis) who were often referred to as 'psychotic', including patients who did not speak, Fromm-Reichmann was often successful. Her particular skill: waiting. 'Waiting was her forte' (Hornstein 2000, p. xv). She sat with people quietly and waited: she 'took to sitting by the beds of psychotic patients, just listening to them' (Hornstein 2000, p. 21). Of course it was not all she did, but the ability to sit and listen was central to her way of being. And whereas 'buried in every psychoanalyst is the wish to be a theorist like Freud' (Hornstein 2000, p. 297), Fromm-Reichmann's 'model of psychotherapy was mundane, more partnership than quest':

> The patient's responsibility was to open the door a crack. Her job was to slip in quietly and bear witness to whatever was there. It was an improvisation, a constant change of frame, responsive to the moment and to the feelings of each person. (Hornstein 2000, p. 228)

This was because she believed that all conditions referred to as mental illness were forms of loneliness, and loneliness was mitigated by a companion. It was in building a relationship with the therapist that 'heals the loneliness that lies at the root of all mental illness' (Hornstein 2000, p. 305). The loneliness suffered by her patients was 'a state of extraordinary anguish in which a person ceases to be able to imagine, much less experience, anyone else being able to enter his experience' (Hornstein 2000, p. 305). The long solitudinous, lonely, path through alienation, conflict, individualism and mass death might be mitigated by therapy, especially by a quiet and patient therapy.

More Silence

Being able to sit quietly and listen to someone, this is a rare skill, especially for someone in a powerful position like a therapist or a teacher. The history educator John Fines says, 'I have in the course of my teaching career learned many hard things but the hardest of all has been to shut up', as 'the instinct to lecture children is profound and we have to chain it, and to learn to listen' (Fines, in Fines and Nichol 1997, p. 231). Quietness is a central theme of this book, and a powerful silence of the kind described by Hornstein of Fromm-Reichmann, or by Fines, also has a musical quality. Silence or pauses in music have a very expressive quality unlike, one might say, 'simple' silence. (There is no such thing as simple silence, but that is for another day.) What musical pauses do, like the pauses of Fromm-Reichmann in her therapeutic sessions, is give an opportunity for rethinking, as well as a form of expression in its own right. Two examples from Bach. In his *St Matthew Passion* (2017), Jesus has just been arrested, having been betrayed, and the Roman soldiers have taken him away. The aria *So ist mein Jesus nun Gefangen* (so my Jesus has now been captured) follows. A soprano and alto (originally sung by a countertenor or boy) sing what seems like a calm and peaceful lament, about Jesus having been captured. They are interrupted by an angry chorus demanding that the soldiers release him. The calm lament continues, and the chorus keeps interrupting. Have thunder and lightning their furies forgotten? May the abyss open and swallow up those who have betrayed Jesus, they proclaim. How is the hellish abyss described musically by Bach? With a bar-long pause, by silence. It is one of the greatest dramatic moments in all classical music. The combination of the calm aria and the increasingly angry chorus builds up the emotional richness, and the sudden silence takes one's breath away. It is followed by breathing again, with another level of more focused anger.

A second example of Bach using silence, an example highlighted by Gardiner, is from the *Actus Tragicus* (Bach 2013). A soprano sings 'Yes, come, Lord Jesus!' (*Ja, komm, Herr Jesu, komm!*) several times, as other voices and instruments fall away. As in the previous example, there follows a full bar of silence. The tonality of the soprano could suggest doubt and uncertainty (like the emotional ambiguity of the passage from *St Matthew Passion*) or could lead to a different tonality of the music following the silence. For Gardiner, 'the most impressive feature of Bach's fusion of music and theology occurs in that central silent bar to which we as listeners are irresistibly drawn' (Gardiner 2013, p. 151). He continues:

> Bach's final, masterly coup – to illustrate the believer's crisis of faith and overwhelming need of divine help – is to leave the soprano's immediately preceding notes tonally ambiguous – her voice just evaporating into that desperate cry. There is no resolution, not even a partial closure that might carry the harmony towards a stable cadence: so it is up to *us* how we interpret it in the silence that follows. If we hear it at face value as a weak perfect cadence …, that would indicate death as a kind of full stop. But perhaps we are being gently nudged to hear the final oscillation between A and B♭ as leading note and tonic respectively, in the key of the movement which follows, B♭ minor. In that case Bach's message is one of hope, the tonal upswing indicating that Christ's intervention guarantees death is only a midway point on our journey, the beginning of whatever comes after.

It is the multiple meanings of silence that attract Bach, and he was a matchless composer of such rich silent ambiguity.

> This planting of uncertainty, or rather ambivalence, is not the same as toying with our expectations, a use of hiatus that Bach (along with many other composers) employs on other occasions to hold our attention and keep us guessing.

Bach's *Actus Tragicus* is music of extraordinary profundity. It comes closer to piercing the membrane of awareness that separates the material world from whatever lies beyond it than any other piece of music in this immensely fecund *fin de siècle* period. (Gardiner 2013, pp. 151–2)

It is not playing with the listener's expectations but, for Gardiner, precisely in expressing ambivalence that makes this a piece of membrane-piercing music.

How do these examples of musical silence illuminate Fromm-Reichmann's therapeutic technique? Being prepared to wait quietly, as she does, is not a simple matter. The sprinter Maurice Greene was interviewed after breaking the 100m world record (achieving 9.79 seconds) in 1999. He was asked what was different, for him, in *this* race. 'I relaxed', he said, 'I took my time'. For most people, relaxing and taking one's time would make for a very slow 100m time. It is only for a top athlete that relaxation could be helpful. For most people, sitting quietly with someone with very serious mental health difficulties would not be helpful. Fromm-Reichmann had many years of experience of remarkably sensitive listening and, when someone talks, responding equally sensitively. It is not Bach's silent bar alone, or Greene's relaxation alone, or Fromm-Reichmann's quiet waiting alone that makes them remarkable, but the placing of the silence (and relaxation) in context. Whilst at medical school, in a large lecture theatre, a patient passing Fromm-Reichmann's seat called out *Bertchen, Bertchen, hab ich dich endlich wieder!* ('Bertie, Bertie, at last I find you again!').

Frieda, who described herself as 'extremely shy', was as astonished as everyone else by this outburst. But without realizing what she was doing, she turned to the patient.

All shyness was gone. 'It' said out of me – not I said, 'It' said: 'Yes, that's fine. I'm very glad too, but you know now the professor wants to talk to you. I'll come and see you later.' I assure you 'It' said this. I had no idea what to do.

Everyone gasped and pointed at her. They were even more amazed when, at the end of the lecture, Frieda stood up and declared: 'I must go and see that man, I have promised him.' Treating the ravings of a mental patient as meaningful communication was unheard of. 'Who would say something to a crazy man, and then do it?' mused Frieda, stunned by her own iconoclasm. (Hornstein 2000, pp. 19–20)

Treating thought-disordered talk as worth listening to and worth responding to rationally and sincerely is more of a commonplace now, but at that time, early in the twentieth century, was indeed iconoclastic.

One Flew Over the Rose Garden

Fromm-Reichmann sat quietly with patients, but was not so quiet about other therapists. She complained that they spoke too soon to patients, and they were usually in a hurry to come to a conclusion. Therapists typically develop a grand theory and are quick to impose that on their patients. The 'waiting' of Fromm-Reichmann was, in contrast, a Keats-like demonstration of 'negative capability', of 'living with uncertainties', her 'model of psychotherapy was mundane, more partnership than quest' (Hornstein 2000, p. 228). Without a theory, there is not a Fromm-Reichmann 'school' of therapy. She wrote up some case notes and wrote some articles, but not a great deal. For our purposes, her most important article is the one she wrote on loneliness (Fromm-Reichmann 1959). Very few psychoanalysts write about loneliness (Melanie Klein was the only other psychoanalyst of the period who wrote on the topic), and yet Fromm-Reichmann said that all serious mental health challenges could be seen as problems of loneliness. All of them. This was not a theory in the conventional sense, but a conclusion based on her clinical experience. Her article explains that she is not referring to 'mild' loneliness or mild mental health difficulties either, but the severest, most existentially challenging, experiences. A failure of relationships as central to mental health issues? This is similar to the personalist 'personal construct' psychologist Salmon who says that 'to understand the development of thought-disordered schizophrenia, we have to look to relational rather than individualistic matters' (Salmon 2004, p. 78). In other words, 'this and other [mental health] problems' should be regarded 'not as residing within people, but between them' (Salmon 2004, p. 76).

If mental health issues (for Fromm-Reichmann) and specifically thought-disordered schizophrenia (for Salmon) are relational problems (loneliness, a failure to relate, respectively), then their mitigation or – if possible – 'cure' would be expected to be relational, too. Now, we are in a post-Postmodern mode of solitude and loneliness, drawing on older traditions, of course, whether *The Anatomy of Melancholy* (Burton 2021), Keats or Goethe. These psychological positions are also distinctive of mid- to late-twentieth-century solitude traditions of therapeutically oriented personalist (rather than individualist) solitudes. Fromm-Reichmann was one of the first in this tradition, and it was one of her patients who wrote her into fiction. Joanne Greenberg was a sixteen-year-old, treated by Fromm-Reichmann. Being with her, quietly listening to Greenberg's description in her invented language and in English, gradually Greenberg began to be able to engage with the 'real world' that Greenberg said she had retreated from. At one point, Greenberg was talking about some of the unfairness of this 'real world', compared to the 'unreal' world Greenberg had spent so much time in. 'Well', Fromm-Reichmann apparently responded, 'I never promised you a rose garden'. This phrase became the title of Greenberg's later novelisation of her treatment and recovery (Greenberg 2009), and the title of a film version of the novel (Page 1977). (As well as being the title of a very successful novel and film, it was also the title of a very successful country song by Joe South, most famously sung by Lynn Anderson, but the lyrics – other than the title – bear no relationship to Greenberg or Fromm-Reichmann, although South later drew on a different psychologist, Eric Berne 1964, for inspiration for his song *Games People Play*.)

By novelising her treatment and recovery, Greenberg found a way to talk about her separation from reality (as she saw it) and her re-emerging into reality through her relationship with the fictionalised Fromm-Reichmann. Whereas some of the anti-psychiatrists described mental health issues in almost heroic ways, with Kesey's hugely popular *One Flew Over the Cuckoo's Nest* (Kesey 2002, made into a movie, Forman 1975) a good example of this, the miserable loneliness of schizophrenia, and the huge relief of coming back into relationships, was the theme of Greenberg's novel. There is more uncertainty than in the more heroic anti-psychiatric accounts. For her novel, Greenberg apparently wanted the title *The Little Maybe*, but the publishers pushed for *I Never Promised You a Rose Garden* (Hornstein 2000, p. 350), with Greenberg's first choice based on how a fellow patient described Fromm-Reichmann's clinic as different from others:

It's different here. I been lotsa joints, lotsa wards. My brother, too; lotsa wards. What's here … there's more scared, more mad; pissin' on the floor and yellin' – but it's because of the maybe. It's because of the little, little maybe. (Greenberg 2009, p. 109, with ellipses in the original)

The novels of Greenberg and Kesey, and the films made of them, could be described as the twin peaks of mid-century literary mental health issues – in terms of public popularity and influence. But it is Greenberg who provides the insight into loneliness through alienation from reality, and of *recovery* through relationship. And I don't think it too fanciful to describe Fromm-Reichmann's role as rather like that of Bach: having the confidence to place silences in the centre of her conversation, silences rich with meaning and possibilities of rich interpretations.

Lonely Dreams

Another example of psychology, therapy and the art of solitude, another good example of post-Postmodernism, is given by *Marianne Dreams* (Storr 1958), mentioned in Chapter 1. This novel for children was one I read myself aged nine or ten, not long after it first came out in paperback. It is one of the novels I remember best from my childhood. The novel describes the frustration and loneliness of solitude, and one way in which a child might cope with it through art/dreams. It describes, particularly well for me, the strange mixing of dreaming and waking, reality and imagination, for any child, anyone, who spends a lot of time alone. With hindsight, reading the book as an adult, I think it also tackles mortality, as Marianne comes to be aware that the boy in the dream may not survive. The book was written by Catherine Storr. Storr's 'day job' was as a doctor and psychologist. The depth of her psychological insight was certainly evident in her novels, though whether her psychological training fed her literary imagination or her storytelling informed her psychology work is too difficult to work out. At one point, Marianne is jealous of the boy in the dream, Mark. She draws eyes on stones to keep watch on him. Surreal and scary, and no doubt intentionally Oedipal, it certainly stayed with me. (I was reminded of Storr's novel when, a few years later, I read some of Freud's cases, and thought them fine short stories.) *Marianne Dreams* was the best book I read on solitude, when I was a child. One of the best books I read on solitude as an adult was the one by psychologist Anthony Storr (1988), to whom Catherine Storr was once married. Perhaps I was inevitably going to find the connection, but it was a surprise when I discovered it. (There was a similar link between *I Never Promised You a Rose Garden*, Frieda Fromm-Reichmann, and the life and work of her patient and for a time husband Erich Fromm.)

There are others who connected solitude and creativity in positive ways. Therapists Clark and Kerry Moustakas wrote of *Loneliness, Creativity and Love: Awakening Meanings in Life* (Moustakas and Moustakas 2004). They see loneliness as a form of suffering, and also as a perhaps necessary stimulus to creativity. Specialising in supporting adolescents, loneliness is a way of separating, albeit an uncomfortable way, that then gives the sufferer the distance and dissatisfaction that can lead to growth and (original) creativity. Hardly the Romantic starving in a garret, more a willingness to break out, and characteristic – in its pain as well as its benefit – of adolescence. Bosacki (2005) writes of adolescents' use of silence, to similar effect, and Horowski (2020) of the need – especially of adolescents and young adults – to be prepared to be lonely, if a person is to hold to their morality or values (as mentioned in Chapter 7). These ideas appear surprisingly often in fiction for children and young people (as mentioned in Chapters 1 and 2). In recent decades, adults have joined in the story, with a Bacharach and David song *Let Me Be Lonely* (https://www.lyrics.com/lyric/7238360/Dionne+Warwick/Let+Me+Be+Lonely sung in 1968 by Dionne Warwick https://www.youtube.com/watch?v=QB8kJQE4KDQ) describing how loneliness is the choice the singer makes, in order to remain faithful to the absent lover.

Creative-therapeutic arts of solitude have become big – or at least mid-sized – business in many countries. Journaling, for example, is recommended as a therapeutic activity (https://www.urmc.rochester.edu/encyclopedia/content.aspx?ContentID=4552&ContentTypeID=1). A development from keeping a diary, journalling often includes sketching, writing affirmations, creating collages from significant everyday objects such as tickets or items cut from magazines. These may also include doodles and particular styles of lettering. Whereas keeping a scrapbook or doodling in a notebook and decorating it with pictures used to be done by young people, it is now more typically an adult activity, and therapeutically framed. The art is not expected to be shown to others, but used as a self-reflective self-help journal. A simpler but similar art-of-solitude for therapeutic purposes, also 'borrowed' from childhoods, is colouring. Shelves in bookshops and supermarkets are filled with colouring books, many explicitly labelled as therapeutic or as aiding mindfulness (e.g. Farrarons 2015, mentioned in Chapter 3). A whole book could be written (or coloured in) on mindfulness, an approach to focussing on the present in order to avoid being over-concerned with the past or the future, an approach adapted from a much broader Buddhist philosophy and practice (Nhất Hạnh 1991; Sedgwick 2003, pp. 153–81), given a therapeutic wash and brush-up and sold on to the lonely and anxious, with its religious features more hidden (e.g. Safran, in Craft et al. 2001, pp. 80–1, Henry, in Csikszentmihalyi and Csikszentmihalyi 2006, p. 125).

Was Cordelia Guilty?

Loneliness is getting closer and closer to being deemed a mental health issue, although as yet it has not appeared in the authoritative DSM (APA 2013). And solitude is more often given as a cure of all kinds of ills, with retreats and isolation tanks increasingly popular. Of course, many of these new practices are old practices rediscovered or repackaged, as with yoga and mindfulness, retreats and withdrawal from the city. This has led to a new appreciation of many of the older arts of solitude, too. Some of the 'rediscoveries' are worth mentioning in some more detail. They are not rediscoveries of underappreciated artists, but rediscoveries of significant solitude themes in generally very well-known artists. And they don't come any better known than the first person to be considered: Shakespeare. In Dumm's subtle book on loneliness (Dumm 2008), he gives an account of Cordelia in Shakespeare's *King Lear* as the first modern truly lonely character. Like Cordelia, 'we too live in the matrix of the missing mother, in the paradoxical context of no context, in the open world of storms into which we moderns have been cast', he tells us, and 'this is the way of loneliness' (Dumm 2008, p. 13).

> What Cordelia seeks is a new way out of her family's drama of counterfeit love, a way into a sense of autonomy, which she tries to find through her attempt to establish a reasonable, rational, thoughtful division of love. She is refused that transition – a transition to a form of adulthood – by her abdicating father, but in spite of and because of that refusal she becomes the first lonely self. For Cordelia, loneliness becomes a way of life. She is thus our first modern person. (Dumm 2008, pp. 13–14)

For Dumm, Cordelia's situation is not wholly a form of suffering; it is also 'marking a path toward the healing of divisions of the self and the social that is, paradoxically, to define the isolated self of the modern era' (Dumm 2008, p. 15). Shakespeare was one of the first writers to use the word 'lonely', but, as described in Chapter 6, this use – in *Coriolanus* – is a description of the eponymous hero in exile, arrogant and plotting his revenge, alone but not (in the modern sense) lonely. Cordelia, however, is certainly a good candidate for loneliness. The third and favourite daughter of Lear, she refuses to ingratiate herself to her father, as he plans to divide his kingdom up as he approaches his death. Tragedy ensues as the other two daughters plot against each other and their increasingly disturbed ('mad'?) father. Cordelia and Lear both die. What makes Cordelia potentially lonely is that she is not simply alone (as many characters are in Shakespeare's plays), and not simply rejected (as many are, including Coriolanus), but has actively chosen a path that has led to her rejection notwithstanding her love of her father, and his of her.

Guilt, more than shame (I suggest), is the consequence of her choice, and her choice is important to her: it is not a mistake. Why is she guilty? She understands the terrible consequences of her decision. Even if it would have been possible for her to paraphrase her comments to her father, in such a way as to avoid making him as angry as he became, this was not done. The audience – at least, the modern audience – might well be wanting to shout advice at Cordelia in Act 1, 'for goodness sake, just tell him how much you really do love him, and don't get trapped into his annoying games'. It is her rejection of the (modern) audience's advice that gives us a sense of her (modern) loneliness. *King Lear* is not, in that sense, a tragedy like the Ancient Greek tragedies. In those – let us say, in Sophocles's *Antigone* (1994), similar in many ways to Cordelia – there is less of a sense of choice. Or rather, all (nominal) choices are the inevitable consequence of the characters of the protagonists. It was, for Cordelia, the annoying 'little maybe' that gives us a sense of the greater range of choice open to her. And therefore, the greater sense of responsibility borne by Cordelia, and the greater sense of self-blame and of guilt. The classical tragedies are not amenable to a little bit of helpful advice. Cordelia is.

Shakespeare's skill – though he needs no compliments from me – is in 'modernising' selfhood. When Polonius advises Hamlet 'to thine own self be true', he is saying something that would have made little sense in earlier centuries or different cultures perhaps even today. As Trilling describes it, this was the emergence in Europe of a modern, fully 'doubled' self, one that could choose 'sincerity', to be 'authentic' to a 'true' self, or not.

> If sincerity is the avoidance of being false to any man through being true to one's own self, we can see that this state of personal existence is not to be attained without the most arduous effort. And yet at a certain point in history certain men and classes of men conceived that the making of this effort was of supreme importance in the moral life, and the value they attached to the enterprise of sincerity became a salient, perhaps a definitive, characteristic of Western culture for some four hundred years. (Trilling 1972, pp. 5–6)

That cultural turn also allows more room for self-blame, guilt and shame. Not simply shame in the eyes of society (or church, or God), but in one's own eyes, becoming *guilt*. Advising Hamlet to be true to himself suggests he could be false to himself. Describing Cordelia as the first modern lonely character suggests a similar doubling. This is Dumm's argument, and he makes the case for an emotional loneliness expressed in literature and art. And of course in life, with the death of Dumm's wife whilst he was writing his book, making the book, and the literature in it, a kind of solitary therapy for the lonely author. The growth in therapeutic approaches to arts of solitude in the later twentieth and early twenty-first centuries has been significant. Just as journalling and colouring are being reframed as therapy, so are older literatures and other arts.

Wandering Again

It is not surprising that Burton's *Anatomy of Melancholy* (2021) is newly appreciated, especially given its surprisingly modern 'confessional' honesty in its depiction of sexuality as well as politics and religion. A novel like Cervantes's *Don Quixote* (2003) is a less obvious choice for revisiting with a therapeutic perspective. Yet it is a masterful book on physical, cognitive and social decline in (relative) old age. Don Quixote speaks to modern concerns about old age and different forms of cognitive decline in particular. Wandering around the country in inappropriate clothing, being manipulated by strangers and misunderstanding situations: these are very modern concerns for isolated old age. When first published, around the same time as *King Lear*, Cervantes's novel was seen as comic, later as social commentary, then as tragedy, then as a story of insanity, then a Freudian battle with reality. More recently it has been described as an encyclopaedia of emotions, and as one of the first modern, subjective, descriptions of loneliness (Mijuskovic 2022, p. 320), and that brings us up to date with an account of an emotionally charged cognitive decline associated with social isolation. Like Shakespeare, Cervantes has broad enough shoulders to bear all of these interpretations and more to come. But as a contribution to the arts of solitude, *Don Quixote* comes into his own.

Another contemporary of Shakespeare, Burton and Cervantes was the poet Góngora. His *The Solitudes* (2011) tells of another wanderer, like Lear or Don Quixote, but one more connected to and aware of his surroundings. Outcast, 'a shipwrecked youth, one scorned and desolate' (Góngora 2011, p. 7), the hero is often welcomed in the places he visits. His is an early (early modern, that is) example of a solitudinous engagement with nature and with different cultures that is, in recent years, seen in a broadly positive light.

> If Góngora's poem has a subject, other than the ongoing exploration of the natural world and its inhabitants, then it is the construction of solitude, the search for that state of mind and body in which a person may find some kind of understanding and peace of mind. Though the quest carries echoes of prophetic Biblical literature and the crying in the wilderness, *The Solitudes* are not jeremiads; they are not conceived as lamentations but rather as songs of praise for the wonders of the world encountered by the exile, from humble human artifacts such as a wooden bowl and fishing nets, to the return of the tired falcons at the end of the *Second Solitude*. (Manguel, in Góngora 2011, pp. xviii–xix)

It is the language of the poetry, the language itself, that mitigates the suffering of exile and constant travelling. The author describes his writing and nature in a single beautiful metaphor, as 'flocks of swift-sailing cranes' which are 'perhaps forming letters on the pellucid / paper of the heavens with / the quill feathers of their flight' (Góngora 2011, pp. 47 and 49). It is a tale of language mitigating the pain of solitude in exile, told in many traditions, as in the Yiddish song *Oyfn Pripetshik* described in Chapter 2. Warshawsky was writing of a nineteenth-century Jewish experience, with the song having even more resonance during and after the Shoah. Yet the idea that literature itself is the comfort of exile, the mitigation of an outcast's loneliness, is expressed – quite differently – by Góngora as by Warshawsky.

Alone Together Again

Being comforted by the written word, by music, by art: that is nothing new. Yet it still seems that the therapeutic value of the arts of solitude has a particular role in post-Postmodern society. From mindfulness colouring books through to the popularity of *King Lear*, via semi-fictional therapists in *I Never Promised You a Rose Garden*, the less-than-perfect isolated individual finding some comfort in art: this is a feature of the age. New solitudes emerge from older arts, with the older arts being reinvented for the purpose, as arts so often are. Bach's solo music for violin and for cello were once considered minor technical exercises, and are newly appreciated as masterpieces. Ovid's *Letters*, previously thought rather insignificant, has come to be regarded as central to his writing. How have we ended up swimming amongst all these solitudes, old and new? Cultures are not straightforwardly cumulative, but they do grow and grow. And in the last couple of decades, the growth – chaotic, biased, unfair, misrepresenting so many people – has been accelerated beyond anyone's imagination by the internet. When I was at school, I used to feel smug as I had access to a multi-volume encyclopaedia to help me with my homework. Now, I can sit on a sofa with a phone and get more information, more art, literature and music, than every encyclopaedia, record, book or gallery I had access to in the first four decades of my life.

Computing has done much more than increase access to information and texts. It has distributed more solitude arts and more solitude mitigation. Some say that computing has isolated people, reducing direct personal interaction and replacing it with more impersonal and separated ways of being. 'Alone together' was a phrase used in 1956 by the philosopher Macmurray (2004, p. 169) to describe how we meet and yet still may feel lonely; 'alone together' was used earlier, by Woolf in *Mrs Dalloway*, to describe a brief moment of marital togetherness for Rezia and Septimus Warren Smith prior to the suicide of Septimus:

> 'There it is,' said Rezia, twirling Mrs. Peters' hat on the tips of her fingers. 'That'll do for the moment. Later ...' her sentence bubbled away drip, drip, drip, like a contented tap left running.
>
> It was wonderful. Never had he done anything which made him feel so proud. It was so real, it was so substantial, Mrs. Peters' hat.
>
> 'Just look at it,' he said.
>
> Yes, it would always make her happy to see that hat. He had become himself then, he had laughed then. They had been alone together. Always she would like that hat.
>
> He told her to try it on. (Woolf 2000a, p. 102)

The phrase was used a third time, quite independently, by Turkle (2011) as the title of her book on the alienating effects of internet use. In my own view, none of these uses quite hit the nail on the head. Aloneness, as I understand it, is central to community, not an alternative to it. Alone together is not necessarily a problematic pairing, but an additional achievement. Alone together is a rallying cry for a good (communal) life that includes opportunities for healthy solitude. And the internet is spectacularly good at facilitating both aloneness *and* togetherness. Much has been written about the art of self-representation, in an age of social media. There is a 'cloneliness' that such online representation encourages, in O'Sullivan's elegant argument, as images are created that are manipulated in such ways that the original cannot possibly live up to the image, rejected as it were by one's own use of filters (O'Sullivan 2019).

Notwithstanding such risks, and such actual harms, the art, literature and music of solitude is now with us like never before, digital or (as it always used to be) analogue. We can manage not only our own images but also our own playlists, galleries and libraries. And the arts are *made* this way too. Hockney used photomontage many years ago, but recently took to creating art on an iPhone and iPad (Hockney and Holzwarth 2021, albeit criticised by Searle 2012, quoted in Chapter 1). There are many solutidinous and socially engaged ways in which such technologies enable writing, art and music-making, as well as reading, observing and listening, at every level from children's contributions (children aged ten or eleven commonly set up YouTube channels these days, reviewing music and movies) through to top professionals like Hockney. Both the 'aloneness' of computing and the 'togetherness' of computing have proliferated. I am not one to talk of the internet as democratising (as democracy is a much heavier political theory than can be captured even by online political activism, the 'smart mobs' of early in the current century, Rheingold 2002), but, to give a musical example, the recent trend to 'layer' musical voices on top of each other within TikTok (making *The Wellerman* an unlikely hit for Evans in 2021) is a good example of solitary creativity that has a strong contribution to community.

Solitude Themes, Positive and Negative

This book started with an account of personalism and how this has influenced my work on solitude and on arts. Computing has undoubtedly changed how personhood is developed and experienced. But personhood has also been affected by increasing concerns with the environment and sustainability, to such an extent that 'posthumanism' is much more mainstream than it has ever been before. This in turn affects how solitude is understood and experienced, with 'animal companions' often used to mitigate isolation and social anxieties – expressed artistically in *His Dark Materials* when the animals accompanying people are their *souls* (Pullman 2012). The book's preface and Chapter 1 both discussed creativity and solitude in history. Although this is not framed as a history book, still, technologies are historically contingent so contemporary creativity is distinguished by newer online experiences. Thematically, these chapters described how different forms of solitude are personal (not 'private', necessarily, but related to *personhood*) and are historically and geographically specific (changing over time and from place to place, and between different groups and communities at any one time and place), rather than being universal and unchanging. This is a problem for researching the topic, but also a positive opportunity to explore solitudes – especially within the arts. It is not only the *product* of the arts that illuminates and helps form our experience of solitude, but the *process* of being creative. How we are creative is, like solitude itself, personal and is placed in space and time. There is an important role for *learning* solitude, just as we learn sociability, from our earliest childhoods, so the emphasis on children's literature at the centre of Chapter 1 is important and gives us even more ways of seeing the formation of new solitude experiences long into the future.

Solitudes of exile, in Chapter 2, clearly have negative forms, the suffering of rejection, being de-cultured, having to survive in a new environment and so on. Ovid's exile represents and creates one of the most powerful models of the solitudinous suffering of exile. Yet we are all, in a sense, exiles and many people base their identities on an exilic history that gives them a joy and a hope for a future – perhaps a future in the 'homeland' or a new, better, future in the land of exile. Along with exile to another country is the 'small' *internal* exile – exile in one's own land, rejected from one's own home and sent to a prison or a hospital, for example, or even, in the case of children, being sent to one's room as a small exile from the company of one's family. Solitudes of exile can be rich creative experiences, even if they are still forms of suffering. But the internal exile experienced by peoples who are colonised is more likely to be a form of silencing, even if anti-colonial movements are able to bring people new voices and power. For Serres, it is exile that is the only route to original creativity, the break-away that creates something new. Into the future, there are continuing exiles based on the age-old pushes of war and oppression, and there are newer exiles – exiles from social media, for example, being as 'real' as other exiles, and migration between platforms almost as significant as between countries.

The ecstasies and enstasies of Chapter 3 draw on arts from Antiquity to the present day, with both ecstasy and enstasy primarily experienced solitudinously. These solitudes are typically *sought*, more than *suffered*, although either might involve suffering along the way – in the desert, in the spiritual practices that might lead to ecstasy or enstasy, or in a coffin-like bricked-in isolated home. There are however, some much more troubled forms of ecstasy and enstasy, and/ or failed forms of ecstasy and enstasy, with Hölderlin a poet struggling with these difficult solitudes for most of his life. Blake's work is often as disturbing as that of Hölderlin, but perhaps in the end more coherently worked-through in a longer active creative life. Other artists have used drugs to give themselves access to forms of ecstasy or enstasy, with more or less success. To explore these solitudes, we can also use the *products* of artists to stimulate our own understandings and generate the possibility of newer solitudes. Notwithstanding the constant development of new drugs and new ecstatic and enstatic practices (new, or newly transferred from one cultural context to another, or newly available online), ecstasies and enstasies of solitude seem less directly influenced by newer technologies. My impression is that these changes have not as yet affected the substance of such arts, although their distribution methods and monetisation (even of ancient practices) continue to change.

Solitary artists seem to have been reinvented online, with home-based music, art and literature, complemented by self-publishing, generating whole new tranches of solitary arts revelling in their bedroom-based contribution to culture, even if the quality of contributions is less consistent. Chapter 4 explored the artist as solitary, and this was always subject to social and economic contexts – with the Romantic 'hero' artists a result as much of the change in Europe from communally embedded, patronage-driven, arts, to individual entrepreneurial opportunities for artists to become stars in their own right. Solitary musicians, and poets seeking solitude not least to help create their own poetic self-image, all encourage a rich and positive theme in the arts of solitude. Yet there was a downside, a loss of connection, in writers such as Clare, or Dickinson, or more recently Beckett, and in artists such as Friedrich. The tension between the solitary individual and the increasingly industrial, commercial, society was elegantly portrayed by Mary Shelley and George Eliot, amongst many others. The positive and negative aspects of the 'solitary artist' are a crucial theme in solitude studies although, as always, the distinction should be made between the artists and their arts: both are thematically interesting, separately – with Awad's recent novel (Awad 2019) an impressive attempt to confuse the distinction.

Solitude's relationship with nature, explored in Chapter 5, is a key area of life that does seem to be unambiguously limited by online culture, and yet is becoming even more important as a source of modern/future solitude. Nature has many meanings and uses, and the solitary arts of nature include a rich seam of ornithological creativity. Larks, nightingales and kestrels are complemented by Icarus's bird-impersonation and Dickinson's fly buzzing. Other solitude searches in nature include those of the musicians Gould and John Luther Adams, and the naturalist-wanderers such as Humboldt, Thoreau, Muir and Shepherd. Bringing together music and nature with an acute sense of silence is the Buddhist-influenced composer Cage, who conducts his 'silent piece' in the middle of a wood. Now, in the twenty-first century, the ability to communicate, to work, to play, to shop and to create without leaving your home has reduced the engagement with nature that used to be at least an incidental consequence of travelling. Commuting is being reduced, with the 'almost in nature' character of many such journeys being missed by many people during the Covid pandemic. The influence of this withdrawal from nature on arts includes a reduction in 'nature' references in arts – as the makers and consumers of arts are less familiar with birdsongs, plant species or even the simple experience of walking in the rain. *The Lost Words* (Macfarlane and Morris 2017) is a brave – and popular – set of poems based precisely on the 'nature' words being lost through reduced access to and use of the countryside as well as the depletion of many species of plants and animals. Using poetry to stand in for nature may seem like a sad compromise, but this was also what Romantic poets were doing capturing Nature for an increasingly urbanised population. It is certainly better than nature simply disappearing, and may help increase a desire to engage with those almost-lost natural plants and animals and landscapes, as well as those almost-lost words. As Mandelshtam said, 'I forgot the word I wanted to say, / And thought, unembodied, / Returns to the hall of shadows' (Mandelshtam, quoted in Daniels 2001, p. 50).

The emotions of alienation explored in Chapter 6 have also had something of a therapeutic refashioning. Alienation of various kinds – related to religion, human nature, and social and economic exploitation – was developed in parallel by philosophers and artists, especially in the first half of the nineteenth century. Alienation and loneliness are rarely paired, and yet they seem, to me, to be swimming together in this period, with the artists concentrating on expressing the emotion of loneliness (and increasingly forms of shame and guilt) and the philosophers concentrating on expressing the different forms of alienation (and increasingly forms of self-consciousness of one's situation). Sexuality is introduced into the mix, with this artistic development taking the artists of the time (later in the nineteenth century and into the twentieth century) beyond the work of the contemporary philosophers, with newer lonely existences emerging from their work. Frank O'Connor writes of short stories as essentially, necessarily, lonely tales, and these – along with sexuality – take us well beyond the philosophical alienations with which the chapter started. What is the future of alienation solitudes? It seems that being 'alien' in one form or another is always with us, as much as being an exile, but the experience of alienation seems to change, as the emotion of loneliness also changes, and both have been drawn into debates on well-being and good mental health. Haddon's *The Curious Incident of the Dog in the Night-Time* (2003) is a popular novel (and play) written from the perspective of a boy who seems to have an autism spectrum condition, and Haddon describes it as a book about an outsider, rather than about autism. Reaction to the book perhaps over-emphasised the autism dimension, yet this was an excellent, largely positive, portrayal of a kind of social isolation that in previous centuries might have been regarded as (or experienced as) far more problematic. *The Reason I Jump* (Higashida 2013) is, as its sometime subtitle, *One Boy's Voice from the Silence of Autism*, suggests, explicitly about the isolation of autism. In an account of being alone, the author distinguishes reasons for being in solitude, and the relationship of aloneness to loneliness.

Do you prefer to be on your own?

'Ah, don't worry about him – he'd rather be on his own.'

How many times have we heard this? I can't believe that anyone born as a human being really wants to be left all on their own, not really. No, for people with autism, what we're anxious about is that we're causing trouble for the rest of you, or even getting on your nerves. *This* is why we often end up being left on our own.

The truth is, we'd love to be with other people. But because things never, ever go right, we end up getting used to being alone, without even noticing this is happening. Whenever I overhear someone remark how much I prefer being on my own, it makes me feel desperately lonely. It's as if they're deliberately giving me the cold-shoulder treatment. (Higashida 2013, pp. 47–8)

The boy, Higashida, is either author of this as autobiography, or stimulus to it as a biography (Fitzpatrick 2013). (The same is true of many best-selling 'autobiographies', most often by celebrities.) Higashida is nonverbal and the book, however written, is a best-seller and a valuable contribution to the literature of alienation deriving from a distinctive cognitive condition. An earlier memoir, *The Diving Bell and the Butterfly* (Bauby 1997), is an autobiography of Bauby who had locked-in syndrome following a stroke. Also made into a film, this was influential in bringing cognitive isolation to a wider audience.

Work-based isolation and alienation have in turn been reinterpreted in terms of computer use, with genuinely new computer-mediated forms of alienation (constant surveillance of the form imagined as science fiction in Orwell's *Nineteen Eighty-Four*, 1949), and some simply reformatted (such as education being 'depersonalised' by computer-facilitated learning, in ways already experienced when books, radio and television were introduced in previous centuries). A television drama like Russell T. Davis's *Years and Years* (2019) is a powerful largely dystopian drama set in the very near future, in which (amongst other things) people are able to upload their brains/minds to a computer to live on beyond their bodies. What is most powerful is the analysis of society that is technically futurist and depressingly recognisable in its portrayal of exile, alienation, economic forces that damage individuality, and the compromises and sacrifices made by people in such circumstances. (*Nineteen Eighty-Four*, first published in 1949, had a similar combination of future and present.)

The theme of Chapter 7 is that of solitude generated by social conflict, both large scale (such as war, civil war and colonialism) and small scale (such as family discord). Whereas short stories have a lonely and perhaps alienated character, the large-scale conflicts are often better or more fully expressed in novels. One of the reasons for separating the theme of conflict from the previous theme of alienation is that at times the arts of conflict attempt to reject emotion altogether, responding with apparent cynicism to the irresolvable conflicts within which we live. Yet discord and concord are not always opposites, and this is particularly well expressed in music, and the changing character of musical discord over time and across cultures. The twentieth-century artistic movements known as Modernism and Postmodernism are central to Chapter 8's theme of individualism and death – as explored in those movements, the 'culmination' of alienating industrialisation and urbanisation of the previous century in the mass slaughters of world wars and genocides. There is humour and joy in some of the solitudes of Modernism and Postmodernism: these are not unremittingly negative. Even an author as death-obsessed as Beckett was full of humour, and his plays are well-liked, and well-performed, by professional comedians. Not only this, but the Modernism and Postmodernism that seem full of extreme forms of individualism and loneliness – especially in Postmodernism – have been re-evaluated through postcolonial as well as feminist and queer theory, having already been 'overcome', to an extent, by post-Postmodern authors from Buber through to Larkin. In the twenty-first century, online life has provided a *new* new, a sense of modern and postmodern for a new generation, utopian and dystopian alike. *The Third Industrial Revolution* of Rifkin (2011) is framed around computing, and follows mechanisation (the Industrial Revolution described by Marx and the later Romantics) and automation (a stimulus for Modernism). Solitudes of the age of the internet are, somewhat oddly, mostly created by being always 'on' and 'connected', creating loneliness out of never being away from the *judgement* of others, or indeed from oneself. It is the inability to have any healthy solitude – away from emails or from social media posts, away from workmates or from friends, away from advertisers and other-generated, targeted, content. Life can be like living in a room with everyone you've ever known and a lot of people you don't know, all talking. Olivia Laing, a good writer of non-fiction on solitude (such as *The Lonely City*, 2016), wrote a novel largely derived from her twitter feed, and written somewhat as we (some of us) create our lives online – with repeated daily statements without much strategy or longer-term editorial control. *Crudo* (Laing 2018) is a kind of stream-of-consciousness for the age of the internet, more modern than Modernists like Woolf, but no less troubling.

A Pause, At Last

Culture, as I've said, is cumulative, but that doesn't mean it is better. As Larkin said (in Chapter 8), addition might mean *increase* or it might mean *dilution*. The various themes highlighted in this chapter include the rediscovery or re-appreciation of older arts of solitude, the move towards more therapeutic arts of solitude, and the distortions created by computing. Our understanding of solitude, silence, loneliness and all the other alonenesses is as always illuminated and to a significant extent created by literature, music and art. My hope is that engagement with the arts of solitude, starting from the very first picture books and nursery rhymes, and working through school into adulthood and old age, can give us the tools to understand and appreciate the positive aspects of solitude, and to mitigate the negative aspects of solitude. But even if there is no salutary benefit from engaging with these arts, even if the arts merely strike us like Kafka's ice axe, at least they may give us pause. And pause itself is, of course, an important form of solitude.

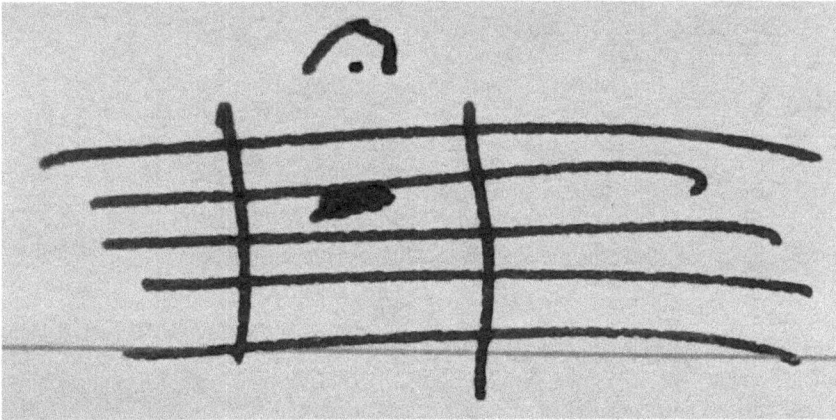

© Julian Stern, 2022

Bibliography

Ackroyd, P. (1996) *Blake*. London: Vintage.

Adams, J. L. (2012) *Songbirdsongs*. New York: Mode Records.

Adams, J. L. (2013) *Inuksuit*. Brooklyn, NY: Cantaloupe Music.

Adams, J. L. (2014) *Become Ocean*. Brooklyn, NY: Cantaloupe Music.

Adams, J. L. (2020) *Silences So Deep: Music, Solitude, Alaska*. New York: Farrar, Straus and Giroux.

Adams, J. L. (2022) *Sila: The Breath of the World*. Brooklyn, NY: Cantaloupe Music.

Albee, E. (1962) *Who's Afraid of Virginia Woolf*. London: Vintage.

Alberge, D. (2022) 'The Cello and the Nightingale: 1924 Duet Was Faked, BBC Admits', *The Guardian*, 8 April 2022, available online at https://www.theguardian.com/media/2022/apr/08/the-cello-and-the-nightingale-1924-duet-was-faked-bbc-admits (accessed 17 July 2023).

Altizer, T. J. J. (2009) 'The Revolutionary Vision of William Blake', *Journal of Religious Ethics*, 37:1, pp. 33–8.

American Psychiatric Association (APA) (2013) *Diagnostic and Statistical Manual of Mental Disorders, Fifth Edition (DSM-5)*. Arlington: American Psychiatric Association.

Andersen, H. C. (2011) *Best Fairy Tales*. London: Macmillan.

Andersen, J. (2005 [2003]) *Hans Christian Anderson: A New Life*. New York: Overlook Duckworth.

Anderson, E. (2008) 'Dancing Modernism: Ritual, Ecstasy and the Female Body', *Literature and Theology*, 22:3, pp. 354–67.

Andreadis, H. (1989) 'The Sapphic-Platonics of Katherine Philips, 1632–1664', *Signs*, 15:1, pp. 34–60.

Anouilh, J. (1987 [1944]) *Antigone*. London: Methuen.

Arendt, H. (1998 [1958]) *The Human Condition: Second Edition*. Chicago: University of Chicago Press.

Ariès, P. (1996 [1960, 1962]) *Centuries of Childhood: A Social History of Family Life*. London: Pimlico.

Athanasius (1980 [356–362]) *The Life of Antony and the Letter to Marcellinus*. Mahwah, NJ: Paulist Press.

Auerbach, E. (2003) *Mimesis: The Representation of Reality in Western Literature*. Princeton, NJ: Princeton University Press.

Awad, M. (2019) *Bunny*. London: Head of Zeus.

Axelrod, J. (n.d.) 'Philip Larkin: "An Arundel Tomb": Does a Notoriously Grumpy Poet Believe in Everlasting Love?', *Poetry Foundation*, available online at http://www.poetr yfoundation.org/learning/guide/237912 (accessed 17 July 2023).

Babyak, J. (1994) *Bird Man: The Many Faces of Robert Stroud*. Berkeley, CA: Ariel Vamp Press.

Bach, J. S. (2013) *Cantatas*. Redhill: SDG.

Bach, J. S. (2017) *St Matthew Passion*. Redhill: SDG.

Bakhtin, M. M. (1981 [1934–41]) *The Dialogic Imagination: Four Essays*. Austin: University of Texas Press.

Barenboim, D. and Said, E. W. (2002) *Parallels and Paradoxes: Explorations in Music and Society*. London: Bloomsbury.

Barker, J., Alldred, P., Watts, M. and Dodman, H. (2010) 'Pupils or Prisoners? Institutional Geographies and Internal Exclusion in UK Secondary Schools', *Area*, 42:3, pp. 378–86.

Barrington, R. (1906) *The Life, Letters and Work of Frederic Leighton, Volume 1*. New York: Macmillan.

Batsleer, J. and Duggan, J. (2021) *Young and Lonely: The Social Conditions of Loneliness*. Bristol: Policy Press.

Bauby, J.-D. (1997) *The Diving-Bell and the Butterfly*. London: 4th Estate.

Baum, L. F. (novel), Langley, N., Ryerson, F. and Woolf, E. A. (screenplay) (1939) *The Wizard of Oz*. Los Angeles, CA: MGM.

The Beatles (2009 [1968]) *The White Album*. London: EMI.

Beckerlegge, G. (ed.) (2001) *The World Religions Reader: Second Edition*. London: Routledge/Open University.

Beckett, S. (2009a [1951] [1955]) *Molloy*. London: Faber and Faber.

Beckett, S. (2009b [1980–9]) *Company / Ill Seen Ill Said / Worstward Ho / Stirrings Still*. London: Faber and Faber.

Beckett, S. (2010a [1951] [1956]) *Malone Dies*. London: Faber and Faber.

Beckett, S. (2010b [1953] [1958]) *The Unnamable*. London: Faber and Faber.

Beckett, S. (2010c [1952]) *Waiting for Godot*. London: Faber and Faber.

Beetles, C. (2021) *Louis Wain's Cats*. Edinburgh: Canongate.

Behrmann, A. (2020) 'A Note on Some of Hölderlin's Epigrams in English Translation', *Studia Metrica et Poetica*, 7:1, pp. 34–46.

Benjamin, W. (1999 [1927–39]) *The Arcades Project*. Cambridge, MA: Belknap Press.

Bennett, A. (1954 [1910]) *Clayhanger*. Harmondsworth: Penguin.

Bennett, A. (1975a [1911]) *Hilda Lessways*. Harmondsworth: Penguin.

Bennett, A. (1975b [1916]) *These Twain*. Harmondsworth: Penguin.

Berne, E. (1964) *Games People Play: The Psychology of Human Relationships*. London: Penguin Books.

Bernstein, L. (1998) *West Side Story*. New York: Sony B0000245HT.

Berry, W. (2018 [1964–2016]) *The Peace of Wild Things*. London: Penguin.

Berryman, J. W. (1991) *Godly Play: An Imaginative Approach to Religious Education*. Minneapolis, MN: Augsburg.

Birkhead, T. (2012) *Bird Sense: What It's Like to Be a Bird*. London: Bloomsbury.

Biss, J. (2020) *Jonathan Biss: Tiny Desk (Home) Concert*. Washington, DC: NPR, available online at https://www.npr.org/2020/12/14/945451489/jonat han-biss-tiny-desk-home-concert?t=1615879202850 (accessed 17 July 2023).

Black Sabbath (2009 [1970–8]) *Greatest Hits*. London: Universal 2705880.

Blake, W. (2000) *The Complete Illuminated Books*. London: Thames & Hudson.

Bloom, H. (1986) 'Freud, the Greatest Modern Writer', *New York Times*, 23 March 1986, section 7, p. 1, available online at https://www.nytimes.com/1986/03/23/books/freud-the-greatest-modern-writer.html (accessed 17 July 2023).

Bosacki, S. L. (2005) *The Culture of Classroom Silence*. New York: Peter Lang.

Bound Alberti, F. (2019) *A Biography of Loneliness: The History of an Emotion*. Oxford: Oxford University Press.

Bowker, J. (ed.) (1997) *The Oxford Dictionary of World Religions*. Oxford: Oxford University Press.

Bowlby, J. (2005 [1979]) *The Making and Breaking of Affectional Bonds*. London: Routledge.

Bradford, R. (2005) *First Boredom, Then Fear: The Life of Philip Larkin*. London: Peter Owen.

Brecht, B. (1962) *Plays: Volume 2*. London: Methuen.

Brontë, C. (2006 [1847]) *Jane Eyre*. London: Penguin.

Brontë, E. (2003 [1847]) *Wuthering Heights*. London: Penguin.

Buber, M. (1958 [1923]) *I and Thou: Second Edition with a Postscript by the Author*. Edinburgh: T&T Clark.

Buber, M. (1999 [1941, 1945]) *Gog and Magog: A Novel*. Syracuse, NY: Syracuse University Press.

Buber, M. (2002a [1965]) *Between Man and Man*. London: Routledge.

Buber, M. (2002b [1908–56]) *The Martin Buber Reader: Essential Writings*. New York: Palgrave Macmillan.

Burton, R. (2021 [1621–51]) *The Anatomy of Melancholy*. London: Penguin Classics.

Cacioppo, J. T. and Patrick, W. (2008) *Loneliness: Human Nature and the Need for Social Connection*. New York: Norton.

Cage, J. (2009 [1968]) *Silence: Lectures and Writings*. London: Marion Boyars.

Campbell, G. (2013) *The Hermit in the Garden: From Imperial Rome to Ornamental Gnome*. Oxford: Oxford University Press.

Camus, A. (2001 [1947]) *The Plague*. London: Penguin.

Camus, A. (2012 [1942]) *The Outsider*. London: Penguin.

Camus, A. (2016 [1946]) *The Human Crisis*. New York: Columbia University, available online at https://www.youtube.com/watch?v=aaFZJ_ymueA (accessed 17 July 2023).

Carson, R. (1962) *Silent Spring*. London: Hamish Hamilton.

Carver, R. (1991) *Where I'm Calling From: The Selected Stories*. London: Harvill Press.

Cascone, S. (2018) 'Damien Hirst Lays Off 50 Employees from His Production Company to "Focus on His Art"', *Artnet, 1,* October 2018.

Cervantes, M. D. (2003 [1616]) *Don Quixote [The Ingenious Hidalgo Don Quixote de la Mancha].* London: Penguin.

Chagall, M. (illustrator) (2007 [2005]) *The Bible: Genesis, Exodus, the Song of Solomon: Illustrations by Marc Chagall.* San Francisco, CA: Chronicle Books.

Chaucer, G. (1992 [c1387–1400]) *Canterbury Tales.* London: Everyman's Library.

Chekhov, A. (1974 [1882–1903]) *Short Stories.* London: Folio.

Chopin, F. (1962) *Selected Correspondence of Fryderyk Chopin by B.E. Sydow and Edited by A. Hedley.* London: Heinemann.

Chopin, F. (2004) Anecdotes, Quotations, and Trivia of Frédéric Chopin, Polish-born Composer and Pianist (1810–1849). http://www.geocities.com/ilian73/composers/chopin.html (accessed 10 August 2004).

Clare, J. (1985) *The Letters of John Clare.* Oxford: Clarendon Press.

Clare, J. (2004) *Major Works.* Oxford: Oxford University Press.

Cocteau, J. (2015 [1922]) *Antigone.* Paris: Folioplus.

Coleridge, S. T. (1994) *Samuel Taylor Coleridge: Selected Poetry.* London: Penguin.

Conrad, J. (1917 [1904]) *Nostromo: A Tale of the Seaboard.* Chapel Hill, NC: Project Gutenberg.

Conrad, J. (2002 [1896–9]) *Heart of Darkness and Other Tales.* Oxford: Oxford University Press.

Courtenay, T. (2003) *Pretending to Be Me: Philip Larkin, a Portrait.* New York: Hachette.

Craft, A., Jeffrey, B. and Leibling, M. (ed.) (2001) *Creativity in Education.* London: Continuum.

Cropley, A. J. (2001) *Creativity in Education & Learning: A Guide for Teachers and Educators.* London: RoutledgeFalmer.

Crotty, P. (2010) *The Penguin Book of Irish Poetry.* London: Penguin.

Csikszentmihalyi, M. and Csikszentmihalyi, I. S. (eds) (2006) *A Life Worth Living: Contributions to Positive Psychology.* Oxford: Oxford University Press.

D'Albert, E. (1992) *D'Albert: Early Recordings by the Composer: The Condon Collection: Rare Recordings.* Noisy-le-Roi: Diffusion Artistique et Musical.

Daniels, H. (2001) *Vygotsky and Pedagogy.* London: RoutledgeFalmer.

Dante Alighieri (2005 [1314]) *The Divine Comedy: Inferno.* The Electronic Literature Foundation (http://www.thegreatbooks.org/) and (http://www.divinecomedy.org/) (both accessed 17 July 2023).

Darabont, F. (director) (1994) *The Shawshank Redemption.* Hollywood, CA: Columbia Pictures.

Davis, E. F. (2019) *Opening Israel's Scriptures.* New York: Oxford University Press.

Davis, R. T. (author) (2019) *Years and Years.* London: BBC.

Dawkins, R. (2006) *The God Delusion.* London: Transworld.

Defoe, D. (2001 [1719]) *Robinson Crusoe.* London: Penguin.

Department for the Economy, Northern Ireland. Higher Education Funding Council for Wales. Research England. Scottish Funding Council [DfENI] (2019) *Guidance on Submissions: REF 2019/01.* http://ref.ac.uk/publications/guidance-on-submissions-201901/ (accessed 31 July 2020).

De Quincey, T. (2013 [1821]) *Confessions of an English Opium-Eater and Other Writings.* Oxford: Oxford University Press.

Descartes, R. (1912 [1637, 1641, 1644]) *A Discourse on Method, Meditations and Principles.* London: Dent Dutton.

Dickens, C. (1955 [1854]) *Hard Times: Hard Times for These Times.* Oxford: Oxford University Press.

Dickinson, E. (1970) *The Complete Poems.* London: Faber and Faber.

Dimitrijević, A. and Buchholz, M. B. (eds) (2022) *From the Abyss of Loneliness to the Bliss of Solitude: Cultural, Social and Psychoanalytic Perspectives.* Bicester: Phoenix.

Disraeli, B. (1906 [1826]) *Vivian Grey.* New York: The Century Co.

Donne, J. (1990) *John Donne: Selections from Divine Poems, Sermons, Devotions, and Prayers.* New York: Paulist Press.

Dostoyevsky, F. (2003 [1866]) *Crime and Punishment.* London: Penguin.

Douglas, A. (2013) *'Two Loves' & Other Poems: A Selection.* East Lancing, MI: Bennett & Kitchel.

Dumm, T. (2008) *Loneliness as a Way of Life.* Cambridge, MA: Harvard University Press.

Duncan, D. (2022) *Index, A History of the: A Bookish Adventure.* London: Penguin.

Dyal, S. (2022) 'Antigone at the Crossroads: The Ethics of Alienation', in *Alone Together 3: International Pandisciplinary Symposium on Solitude in Community,* Szczecin, Poland: University of Szczecin, March 2022.

Eagleton, T. (2022) *Critical Revolutionaries: Five Critics Who Changed the Way We Read.* New Haven, CT: Yale University Press.

Eco, U. (ed.) (2011) *On Ugliness.* London: MacLehose Press.

Eliot, G. (1878) *The Legend of Jubal and Other Poems.* London: William Blackwood.

Eliot, G. (1965 [1871]) *Middlemarch.* Harmondsworth: Penguin.

Eliot, G. (1999 [1861]) *Silas Marner: The Weaver of Raveloe.* Ware: Wordsworth.

Eliot, T. S. (2015) *The Poems of T S Eliot: Volume I: Collected and Uncollected Poems.* London: Faber & Faber.

Ellwand, D. (2001) *10 in the Bed: A Counting Book.* London: Templar Books.

Engelberg, E. (2001) *Solitude and Its Ambiguities in Modernist Fiction.* New York: Palgrave.

Engels, F. (1972 [1884]) *The Origin of the Family, Private Property and the State.* London: Penguin.

Evans, N. (2021) *The Wellerman.* Hilversum: Universal Music.

Farrarons, E. (2015) *The Mindfulness Colouring Book: Anti-Stress Art Therapy for Busy People.* London: Boxtree.

Feeney, D. (2006) 'I shall be read', *London Review of Books*, 28:16, pp. 13–15.

Feuerbach, L. (1855 [1841, 1843]) *The Essence of Christianity: Second Edition*. New York: Calvin Blanchard.

Fines, J. and Nichol, J. (1997) *Teaching Primary History: Nuffield Primary History Project*. Oxford: Heinemann.

Fitzgerald, F. S. (2013 [1922]) *Tales of the Jazz Age*. London: Harper.

Fitzpatrick, M. (2013) 'Michael Fitzpatrick Isn't Convinced by a Much Raved-About Autism Memoir', *Spiked*, available online at http://www.spiked-online.com/newsite/ article/autistic_children_are_not_the_spiritual_saviours_of_mankind/13950#.Ur0y rcuYbDe (accessed 17 July 2023).

Forman, M. (director) (1975) *One Flew Over the Cuckoo's Nest*. Hollywood, CA: United Artists.

Foster, C. (2016) *Being a Beast: An Intimate and Radical Look at Nature*. London: Profile Books.

Frankenheimer, J. (director) (1962) *Birdman of Alcatraz*. Hollywood, CA: United Artists.

Fromm-Reichmann, F. (1959) 'Loneliness', *Psychiatry*, 22:1, pp. 1–15.

Fugard, A. (1999 [1958–74]) *Township Plays*. Oxford: Oxford University Press.

Gaddis, T. E. (1955) *Birdman of Alcatraz*. Mattituck, NY: Aeonian Press.

Gardiner, J. E. (1996) *Londonderry Air: The Music of Percy Grainger*. London: Philips.

Gardiner, J. E. (2013) *Music in the Castle of Heaven: A Portrait of Johann Sebastian Bach*. London: Penguin.

Georgianna, L. (1981) *The Solitary Self: Individuality in the* Ancrene Wisse. Cambridge, MA: Harvard University Press.

Gershwin, G. (2004) *Masters of the Piano Roll: Gershwin Plays Gershwin*. Perrivale, Middlesex: Dal Segno.

Góngora, L. D. (2011 [1613]) *The Solitudes: A Dual-Language Edition with Parallel Text*. New York: Penguin.

Gould, G. (1983) *The Glenn Gould Legacy: Vol I: J.S. Bach (1685–1750)*. New York: CBS Records.

Gould, G. (2003 [1967, 1969, 1977]) *Glenn Gould's Solitude Trilogy: Three Sound Documentaries*. Toronto: CBC Records (catalogue PSCD 2003-3).

Grave, J. (2017) *Caspar David Friedrich*. Munich: Prestel.

Greenberg, J. (2009 [1964]) *I Never Promised You a Rose Garden: With a New Afterword by the Author*. New York: St Martin's.

Griswold, J. (2005) 'Hans Christian Andersen (and Sex): The Original Ugly Duckling', *Los Angeles Times Book Review*, 3 April 2005.

Guignon, C. (2004) *On Being Authentic*. Abingdon: Routledge.

Haddon, M. (2003) *The Curious Incident of the Dog in the Night-Time*. London: Vintage.

Hall, R. (1982 [1928]) *The Well of Loneliness*. London: Virago.

Hamer, R. (ed. and trans.) (1970) *A Choice of Anglo-Saxon Verse*. London: Faber and Faber.

Hardy, T. (1912a [1874]) *Far from the Madding Crowd*. London: Folio.

Hardy, T. (1912b [1891]) *Tess of the d'Urbervilles: A Pure Woman*. London: Folio.

Hardy, T. (1989 [1872]) *Under the Greenwood Tree or the Mellstock Quire: A Rural Painting of the Dutch School*. London: Folio.

Hardy, T. (1993) *Jude the Obscure*. Ware: Wordsworth.

Hatfield, E. (2004) *Feeling Included? A Critical Analysis of the Impact of Pedagogy on Inclusion in a Primary School*. Hull: unpublished MA dissertation, University of Hull.

Hegel, G. W. F. (1977 [1807]) *Phenomenology of Spirit*. Oxford: Oxford University Press.

Hegel, G. W. F. (1988 [1832]) *Lectures on the Philosophy of Religion*. Berkeley: University of California Press.

Hendrick, H. (1992) 'Children and Childhood', *ReFresh*, 15, pp. 1–4.

Higashida, N. (2013) *The Reason I Jump*. London: Sceptre.

Hildegard of Bingen (2001 [1151–73]) *Selected Writings*: London: Penguin.

Hockney, D. and Holzwarth, H. W. (eds) (2021) *David Hockney: A Chronology*. Köln: Taschen.

Hogg, J. (1996 [1822]) *The Three Perils of Man*. Edinburgh: Canongate.

Hölderlin, F. (1990) *Hyperion and Selected Poems*. New York: Continuum.

Hölderlin, F. (2009) *Essays and Letters*. London: Penguin.

Hornstein, G. A. (2000) *To Redeem One Person Is to Redeem the World: The Life of Frieda Fromm-Reichmann*. New York: Other Press.

Horowski, J. (2020) 'Education for Loneliness as a Consequence of Moral Decision-Making: An Issue of Moral Virtues', *Studies in Philosophy and Education*, 39, pp. 591–605.

Hugo, V. (1976 [1862]) *Les Miserables*. London: Penguin.

Hugo, V. (2004 [1831]) *Notre-Dame de Paris*. London: Penguin.

Hutcheson, E. (1975) *The Literature of the Piano: A Guide for Amateur and Student: Second Edition Revised by Rudolph Ganz*. London: Hutchinson.

Huxley, A. (1950 [1931]) *Music at Night and Other Essays*. Edinburgh: Penguin in association with Chatto & Windus.

Ifrah, G. (1998) *The Universal History of Numbers: From Prehistory to the Invention of the Computer*. London: Harvill.

Ingleheart, J. (ed.) (2011) *Two Thousand Years of Solitude: Exile after Ovid*. Oxford: Oxford University Press.

Jantzen, G. (2000) *Julian of Norwich: Mystic and Theologian: New Edition*. London: SPCK.

Johnson, R. (2008 [1936–1937]) *The Complete Recordings*. New York: Sony Music.

Jones, D. (ed.) (2019) *The Philosophy of Creative Solitudes*. London: Bloomsbury.

Joyce, J. (1961 [1914]) *The Dubliners*. New York: The Modern Library.

Joyce, J. (2000 [1920, 1922]) *Ulysses*. London: Penguin.

Julian of Norwich (1966 [1373–1416, 1670]) *Revelations of Divine Love*. Harmondsworth: Penguin.

Kafka, F. (1961 [1916–31]) *Metamorphosis and Other Stories*. Harmondsworth: Penguin.

Kafka, F. (2015 [1925]) *The Trial*. London: Penguin.

Kagge, E. (2017) *Silence in the Age of Noise*. London: Penguin Random House.

Keats, J. (1956) *Keats Poetical Works*. Oxford: Oxford University Press.

Keats, J. (2007) *Selected Poems*. London: Penguin.

Kesey, K. (2002 [1962]) *One Flew Over the Cuckoo's Nest*. London: Penguin.

Kierkegaard, S. (1985 [1843]) *Fear and Trembling*. Harmondsworth: Penguin.

Kierkegaard, S. (2000 [1978–2000] [1835–55]) *The Essential Kierkegaard*. Princeton, NJ: Princeton University Press.

King, S. (1982) *Different Seasons*. London: Hodder & Stoughton.

Koch, P. (1994) *Solitude: A Philosophical Encounter*. Chicago: Open Court.

Kusama, Y. (2019) *All about My Love*. London: Thames & Hudson.

Lahr, J. (2023) 'Buster Keaton's Star Turn', *London Review of Books*, 45:2, 19 January 2023, pp. 3–6.

Laing, O. (2016) *The Lonely City: Adventures in the Art of Being Alone*. Edinburgh: Canongate.

Laing, O. (2018) *Crudo*. London: Picador.

Laing, R. D. (1971 [1961]) *Self and Others*. Harmondsworth: Penguin.

Laing, R. D. (1999 [1970]) *Knots*. London: Routledge.

Larkin, P. (ed.) (1973) *The Oxford Book of Twentieth Century English Verse*. Oxford: Oxford University Press.

Larkin, P. (1988) *Collected Poems*. London: The Marvell Press and Faber and Faber.

Lau, B. (2004) 'Placing Jane Austen in the Romantic Period: Self and Solitude in the Works of Austen and the Male Romantic Poets', *European Romantic Review*, 15:2, pp. 255–267.

Lavin, M. (2011 [1969]) *Happiness And Other Stories*. Stillorgan: New Island Books.

Leavis, F. R. (1948) *The Great Tradition: George Eliot • Henry James • Joseph Conrad*. London: Chatto & Windus.

Leavis, F. R. and Leavis, Q. D. (1969) *Lectures in America*. London: Chatto & Windus.

Lees, H. E. (2012) *Silence in Schools*. Stoke-on-Trent: Trentham.

Lewis, K. (2009) *Lonesome: The Spiritual Meanings of American Solitude*. London: I. B. Tauris.

Lewis, S. (1963 [1935]) *It Can't Happen Here*. New York: Penguin Random House.

Lindén, A. (2018) *On Sheep: Diary of a Swedish Shepherd*. London: Quercus.

Liszt, F. (composer), Bolet, J. (pianist) (2001) *Liszt: Piano Works*. London: Decca.

London Review of Books (2022) *That Year Again: Writing asbout 1922 from the* London Review of Books. London: London Review of Books.

Losseff, N. and Doctor, J. (eds) (2007) *Silence, Music, Silent Music*. London: Routledge.

Lurie, A. (1967) *Imaginary Friends*. New York: Henry Holt.

Lurie, A. (1990) *Don't Tell the Grown-Ups: Subversive Children's Literature*. London: Bloomsbury.

MacCulloch, D. (2013) *Silence: A Christian History*. London: Penguin.

Macfarlane, R. (text) and Morris, J. (illustrations) (2017) *The Lost Words: A Spell Book*. London: Hamish Hamilton.

McGeachy, M. G. (2006) *Lonesome Words: The Vocal Poetics of the Old English Lament and the African-American Blues Song*. New York: Palgrave Macmillan.

McKee, D. (1980) *Not Now, Bernard*. London: Red Fox.

Macleod, D. (1992) 'Patten in Favour of Japanese Work Ethic', Independent, 15 July 1992, available online at http://www.independent.co.uk/news/uk/politics/patten-in-favour-of-japanese-work-ethic-1533594.html (accessed 17 July 2023).

Macmurray, J. (1991 [1961]) *Persons in Relation: Volume 2 of The Form of the Personal*. London: Faber.

Macmurray, J. (2004) *John Macmurray: Selected Philosophical Writings, Edited and Introduced by Esther McIntosh*. Exeter: Imprint Academic.

Macpherson, C. B. (1962) *The Political Theory of Possessive Individualism: Hobbes to Locke*. Oxford: Clarendon Press.

Mann, T. (1991) *Death in Venice and Other Stories*. New York: Knopf.

Marcuse, H. (1991 [1964]) *One-Dimensional Man: Studies in the Ideology of Advanced Industrial Societies*. London: Routledge.

Marx, K. (1973 [1858]) *Grundrisse: Foundations of the Critique of Political Economy (Rough Draft)*. Harmondsworth: Penguin.

Marx, K. (1976 [1867]) *Capital: A Critique of Political Economy: Volume 1*. London: Penguin.

Marx, K. (2009 [1844] [1932] [1959]) *Economic & Philosophic Manuscripts of 1844*. https://www.marxists.org/archive/marx/works/download/pdf/Economic-Philosophic-Manuscripts-1844.pdf (accessed 17 July 2023).

Marx, K. and Engels, F. (1970 [1846]) *The German Ideology: Students Edition*. London: Lawrence & Wishart.

Maupassant, G. D. (1996) *Best Short Stories: A Dual-Language Book*. New York: Dover.

Melville, H. (2016a [1853–91]) *Billy Budd, Bartleby and Other Stories*. New York: Penguin.

Melville, H. (2016b [1851]) *Moby-Dick, or The Whale*. London: Macmillan.

Merback, M. B. (2017) *Perfection's Therapy: An Essay on Albrecht Dürer's Melencolia I*. Brooklyn, NY: Zone Books.

Michalski, P. (2017) 'The Significance of Silence in the Poetry of T. S. Eliot', in *Verschwiegenes, Unsagbares, Ungesagtes sagbar machen: Der Topos des Schweigens in der Literatur [Making the Silent, the Unsayable, the Unsaid Sayable: The Topos of Silence in Literature]*, edited by Bednarowska and Kołodziejczyk-Mróz. Berlin: Weidler Buchverlag, pp. 73–83.

Mijuskovic, B. L. (2022) *Metaphysical Dualism, Subjective Idealism, and Existential Loneliness: Matter and Mind*. London: Routledge.

Milton, J. (1980) *The Complete Poems*. London: J. M. Dent.

Molinos, M. D. (2010 [1675]) *The Spiritual Guide*. New York: Paulist Press.

Mounier, E. (1952) *Personalism*. Notre Dame, IN: University of Notre Dame Press.

Moustakas, C. and Moustakas, K. (2004) *Loneliness, Creativity & Love: Awakening Meanings in Life*. Bloomington, IN: Xlibris.

Muir, J. (2017) *Selected Writings*. New York: Everyman's Library.

Murdoch, I. (2014 [1971]) *The Sovereignty of Good*. Abingdon: Routledge.

Murray, C. J. (ed.) (2004) *Encyclopedia of the Romantic Era, 1760–1850*. New York: Taylor & Francis.

Naess, A. (2008) *Ecology of Wisdom*. London: Penguin.

Nagata, K. (2017) *My Lesbian Experience with Loneliness*. Los Angeles, CA: Seven Seas.

Nancarrow, C. (1999) *Studies for Player Piano*. Mainz: Wergo B000031W5A.

Neugroschel, J. (ed. and trans.) (2006) *The Golem: A New Translation of the Classic Play and Selected Short Stories*. New York: W. W. Norton.

Newton, K. M. (1981) *George Eliot: Romantic Humanist: A Study of the Philosophical Structure of Her Novels*. Basingstoke: Macmillan.

Nhất Hạnh, T. (1991) *Peace Is Every Step: The Path of Mindfulness in Everyday Life*. London: Rider.

O'Connor, F. (1957) *My Oedipus Complex and Other Stories*. London: Penguin.

O'Connor, F. (1968 [1963]) *The Lonely Voice: A Study of the Short Story: Special Anthology Edition*. New York: Bantam.

Oosthuizen, A. (1981) *Loneliness and Other Lovers*. London: Sheba.

Orwell, G. (1949) *Nineteen Eighty-Four: A Novel*. London: Secker & Warburg.

Ostwald, P. F. (1997) *Glenn Gould: The Ecstasy and Tragedy of Genius*. New York: W. W. Norton.

O'Sullivan, M. (2019) *Cloneliness: On the Reproduction of Loneliness*. New York: Bloomsbury.

Ovid (2004 [8 CE]) *Metamorphoses*. London: Penguin.

Ovid (2005 [8–18]) *The Poems of Exile: Tristia and The Black Sea Letters*. Berkeley: University of California Press.

Oxford English Dictionary (OED) (2005) *The Oxford English Dictionary: Third Edition*. Oxford: Oxford University Press.

Page, A. (director) (1977) *I Never Promised You a Rose Garden*. Atlanta, GA: New World Pictures.

Pärt, A. (2000) *Litany*. Munich: ECM.

Pärt, A. (2021) *The Collection*. Leeuwarden, Netherlands: Brilliant Classics.

Patinkin, M. (1998) *Mamaloshen*. New York: Nonesuch 7559–79459–2.

Paul, C. (2022) 'At the Courtauld: Edvard Much', *London Review of Books*, 44:15, 4 August 2022, p. 10.

Pearce, D. (1965) *Cool Hand Luke*. New York: Scribner.

Perrin, C. (2020) 'Some Notes on the Phenomenon of Solitude', *Paedagogia Christiana*, 45:1, pp. 11–22.

Peters, G. (2013) 'Affirming Solitude: Heidegger and Blanchot on Art', *Eidos*, 19, pp. 11–38.

Philips, K. (1710) *Poems by the Most Deservedly Admired Mrs Katherine Philips, the Matchless Orinda: To Which Is Added Monsieur Corneille's Tragedies of Pompey and Horace, With Several Other Translations out of French*. London: Jacob Tonson.

Phillips, A. (1999) 'Promises, Promises', *Contemporary Psychoanalysis*, 35:1, pp. 81–9.

Piaget, J. (1950 [1947]) *The Psychology of Intelligence*. London: Routledge.

Plamper, J. (2015) *The History of Emotions: An Introduction*. Oxford: Oxford University Press.

Plato (1997) *Complete Works*. Indianapolis, IN: Hackett.

Polanyi, M. (1962) *Personal Knowledge: Towards a Post-Critical Philosophy*. London: Routledge.

Pope, A. (1994) *Essay on Man & Other Poems*. Mineola, NY: Dover.

Prawer, S. S. (1978) *Karl Marx and World Literature*. Oxford: Oxford University Press.

Pullman, P. (2012 [1995] [1997] [2000]) *His Dark Materials: Books 1–3: Northern Lights: The Subtle Knife: The Amber Spyglass*. London: Scholastic.

Putnam, H., Saito, N. and Standish, P. (2014) 'Hilary Putnam Interviewed by Naoko Saito and Paul Standish', *Journal of Philosophy of Education*, 48:1, pp. 1–27.

Rayborn, T. (2016) *A New English Music: Composers and Folk Traditions in England's Musical Renaissance from the Late 19th to the Mid-20th Century*. Jefferson, NC: McFarland.

Rée, J. (2019) 'The Young Man One Hopes For: Wittgenstein's Family Letters: Corresponding with Ludwig', edited by Brian McGuinness, translated by Peter Winslow, *London Review of Books, 41:22*, 21 November 2019, pp. 7–8.

Reisman, D. with Glazer, N. and Denney, R. (2000 [1961]) *The Lonely Crowd*. New Haven, CT: Yale Nota Bene.

Rheingold, H. (2002) *Smart Mobs: The Next Social Revolution: Transforming Cultures and Communities in the Age of Instant Access*. Cambridge, MA: Perseus.

Rifkin, J. (2011) *The Third Industrial Revolution: How Lateral Power Is Transforming Energy, the Economy, and the World*. New York: St Martin's Press.

Rilke, R. M. (2009 [1910]) *The Notebooks of Malte Laurids Brigge*. London: Penguin Books.

Robert, M. (1974) *Loneliness in the Schools (What to Do about It)*. Niles, IL: Argus.

Romano, J. (1979) 'Lonely Sharer', *New York Times*, 11 February 1979, section BR, p. 1.

Rosen, C. (1995) *The Romantic Generation*. Cambridge, MA: Harvard University Press.

Rosenberg, S. (director) (1967) *Cool Hand Luke*. Burbank, CA: Warner Bros.-Seven Arts.

Rosenzweig, F. (1999 [1921]) *Understanding the Sick and the Healthy: A View of World, Man, and God*. Cambridge, MA: Harvard University Press.

Rouner, L. S. (ed.) (1998) *Loneliness*. Notre Dame, IN: University of Notre Dame Press.

Rufus, A. (2003) *Party of One: The Loners' Manifesto*. Cambridge, MA: Da Capo.

Rumi (1995) *The Essential Rumi*. Harmondsworth: Penguin.

Sacks, J. (2003) *The Dignity of Difference: How to Avoid the Clash of Civilizations: Second Edition*. London: Continuum.

Sacks, J. (2021) *Studies in Spirituality: A Weekly Reading of the Jewish Bible*. New Milford, CT: Maggid Books.

Said, E. W. (2008) *Music at the Limits: Three Decades of Essays and Articles on Music*. London: Bloomsbury.

Saint-Saëns, C. (1994) *The Best of Saint-Saëns*. Philips ASIN: B0000041AP.

Salmon, P. (1988) *Psychology for Teachers: An Alternative Approach*. London: Hutchinson Education.

Salmon, P. (2004) 'The Schizococcus: An Interpersonal Perspective', *Personal Construct Theory & Practice*, 1, pp. 76–81.

Salzberger-Wittenberg, I., Henry, G. and Osborne, E. (1983) *The Emotional Experience of Learning and Teaching*. London: Routledge & Kegan Paul.

Sarton, M. (1973) *Journal of a Solitude*. New York: Norton.

Sarton, M. (1974) 'No Loneliness: Solitude Is Salt of Personhood', *The Palm Beach Post*, 3 May 1974, p. A19.

Sarton, M. (2014) *Coming into Eighty: Poems*. New York: Open Road Integrated Media.

Sartre, J.-P. (2000 [1938]) *Nausea*. London: Penguin.

Savage, A. and Watson, N. (trans.) (1991) *Anchoritic Spirituality: Ancrene Wisse and Associated Works*. Mahwah, NJ: Paulist Press.

Schiller, F. (1967 [1795]) *On the Aesthetic Education of Man in a Series of Letters*. Oxford: Clarendon.

Schiller, F. (1988) *Poet of Freedom: Volume II*. Washington, DC: Schiller Institute.

Schmitz, M. (2012) *Caspar David Friedrich: His Life and Work*. Whitefish, Montana: Literary Licensing, LLC.

Schopenhauer, A. (1995 [1818]) *The World as Will and Idea*. London: Everyman.

Schutz, A. (1976) *Collected Papers II: The Problem of Social Reality*. Martinus Nijhoff: The Hague.

Searle, A. (2012) 'David Hockney Landscapes: The Wold Is Not Enough', *Guardian*, 16 January 2012, available online at https://www.theguardian.com/artanddesign/2012/jan/16/david-hockney-landscapes (accessed 17 July 2023).

Sedgwick, E. K. (2003) *Touching Feeling: Affect, Pedagogy, Performativity*. Durham, NC: Duke University Press.

Sendak, M. (1963) *Where the Wild Things Are*. London: Random House.

Sennett, R. (1978) *The Fall of Public Man*. London: Penguin.

Serres, M. (1997) *The Troubadour of Knowledge*. Ann Arbor: University of Michigan Press.

Serres, M. (2022 [2019]) *Religion*. Stanford, CA: Stanford University Press.

Seth, V. (2000) *An Equal Music: Music from the Bestselling Novel*. London: Decca (466 945-2).

Shelley, M. W. (1999 [1818]) *Frankenstein*. London: Wordsworth.

Shelley, M. W. (2004 [1826]) *The Last Man*. Ware: Wordsworth.

Shelley, P. B. (2017) *Selected Poems and Prose*. London: Penguin.

Shepherd, N. (2011 [1977]) *The Living Mountain*. Edinburgh: Canongate.

Shikibu, M. (2001 [c1008]) *The Tale of Genji*. New York: Penguin.

Shorter Oxford English Dictionary Sixth Edition (SOED) (2007) *Shorter Oxford English Dictionary Sixth Edition*. Oxford: Oxford University Press.

Siegel, J. (writer) and Shuster, J. (illustrator) (2006 [1938–9]) *The Superman Chronicles: Volume One*. New York: DC Comics.

Sillitoe, A. (1958) *The Loneliness of the Long-Distance Runner*. London: Star.

Simpson, G. and Stern, L. J. (2018) 'The Educational Use of Holocaust Novels', *Other Education: The Journal of Educational Alternatives*, 7:2, pp. 38–54.

The Simpsons (1998) *Songs in the Key of Springfield*. Los Angeles, CA: Rhino B0000033Z8.

Sinclair, U. (1988 [1906]) *The Jungle*. Harmondsworth: Penguin.

Smiley, J. (preface) (2000) *The Sagas of Icelanders: A Selection*. New York: Penguin.

Smith, T. W. (2015) *The Book of Human Emotions: An Encyclopaedia of Feeling from Anger to Wanderlust*. London: Profile Books [Kindle edition].

Solzhenitsyn, A. (1963) *One Day in the Life of Ivan Denisovich*. London: Penguin.

Sophocles (1994 [441, 429, 420 BCE]) *Antigone, Oedipus the King*, and *Electra*. Oxford: Oxford World Classics.

Spinoza, B. (1955 [1677]) *The Ethics*. New York: Dover.

Spinoza, B. (2000 [1677]) *Ethics*. Oxford: Oxford University Press.

Spinoza, B. (2020 [1677]) *Spinoza's Ethics: Translated by George Eliot*. Princeton, NJ: Princeton University Press.

Spurr, B (2008) 'Alienation and Affirmation in the Poetry of Philip Larkin', *Sydney Studies in English*, 14, pp. 52–71.

Starr, G. A. (1965) *Defoe & Spiritual Autobiography*. Princeton, NJ: Princeton University Press.

Steiner, G. (1967) *Language and Silence: Essays on Language, Literature, and the Inhuman*. New Haven, CT: Yale University Press.

Stern, L. J. (2009) *The Spirit of the School*. London: Continuum.

Stern, L. J. (2014a) *Loneliness and Solitude in Education: How to Value Individuality and Create an Enstatic School*. Oxford: Peter Lang.

Stern, L. J. (2014b) 'Dialogues of Space, Time and Practice: Supporting Research in Higher Education', *Other Education: The Journal of Educational Alternatives*, 3:2, pp 3–21.

Stern, L. J. (2018) 'Missing Solitude: Macmurray, Buber and the Edges of Personalism', in *Looking at the Sun: New Writings in Modern Personalism*, edited by A. Castriota and S. Smith. Wilmington: Vernon Press, pp. 157–72.

Stern, L. J. (2021a) 'A Self Rejected: Childhood Loneliness and the Experience of Alienation', in *The Bloomsbury Handbook of Culture and Identity from Early Childhood to Early Adulthood: Perceptions and Implications*, edited by R. Wills, M. de Souza, J. Mata-McMahon, M. Abu Baka and C. Roux. London: Bloomsbury, pp. 49–59.

Stern, L. J. (2022a) 'Introduction: Personhood, Alone and Together – Solitude, Silence and Loneliness in Context', in *The Bloomsbury Handbook of Solitude, Silence and Loneliness*, edited by L. J. Stern, C. A. Sink, M. Wałejko and Wong P. H. London: Bloomsbury, pp. 1–9.

Stern, L. J. (2022b) 'The Art, Music and Literature of Solitude', in *The Bloomsbury Handbook of Solitude, Silence and Loneliness*, edited by L. J. Stern, C. A. Sink, M. Wałejko and Wong P. H.. London: Bloomsbury, pp. 89–103.

Stern, L. J. (2022c) 'Conclusion: Lifelong Learning of Aloneness', in *The Bloomsbury Handbook of Solitude, Silence and Loneliness*, edited by L. J. Stern, C. A. Sink, M. Wałejko and P. H. Wong. London: Bloomsbury, pp. 323–33.

Stern, L. J. and Buchanan, M. T. (2021) 'RE Leader Connectedness: A Theology of the Lived Reality of Catholic Education', *Journal of Beliefs and Values*, 42:3, pp. 378–92.

Stern, L. J. and Shillitoe, R. (2018) *Evaluation of Prayer Spaces in Schools: The Contribution of Prayer Spaces to Spiritual Development*. York: York St John University, available online at https://prayerspacesinschools.com/prayer-spaces/resea rch/ (accessed 17 July 2023).

Stern, L. J. and Shillitoe, R. (2019) 'Prayer Spaces in Schools: A Subversion of Policy Implementation?', *Journal of Beliefs and Values*, 40:2, pp. 228–45.

Stern, L. J. and Wałejko, M. J. (2020) 'Solitude and Self-Realisation in Education', *Journal of Philosophy of Education*, 54:1, pp. 107–23.

Storr, A. (1988) *Solitude*. London: HarperCollins.

Storr, C. (1958) *Marianne Dreams*. London: Faber and Faber.

Szasz, T. S. (2010 [1961]) *The Myth of Mental Illness: Foundations of a Theory of Personal Conduct*. New York: Harper Perennial.

Szynkaruk, O. (2020) 'The Exile's Lament. Solitude and Togetherness in Ovid's Later Works', *Paedagogia Christiana*, 45:1, pp. 217–24.

Tan, S. (2006) *The Arrival*. London: Hodder.

Tauber, A. I. (2012) 'Freud's Social Theory: Modernist and Postmodernist Revisions', *History of the Human Sciences*, 25:4, pp. 43–72.

Taylor, C. (1989) *Sources of the Self: The Making of the Modern Identity*. Cambridge: Cambridge University Press.

Taylor, C. (1991) *The Ethics of Authenticity*. Cambridge: Cambridge University Press.

Terezin Music Memorial Project (1998) *Al S'fod: Do Not Lament*. Port Washington, NY: Koch.

Thoreau, H. D. (2006 [1854]) *Walden*. New Haven, CT: Yale University Press.

Thwaite, A. (ed.) (1992) *Selected Letters of Philip Larkin: 1940–1985*. London: Faber and Faber.

Trilling, L. (1972) *Sincerity and Authenticity: The Charles Eliot Norton Lectures, 1969–1970*. Cambridge, MA: Harvard University Press.

Tromans, N. (2011) *Richard Dadd: The Artist and the Asylum*. London: Tate.

Turgenev, I. (1991 [1862]) *Fathers and Sons*. Oxford: Oxford University Press.

Turgenev, I. (2013 [1852]) *Sketches from a Hunter's Album: The Complete Edition.* Hollywood, FL: Simon & Brown.

Turkle, S. (2011) *Alone Together: Why We Expect More from Technology and Less from Each Other.* New York: Basic Books.

Twain, M. (2001 [1876, 1884]) *Tom Sawyer & Huckleberry Finn.* Ware: Wordsworth.

Vaughan, W. (1980) *German Romantic Painting.* New Haven, CT: Yale University Press.

Waiblinger, W. (2018 [1831]) *Friedrich Hölderlin's Life, Poetry and Madness.* London: Hesperus.

Webb, D. (2007) *Privacy and Solitude in the Middle Ages.* London: Continuum.

Weber, M. (1978) *Max Weber: Selections in Translation.* Cambridge: Cambridge University Press.

Wegener, P. (writer/director) (1920) *Der Golem: The 1920 Horror Masterpiece* [originally *Der Golem, wie er in die Welt kam* or *The Golem: How He Came into the World*]. Eureka! EKA40065.

Weiss, R. S. (1973) *Loneliness: The Experience of Emotional and Social Isolation.* Cambridge, MA: MIT Press.

Whale, J. (director) (1931) *Frankenstein.* Hollywood, CA: Universal Pictures.

Wilde, O. (1966) *Complete Works of Oscar Wilde.* London: Collins.

Williams, W. C. (1976) *Selected Poems.* London: Penguin.

Wimbush, A. (2020) *Still: Samuel Beckett's Quietism.* Stuttgart: Ibidem.

Winnicott, D. W. (2017) *The Collected Works of D. W. Winnicott: Volume 5: 1955–1959: Edited by Lesley Caldwell and Helen Taylor Robinson.* Oxford: Oxford University Press.

Wittgenstein, L. (1961 [1922]) *Tractatus Logico-Philosophicus.* London: Routledge & Kegan Paul.

Wohlleben, P. (2017) *The Inner Life of Animals: Surprising Observations of a Hidden World.* London: Bodley Head.

Wolf, N. (2003) *Caspar David Friedrich: 1774–1840: The Painter of Stillness.* Köln: Taschen.

Woolf, V. (1929, 1938) *A Room of One's Own* and *Three Guineas.* London: Vintage.

Woolf, V. (1982 [1953–4]) *A Writer's Diary: Being Extracts from the Diary of Virginia Woolf.* San Diego, CA: Harvest.

Woolf, V. (2000a [1925]) *Mrs Dalloway.* London: Vintage.

Woolf, V. (2000b [1931]) *The Waves.* London: Vintage.

Woolf, V. (2000c [1937]) *The Years.* London: Vintage.

Woolf, V. (2022a [1922]) *Jacob's Room.* London: Vintage.

Wordsworth, W. (1994 [1786–1850]) *The Collected Poems of William Wordsworth.* Ware: Wordsworth.

World Music Network (1999) *The Rough Guide: Irish Folk.* London: World Music Network.

Wulf, A. (2015) *The Invention of Nature: The Adventures of Alexander von Humboldt, the Lost Hero of Science.* London: John Murray.

Yang, K. (2019) *Loneliness: A Social Problem*. London: Routledge.

Yates, R. (2008 [1962]) *Eleven Kinds of Loneliness*. London: Vintage.

Yeats, W. B. (ed.) (1936) *The Oxford Book of Modern Verse: 1892–1935*. London: Oxford University Press.

Yeats, W. B. (2002) *W. B. Yeats: Selected Poems*. London: Orion.

Zaehner, R. C. (ed. and trans.) (1969) *The Bhagavad-Gītā*. London: Oxford University Press.

Zaehner, R. C. (ed. and trans.) (1992) *Hindu Scriptures*. London: Everyman.

Zola, É. (1993) *Germinal*. Oxford: Oxford University Press.

Index

Art, literature, music and solitude are addressed throughout the book and do not therefore appear in the index.